To Annie

With All my love
And the love Barclay will
give you,
                Mommy
                        1985

# THE NEW COMPLETE GOLDEN RETRIEVER

Pele of Flarewin's Gold Falcon, owned by David Elliott,
graces the scenic Maine coast with his own special beauty.
This photogenic Golden was bred by Jack Martin.

FC-AFC Tigathoe's Kiowa II (FC-AFC, CFC Bonnie Brooks Elmer ex Tigathoe's Chicka-saw***), owned by Pat Sadler, is a noted trial dog with numerous placements and the sire of many excellent performers. Kiowa is a three-time winner of the Ralph Boalt award and also won the Gilnockie Challenge Cup in 1977.

*Jim Doersam*

# The New Complete
# Golden Retriever

by

GERTRUDE FISCHER

SECOND EDITION
Second Printing — 1984

HOWELL BOOK HOUSE INC.
230 Park Avenue
New York, N.Y. 10169

Ch. Cragmount's Hi-Lo (Ch. Golden Pine's Ace High ex Ch. Cragmount's Tiny Cloud), owned and bred by Jane Engelhard. Hi-Lo was one of the top show dogs in the breed. He was Golden of the Year in 1965 and 1966, and, to date, is the only one of his breed to have won the Sporting Group at Westminster. *William Gilbert*

**Library of Congress Cataloging in Publication Data**

Fischer, Gertrude.
    The new complete golden retriever.

    Rev. ed. of: The complete golden retriever. 1974.
    Bibliography: p. 299
    1. Golden retrievers.  I. Fischer, Gertrude.  Complete golden
retriever.  II. Title.
SF429.G63F57  1984      636.7'52      84-700
ISBN 0-87605-185-9

Gerald R. Ford, 38th President of the United States, is among the many thousands who enjoy the companionship of the personable Golden Retriever. Here the President takes a moment from the affairs of state to relax with Liberty in the oval office.

# Contents

# The Author

GERTRUDE FISCHER brings to this book an authority that melds outstanding educational qualifications with over 35 years of practical experience in the breeding and exhibiting of Golden Retrievers—during which time there has been at least one champion from every litter bred in her kennel.

Raised in Iowa, Mrs. Fischer grew up around animals of every variety. This interest was developed with a Bachelor of Science degree from Iowa University, and a Masters from the University of California.

Her experience covers involvement in every phase of dog management—genetics, nutrition, care, training. She has held many offices with both the Golden Retriever Club of America and the NorCal Golden Retriever Club, and for nearly 30 years has been the official columnist for the parent club in *Pure-Bred Dogs—American Kennel Gazette,* published by the American Kennel Club.

In making this a book that more satisfyingly and more completely serves the Golden Retriever enthusiast than any that has gone before, Mrs. Fischer has complemented her own expertise with chapters by some of the most highly respected writers on the breed: Elma Stonex writes on the Golden in Britain and other lands; Rachel Page Elliott discusses the Standard in depth. The chapter on early field training by the late Dr. Forrest Flashman remains unchanged in this edition, as does the chapter on Field Trials in the British Isles, by Dora Gostyn. The contribution by Ann F. Walters provides full understanding of field training; and the well-known Edith E. Munneke offers two expertly-written chapters on obedience. Both these experts have updated their material since the first edition. In addition, Jennifer Bassing, an officer with Guide Dogs for the Blind, has added some new material to the chapter on the Golden Retriever as a Dog for Leading the Blind. Jeannie Fox, an obedience judge and currently working her own dogs, has contributed material to the History of Great Obedience Dogs, 1945-1983. Together, they have provided a classic work that everyone interested in this fine breed will long, long cherish.

Ch. Goldwing True Bear, OS (Ch. Gold Rush Great Teddy Bear, OS, ex Ch. Goldwing Rhythym-N-Blue, OD), owned, bred and handled by Leslie Dove, he is a multiple Specialty and BIS winner and the sire of numerous winners in conformation. *Alverson*

# Foreword to the Second Edition

*by Nick and Suse Hammond*

---

**W**HEN we first met Dr. and Mrs. Donovan Fischer at the Western Regional Specialty in 1963, we would have never imagined that almost 20 years later to the day, we would be asked to write the Foreword to the Second Edition of her outstanding book *The Complete Golden Retriever*. Since it was first published, Mrs. Fischer's shining tribute to our wonderful, versatile breed has been recommended as the best single information source by successive Secretaries of the Golden Retriever Club of America to the many, many hundreds of inquiries received each year.

Mrs. Fischer—Gertrude—has that rare combination of a structured formal education, obtained with her advanced degrees in science, and the ability to put words together that are easily understandable to a novice in the dog fancy. Her 25-plus years as our Golden columnist for *Pure-Bred Dogs—American Kennel Gazette* have certainly honed her skills and have identified her as the voice of American Golden happenings throughout the world.

In this Second Edition, Gertrude has kept intact the historical portions of her book along with the vitally important pictures of those dogs that were the basis of the marvelous animals we have in the U.S.A. and Canada today. Those chapters by the experts, chosen by Gertrude for the coverage of the various activities our Goldens do so well, are still intact and as pertinent today as 10 years ago when they were written by the giants of our breed: Pagey Elliott, Edi Munneke, Ann Walters, Forrest L. Flashman, M.D. and Mardy Perry. All but Dr. Flashman are still active in our breed. Numerous pictures of the outstanding dogs of the past two decades have been added along with a thumbnail history on each describing their accomplishments.

All of us who know and love Gertrude are constantly amazed by her stamina and iron will that have helped her overcome a number of serious physical handicaps, including a triple by-pass heart operation, that would have made invalids of most of us. She still is out there at dawn to see the first series of the Open All-Age stake, and there she is late in the same day in the hospitality room passing on to us neophytes some of the benefits of her years of research backed by that all-important actual experience. She is never too busy to help and always willing to be a "worker." Her devotion to the betterment of dogs in general is known throughout the dog fancy. She has always turned over all royalties from *The Complete Golden Retriever* to canine research and primarily to the University of California at Davis for canine cancer research. Hopefully each of you that becomes interested in our great Goldens will have the opportunity to talk with this LADY and come away with some of the devotion to and understanding of Goldens that she instills. Surely this book will enhance the "Golden magic" that envelopes all who talk with her.

The thousands that have crossed her path are better for the experience.

—SUSE AND NICK HAMMOND
Secretaries, Golden Retriever Club of America, Inc., 1975 -

Golden Glo's Bit O'Honey, owned by Don and Marilyn Sturz, dripping wet and with nothing to hide. Note the exceptional conformation, angulation and balance on this lovely Golden.

# Introduction

WHEN Mr. Elsworth Howell first asked me to write this book, I thought it would be a simple task, as I had prepared some manuscripts and had been writing articles for magazines for several years, including the Golden Retriever column for *Pure-Bred Dogs—American Kennel Gazette*. But the book was delayed for several reasons—first, due to my late husband's long illness, and then, changes in thoughts as to how I wished the book to read. I did not want the book to reflect only one person's opinion, so I asked others to join me, which they graciously did.

This second edition took a long time to complete as well. There has been an increasing interest in Goldens and their activities in field, show, and obedience competition which has resulted in a large body of information to review. At the time of the first edition, there were approximately 5,000 registered Goldens—today, there are nearly 50,000 which are participating in growing numbers in rescue work and in leading the blind. Major revisions, therefore, have been required and the charts and kennel lists from the first edition have been dropped to make room for new and updated materials. The great expansion and success of the breed has increased my interest and appreciation for the Golden and has led to the formation of many lasting friendships.

My own background includes a Bachelor of Science and a Master's degree with several courses in genetics and nutrition and other types of research. Several close friends were doing research in animal nutrition and shared the results with me.

As a child, I always had horses and dogs, my parents thinking that care of animals helped develop responsibility in children. They also felt that such things as taking care of collections of fancy rabbits and pigeons, and the training of horses and dogs kept my two brothers and me out of mischief. My father's hobbies were purebred cattle and saddlebred horses (mostly gaited horses for the family), so I had a start in having quality animals around. This did not prevent us as children from having a variety of dogs. Some were purebreds; there was also one top-flight mixed breed known as Badge, for Badge of Honor, who so stood alone that we were never able to name another dog for him.

In 1947, I decided to acquire a dog which I could enjoy in late evening walks around the hedges and lanes where I lived. After viewing several attractive breeds, I came down to two. The Golden Retriever was one of them. My brother, a geneticist, reviewed my choices and ordered for my Christmas gift, a beautiful Golden Retriever bitch from a well-known Eastern kennel. She was related to the kennel-mate of Ch. Czar of Wildwood, who, although the only Golden entered, had won a Best in Show at Golden Gate in San Francisco. Soon thereafter I acquired another one who was to become my first champion. These two, Candy and Flare, were delightful friends and companions.

In time, Candy and Flare had puppies, and lots of time and thought were put into the selection of their mates, and special care for their litters. Flare was my first champion, in 1950, and her great granddaughter received her championship in 1970, with majors to spare. In each litter there were excellent field dogs, one or more champions, and obedience workers.

I was fortunate in that my late husband, Dr. Donovan D. Fischer, Professor of Western Civilization and Dean of Humanities at Menlo College, had great acumen for assessing and selecting animals of quality and enjoying Goldens for themselves. He had an unusual eye and feeling for selecting the animal that would have the personality and quality to grow into a fine personal dog and also often a show or field winner. He also felt strongly that no retriever should be shown on the bench unless it could retrieve long singles and doubles on land and water.

One day in 1954, someone asked me to write some articles on Golden Retrievers for a local magazine; so I became even more involved. It was interesting to listen to others and exchange information. I became a member of several retriever clubs and enjoyed the contacts I made.

Breeding and rearing Golden Retrievers, and exchanging information about them from all over the world has been a balance to my academic interests and other hobbies which include collecting sporting prints (old and new), and some forms of Oriental art and ceramics. While I enjoy looking at these pieces, there is nothing quite like the company of that Golden friend, or the rush to show me how each can retrieve, or just being there with their lovely presence, and sometimes their mischief, to give life a little spice.

GERTRUDE FISCHER

# Acknowledgements

$S$INCE so few books on Golden Retrievers have been written in the United States, it seemed to me that people interested in the breed should have the opportunity and pleasure of meeting some of the individuals who have contributed in various ways to the research and breeding of Goldens for field, show, and obedience. This book includes contributors who have enjoyed success with Goldens over a long period of time as well as more recent enthusiasts who have also done well with their dogs.

**Elma Stonex (Mrs. H. T.)** of Somerset, England, a world authority on Goldens, has contributed important and valuable material in her chapters on the "Origin of the Breed" and "Goldens in Other Lands." She has been a recognized judge in England and the owner of the Dorcas Goldens.

**Rachel Elliott (Mrs. Mark D.)**, who has written for this book the critique of the breed Standard, was the first to qualify a Golden for Open All-Age field stakes in New England, and trained and handled her own Goldwood Toby, UD, the first Golden to obtain the Utility Dog title. She is also a past president and historian of the Golden Retriever Club of America, and the author of both editions of the classic book on gait, *Dogsteps*.

**Marjorie B. Perry (Mrs. Arthur)** has owned and trained several Goldens; one of her first was Featherquest Trigger, UDT, son of Goldwood Toby, UD. She has done the official drawings for the Golden Retriever Club of America's brochure on the Standard and also executed the revised drawings on the critique of the breed Standard for this book.

15

For the chapters on "Early Field Training" by **the late Dr. Forrest L. Flashman** and "Training for Retriever Field Trials" by Ann F. Walters, special acknowledgements are due. Dr. Flashman was devoted to Golden Retrievers, believed in a dual purpose Golden, and was interested in all aspects of the breed. He was a judge of National Open field trials and supported the breed in many ways. The fancy lost a great advocate with his untimely death.

**Ann Fowler Walters (Mrs. D. L.)** was an amateur trainer and trained several of her Goldens which qualified for the National Open and the National Amateur stakes. She, like her husband, is now a professional trainer and her chapter is one of great interest as the Walters are both highly successful with Goldens and other retriever breeds.

**Dora Gostyn (Mrs. Eric)** of Lancashire, England, has run her Goldens in field trials in the British Isles. Both she and her husband enjoy the Goldens for themselves and have had great success both in the conformation ring and in the field.

**Edith and the late Albert Munneke** have been considered leaders in obedience training, having trained their own Goldens as well as other breeds with high success as attested by the unequalled American Kennel Club record of their Golden Retriever, Am., Can. Ch. Sundance's Rusticana, Am. UDT, Can. UD. Mrs. Munneke continues to judge, hold clinics, and writes an obedience column for *Dog World* magazine. She has been kind enough to share her knowledge with the novice obedience trainee and those interested in tracking.

**The late Ralph Boalt** deserves much credit for his contributions concerning the early Golden and the use of his unique and very complete pedigree record of the Stilrovin and related Goldens. At his death, his son donated a substantial sum from the estate towards the establishment of the perpetual Ralph Boalt Stilrovin Trophy.

**Christopher R. Burton** has been kind enough to contribute information on some of the great dogs of Canada. He was a close friend of Samuel Magoffin; he has owned and maintained a keen interest in Golden Retrievers for many years.

**Jennifer Bassing** has added new material on Goldens trained to lead the blind; **Jeannie Fox,** an obedience judge, has contributed to the chapter tn "A Short History of Great Obedience Dogs from 1945 to the Present."

The cooperation and kindness of those who have supplied so many pictures and other information for the first and second editions could not be equalled. While it is not possible to name them all in these pages, some deserve special mention. **Miles Midloch** was invaluable in reading and making suggestions for both the first and second manuscripts. **Kerry Wood,** a professor of English, author and Golden owner, also donated his time and talent in the preparation of this second edition. And a special thanks is extended to **Dorothy Carter,** who so kindly helped review and crop the many photographs and who also took the picture for the back cover. I feel sure you will enjoy considering the viewpoints of the many Golden people contributing to this book. Each is qualified to speak for at least one, if not many, aspects of the breed.

I also deeply appreciate the cooperation of **Marjorie Schallau, Joy Clemens,** and **Sam Nelson** for their help in typing and assembling the contents of this second edition.

Any royalties due the author or authors are to be donated to canine research foundations. To each of you who purchases this book, we wish you joy in its content, pleasure in its pictures, and satisfaction in the knowledge of your contribution to the welfare of all dogs.

"Mom, give me the wing!"
Ch. Poppygold Ginger Ripple*, UDT with her daughter, Doo-Da Day, who grew up to earn two stars and a CD degree. Mother and daughter are owned by Bill and Dorothy Carter. This appealing photo is the work of Mrs. Carter whose lovely camera studies will be found throughout this book.

Oil painting of a water dog, by John Charlton. The model is thought to resemble the now extinct Tweed Water Spaniel on the basis of early descriptions and research. Original painting owned by Rachel Page Elliott.

Water Spaniels, an early rendering, published in London, 1820, by T. McLean.

# 1

# How the Retrievers Began

*by Elma Stonex*

---

$T$O SOME GUNDOG BREEDERS perhaps the origin of their particular breed does not seem to matter very much. To them it is the best one, and they don't feel concerned with how it came into being. But in the last few years I have been struck by the interest shown by numbers of people, from many countries, in the origin of the retriever, which Sir Ralph Payne-Galley in 1885 called "the king of all sporting dogs," and felt that to try to set out a few facts I have learned might be helpful. It is now 25 years since I started to look seriously into the more than half-century-old arguments on Golden Retriever origin, and in continuing researches since became very interested in the history of all the retriever breeds.

As early as the fourteenth century spaniels of some sort were used for driving game, and it is known that they were taught to retrieve to hand in the sixteenth century. But that is rather too far back to start tracing in detail.

## The First Retrievers

At the beginning of the nineteenth century the setters and pointers were often trained to retrieve, as well as to perform their ordinary work, but it was not until about 1840 that real attention was given to making a new breed which would only be used to find and bring back wounded and dead game. The aims for this working dog's makeup of course were brains, first-rate nose, tender mouth, biddability, stamina, and pace, but with less disposition to hunt than the setters and spaniels. Looks were not really considered at this time. There is a picture, *The Earl of Lichfield's Shooting Party,* painted as early as 1840 by Sir Francis Grant, which, besides four broken-colored spaniels, shows two dogs of retriever type. One, standing carrying a black cock, is light fawn or sandy-colored, with a real Golden's head but rather heavy in ear, big and very strongly made, with a short coat without wave and very little feathering. Apart from the head it is very like a small Bloodhound. The other, lying down, is wavy-coated and apparently black, with light-colored throat, chest, forelegs to the knees and inside flanks. It has a Collie look.

What can authorities tell us of how the retriever breed was evolved in the first place before its varieties evolved? General Hutchinson in his classic *Dog Breaking,* first published in 1847, wrote, "From education there are a good many retrievers of many breeds, but it is generally allowed that as a rule the best retrievers are bred from a cross between the setter and the Newfoundland, or the strong spaniel and the Newfoundland. I do not mean the heavy Labrador whose weight and bulk is valued as it adds to his power of draught, nor the Newfoundland increased in size at Halfax and St. John's to suit the taste of the English purchaser; but the far slighter dog reared by the settlers of the coast. Probably a cross from the long heavy-headed setter, who, though so wanting in pace, has an exquisite nose, and the true Newfoundland, makes the best retriever. Nose is the first desideratum." The wood-cut frontispiece to General Hutchinson's book is, I think, of the greatest interest. Called *Various Retrievers,* it shows three dogs lying down. At the top, *Cross between Water-Spaniel and Newfoundland,* a brownish-colored dog, plain in head with a rather pointed muzzle and not much stop, fairly large but not long ears; entirely covered with tight curls except on the face, which is bare from about two inches above the eyes, no top-knot, cat-feet, and a curly, feathered tail. Below on the left, *Cross between Water-Spaniel and Setter,* brown again, a handsome broad-headed dog with well-defined stop, deep square muzzle, long ears, heavy bone, wavy coat which curls on the quarters, and plenty of feathering. Its nearest resemblance is to an old-fashioned Irish Setter. Below on the right, *Cross between Setter and Newfoundland,* a black dog with rounded skull, not much stop, strongish muzzle, small ears, wavy coat. Its nearest resemblance would be a Flat-Coat. General Hutchinson also shows a retriever with a Bloodhound cross in another picture, but only its heavy head, a little reminiscent of a Gordon Setter, can be seen.

Stonehenge (J. H. Walsh, editor of *The Field*) wrote in *British Rural Sports* about ten years later:

> "The modern retriever is now almost always a cross of the Setter and Newfoundland (showing the smooth or wavy coat) or of the Water-Spaniel (generally Irish) with the same dog, in which case the coat is curly. Very often the two kinds are intermixed, the result of which is a coat showing more or

less of each texture. My own impression is in favour of the smooth wavy coat, indicative of the Setter origin rather than the Spaniel, as I believe this cross is more docile and better fitted to be broken to the extent of implicit obedience which is required. It is a great nuisance to have to work a retriever in a slip, but there are very few curly-coated dogs with which it can be dispensed, whereas it is comparatively easy with the smooth kind—Colour either jet black without white, or liver also without white, or black and tan, or black with brindled legs, or lastly whole brindled. The height should be at least twenty-four inches, weight from seventy to eighty pounds."

Other authorities mention the Old English Water Spaniel and the Irish Water Spaniel, with Setters, Collies, and the smaller Newfoundland, as having been used in various crosses.


## The Newfoundland Influence

The repetition of Newfoundland is rather confusing. My childhood's memory of the first retriever I ever knew is what I think would have been casually called "rather like a Newfoundland." A big black dog (he seemed enormous to me), very powerful and strongly made, with a broad skull and heavy muzzle, small ears, curly-coated all over, but not tight curls, fairly profuse feathering, and long tail.

We can go a long way back for a clear picture of the early nineteenth century Newfoundland, to Colonel Hawker's *On Shooting,* written about 1820. He said:

"NEWFOUNDLAND Dogs. Here we are a little in the dark. Every canine brute, that is nearly as big as a jackass, and as hairy as a bear is denominated a *fine Newfoundland dog.* Very different, however, is the proper Labrador and St. John's breed of these animals—. The one is very large, rough-haired— kept in that country for drawing sledges, and also very useful by his immense strength and sagacity among wrecks and other disasters in boisterous weather. The other, *by far the best for every kind of shooting,* is oftener black than any other colour and scarcely bigger than a Pointer. He is made rather long in the head and nose, pretty deep in the chest, very fine in the legs, has short or smooth hair; does not carry his tail as much as the other and is extremely quick and active in running, swimming and fighting—. For finding wounded game, of every description, there is not his equal in the canine race."

These two types of Newfoundland are also referred to by Stonehenge who said the large one was most common in England, and that the colors were black or black and white, but occasionally brindled or chestnut. So that reading *Newfoundland* we must not picture that breed as it is today.


## The Water Spaniel Influence

Another chief component of those first Retrievers was the Water Spaniel. Richard Lawrence, a veterinary surgeon, described the Water-

Wavy Coated Retrievers, Paris and Melody.

A retriever/setter cross

The above drawings are from THE COMPLETE LABRADOR RETRIEVER by Helen Warwick, copyright © 1965, 1964 by Howell Book House Inc. and reprinted here with the permission of the publisher.

Dog, in his 1816 book *The Complete Farrier and British Sportsman,* as the ancestor of the Water Spaniel. It was big and unusual looking, of various colors but black with white feet considered the best, and he thought probably descended from "the Greenland dog blended with some particular English race." He wrote:

"The head is rather round, the nose short, the ears long, broad and pendulous; the eyes full and lively; the neck thick and short; the shoulders broad; the legs straight, the hind-quarters round and firm; the pasterns strong and dew-clawed, the forefeet long but round, with the hair in natural short curls. During his puppyhood this dog displays a strong inclination to be busy; he takes delight in removing shoes, boots, mops, brooms, patterns, etc. At this time he should be taught to fetch and carry sticks, or any other article of which he is capable of retrieving; also, to bring sticks, etc., out of waters of every depth and description. Upon the sea-coast this breed is principally propagated. Along the rocky shores and dreadful declivities beyond the junction of the Tweed with the sea of Berwick, Water-Dogs have derived an addition of strength from the experimental introduction of a cross with the Newfoundland dog, which has rendered them completely adequate to the arduous difficulties and diurnal perils in which they are systematically engaged."

He went on to describe how their peasant owners supported themselves by shooting the many kinds of wild-fowl there, and depended entirely on "the persevering exertions" of these dogs for retrieving them from the most inaccessible places. It sounds as if it was a pretty exciting way of earning a living.

Lawrence said that Water Spaniels came from a cross between the Water-Dog and the Springing Spaniel, that some people considered the blacks the hardiest, the pied had the best noses, and the liver-colored ones the best in water and fastest on land. (A retrieving Water Spaniel was mentioned by Shakespeare three centuries earlier.) Stonehenge gave their varieties as "English, Irish, and the Tweedside breed."

These are the mixed background origins of the retriever breeds in the early nineteenth century. From them shooting men slowly produced, without any clear plan for the most part, separate types by breeding from the workers they liked best.

Gulsachan House, the home of Lord Tweedmouth, in the ruggedly beautiful county of Inverness in the north Scottish highlands. It was here that the first Yellow Retrievers were bred and raised. *From a sketch by Nathanial Green.*

# 2

# Development of the Breed in Great Britain and Other Lands

*by Elma Stonex*

---

W AS THE GOLDEN RETRIEVER descended from a troupe of Russian circus dogs bought in Brighton in 1858 by Sir Dudley Marjoribanks, first Lord Tweedmouth, of Guisachan (pronounced *Gooeesicun*), Inverness-shire, Scotland, or had it been haphazardly evolved from the yellow "sports" known to occur in some strains of black Flat or Wavy-coated Retrievers?

## The Golden's True Origin

Arguments went on in England for half a century. The bombshell answer came at last in 1952 when the sixth Earl of Ilchester, historian and sportsman, published his researches into his great-uncle Lord Tweedmouth's kennel record book in a *Country Life* article. This showed that Lord Tweedmouth bought his first yellow Retriever, only one, Nous (i.e. Wisdom) in Brighton in 1865. He is said to have told his grandson it was a "sport" in a litter of blacks, and Nous is recorded as bred by the Earl of Chichester. Photographed about 1870 he looks a very handsome, biggish Golden of medium color, with a very wavy coat. In the record book, started in 1835 and continued until 1890, there is no mention of any Russian dog at all, and only single retrievers were bought at any time.

The Hon. Mary Marjoribanks (daughter of the First Lord Tweedmouth) on "Sunflower." With her is a Yellow (Golden) Retriever bitch. It was whelped in 1868 and was a member of the very first litter of Yellow Retrievers bred by Miss Marjoribanks' father. The sire was "Nous," a Yellow Retriever, and the dam was "Belle," a Tweed Water Spaniel. The bitch was named either "Cowslip" or "Primrose."

This painting, by Gourlay Steele, was done in 1871, and shown at the International Exhibition, London, 1872. Afterward it hung in the dining room at Gulsachan House, Invernessshire, Scotland. *Photograph reproduced by the kind permission of Marjorie Lady Pentland (Lord Tweedmouth's daughter).*

Two years after Nous' arrival at Guisachan, Lord Tweedmouth's cousin, Mr. David Robertson, M.P. of Ladykirk on the river Tweed, gave him a Tweed Water Spaniel named Belle. Stonehenge describes Tweed Water Spaniels as "Like a small English Retriever of a liver colour." Other authorities say they were usually curly-coated and had a more pointed skull and heavier muzzle than the Irish variety. (Liver apparently was a term covering all the sandy, fawn, and brown shades.) They were almost certainly descendants of the "Water-Dogs."

In 1868 Nous and Belle produced four yellow puppies, Crocus, Cowslip, Primrose and Ada. Paintings and photographs of these show them of quite modern type and size, and medium lightish color. Ada was given to the fifth Earl of Ilchester and founded his Melbury strain, in which he mixed black Flat- or Wavy-Coats, and Labradors. Cowslip was really the kingpin of Lord Tweedmouth's carefully worked-out plan to make a yellow retriever breed. In 1873 she was mated to another Tweed Water Spaniel, given by David Robertson the year before, and a bitch puppy, Topsy (thus three-quarters Tweed Water Spaniel), retained. In 1876 Jack, sired by a red Setter out of Cowslip, was kept. In 1877 Topsy, mated to Sir Harry Meux's (presumably black) Retriever Sambo, had Zoe, who in due course had two litters by Sweep (presumably black) a descendant of Ada, bred by Lord Ilchester, and a third litter by Jack in 1884. Linebreeding like this was unusual then, but the last yellow puppies entered in the record book in 1889 had the most interesting pedigree of all, showing four lines to Cowslip in five generations. Called Prim and Rose, they were by a second Nous, a son of Jack and Zoe, out of Queenie, a black daughter of the black Flat-coat, Tracer (full-brother to Ch. Moonstone) and Gill, litter-sister to the second Nous. What a pity Lord Tweedmouth did not live to pursue his scientific breeding operations to the next generation! A loose note recording the use of a Bloodhound has unfortunately been lost, for the late Lord Ilchester well remembered the very big (some rather savage) dogs, clearly showing this cross in looks, at Guisachan in the 1890's. The second Lord Tweedmouth did not keep any records, though the yellow retrievers continued to be bred and worked at Guisachan until it was sold in 1905. None of them having been registered it is very difficult definitely to connect them to the backs of our pedigrees. But there is one outstanding link.

With her grandfather's record book, so kindly lent to me by Marjorie, Lady Pentland, were other papers; among them I found a letter written to her by John MacLennan, one of the family of Guisachan keepers, which said the first Viscount Harcourt had bought his first two puppies from a litter MacLennan bred out of a daughter of Lady, a bitch belonging to Lord Tweedmouth's youngest son, the Hon. Archie Marjoribanks. The latter, who later had a ranch in Texas, took Lady out to Ottawa in 1894 when he stayed with his sister the Marchioness of Aberdeen, wife of the then Governor-General of Canada. Whether Lady had any litters in Canada, or in Texas, I don't know; in the 1894 photograph she looks about four.

Her Excellency Lady Aberdeen (Ishbel Marjoribanks), youngest daughter of the First Lord Tweedmouth, with her children and her brother, the Hon. Archie Marjoribanks. The Golden dozing in the foreground is Lady.

Lady Aberdeen.

28

## The First Exhibitors

Lord Harcourt of the famous Culham Kennel was the first to show Goldens in England (as Flat-coats, Golden) at the Crystal Palace show in 1908, and his great sires Culham Brass (registered 1903) and Culham Copper (1905) are behind the whole breed today. Behind them are such names as Dust and Chlores (1901), Sulphur and Melody. There is a tantalizingly small time-gap between those and Lady (just as there is between Lady and the record book), but in spite of much effort to bridge it I have failed. Everyone who might have known is now dead. Lord Tweedmouth gave many puppies he bred to friends, others were put out with keepers and bred from, so that the yellow retrievers in the hands of gundog men, at that time seldom interested in pedigrees but only in how their dogs worked, would have been crossed with black retrievers or with setters, without compunction. Whatever did happen, Lord Tweedmouth's systematic yellow linebreeding in Scotland laid the firm foundation of the Golden Retriever as a breed.

Mrs. W. M. Charlesworth joined Lord Harcourt as an exhibitor in 1909, having obtained an unpedigreed bitch named Normanby Beauty, a wonderful worker. Her next exhibits were by Culham sires, and in 1912 she bred the first champion Noranby Campfire, from Culham Copper and Beauty. In 1913 with a few other enthusiasts the Golden Retriever Club (of England) was formed.

## The First Field Trials

The first field trial meeting for retrievers, held in 1899, was won by a black Flat-coat, and in 1900 Rust, a liver-colored grand-daughter of the black Flat-coat Ch. Taut, but whose dam was a liver, won the Retriever Society's All-Aged stake. Four years later the International Gundog League's open stake of 19 runners was won by Rust's son, Mr. A. Williams' Don of Gerwyn, given on the card as a "liver Flat-coat, sired by Lord Tweedmouth's Golden Flat-Coat Lucifer (unregistered)." Can this be claimed as a Golden win? Almost I feel, for Goldens of course were registered as Flat-Coats and defined only by color until 1913 when they were called "Golden or Yellow Retrievers," and the title "Golden Retrievers" only came in 1920. (It should be remembered that Flat-Coat and Labrador history is closely interwoven. Labradors were registered under Flat-Coats until 1903 when a separate register was started for them. So that Flat-Coat progeny in fact became the first official Labradors.) In 1912 Capt. H. F. Hardy's Vixie took second in an open stake, and Mrs. Charlesworth's Noranby Sandy (1910) and Noranby Tweedledum won certificates of merit, the first successes scored by Golden Flat-Coats. The last two were both out of Mr. W. Hall's Yellow Nell, a famous ancestress, said to have been of close Guisachan descent. Her parents were Ingestre

Noranby Tweedledum with Mrs. W. M. Charlesworth at the I.G.L. Trials, 1913. This dog was the second Golden to run in British trials and won a Certificate of Merit in open trials.

Culham Brass, owned by the First Viscount Harcourt, retrieving to a gamekeeper in Nuneham Park, Nuneham Courtenay, Oxfordshire. The picture was taken about 1908 or 1909.

Scamp (1906) and Ingestre Tyne (1905), and she was bred by Mr. W. Macdonald, keeper to the Earl of Shrewsbury. Macdonald, who went on breeding until 1915, is said to have started with a "liver Flat-Coat bitch," and from registrations of his Ingestres, seems early on more than once to have used black sires on his Goldens. Several of Scamp and Tyne's progeny got show reports as "very dark" or "too red." Another famous Ingestre-bred was Noranby Dandelion, by Ingestre Dred ex Ingestre Luna, a 1913 winner which mated to Ch. Noranby Campfire was dam of the Hon. Mrs. Grigg's Binks of Kentford, sire of two all-time famous ancestors Ch. Flight of Kentford, (sire of Chs. Banner and Vic of Woolley, Noranby Jeptha and Sh. Ch. Sewardstone Tess); and Mrs. Evers-Swindell's Ch. Cornelius (sire of F.T. Ch. Anningsley Crakers, Chs. Bruce of Dewstraw and Wilderness Maud, and Sh. Ch. Speedwell Emerald). Mrs. Grigg's Kentford kennel played a big part early on. She also owned F.T. Ch. Eredine Rufus (grandson of Culham Copper) winner of five field trials firsts, including two of the top A.V. open stakes, Chs. Kib and Mischief of Kentford, and made the breed's first bitch champion Bess of Kentford in 1923.

### Prewar Fanciers and Dogs

We must not by-pass Mrs. Charlesworth and her Noranby (first Normanby) kennel. The breed owes her much for nearly fifty years enthusiastic determination to preserve and further its working ability combined with true type and soundness. She certainly set an example for all to follow in the lovely-headed, powerfully-made but active, and absolutely sound dogs she bred, which not only worked hard and won in trials, but also took the highest honors on the bench. From her kennel came Mr. W. Hunt's Normanby Balfour (grandsire of Ch. Michael of Moreton, and Chs. Heydown Gunner and Grip), Chs. Noranby Campfire, Noranby Daydawn, Noranby Jeptha, Noranby Diana, Noranby Dutiful and Noranby Deirdre. Finally, when she was over seventy she handled Ch. and F.T. Ch. Noranby Destiny to the dual title.

One of the most famous and influential ancestors the breed has known was Mr. R. Hermon's Ch. and F.T. Ch. Balcombe Boy, bred by Lord Harcourt from Culham Tip and Culham Amber II, who completed both titles in 1922. His mating to Balcombe Bunty (great-grand-daughter of Yellow Nell) produced Ch. Haulstone Dan, Haulstone Rusty (great grand-dam of Gilder, only Golden ever to sire eight champions, Yelme kennel), Amber Dimple (grand-dam of Gilder) and Onaway (dam of Ch. Cubbington Diver, sire of seven champions). Boy also sired Ch. Noranby Daydawn.

Space unfortunately does not allow mention by name of the many notable kennels between the wars, whose dogs lie closely behind the grand, dual-purpose Goldens we have today.

What were Goldens like up to 1930? Roughly speaking bigger all over with great bone, often longer in leg ("showing more daylight"), sometimes rather plain in head with a heavy ear, sometimes light eyes, inclined to long backs. They were not cumbersome, as some had been earlier, but they did not look—and were not—fast in the field. They were noted for excellence in water and for delightful dispositions and trainability. One or two early champions show a Flat-Coat background in other points beside coat. Color tended to be a good deal darker when I started showing in 1931, and light ones were frowned on by some all-round judges until 1936 when the breed Standard was altered to include cream, and from then on the lighter shades became more popular. One of the troubles in the 1920's was white. Big splashes of white, perhaps on the skull or muzzle (I saw a bitch with both as late as 1947), larger ones down the chest, and white paws. I have even heard of white "socks" to just below the knee-joint!

When shows and trials restarted in 1920 after the first World War a good many new breeders took up Goldens and numbers steadily increased. In 1920 registrations first reached three figures, three years later they were trebled, and by 1938 (the last full year before the second World War) they were just over a thousand. Entries at Crufts show, only 34 in 1921, averaged between 222 and 263 from 1925 to 1939. The Golden Retriever Club ran its first breed trials in 1921, and records that in 1928 members' dogs won 27 trial awards. This rose to 63 awards in 1938.

Type and quality steadily improved through the 1930's with the larger and more closely contested classes, and there were some noteworthy any variety wins in trials. The breed's second dual champion, Mr. Venables Kyrke's Ch. and F.T. Ch. Anningsley Stingo was made up (completed his championship) in 1936.

## World War II and Beyond

There were no championship shows or field trials during the second World War but luckily a few breeders just kept their strains going. A good deal of breeding for high "pet" prices was done by others with scant attention paid to breed type or proper rearing, with very mixed results seen when three big breed championship shows were held in 1946, and at first when general shows and trials restarted in 1947. Some pre-war breeders and several keen and thoughtful newcomers were there to help re-establish type, so before very long Goldens were again not only on the up-grade in registrations—from 1385 in 1945 to 2653 in 1947—and numbers at shows and trials, but most important of all in growing evenness of type and quality.

The second post-war Crufts in 1950 had 448 entries in twenty-two classes which remained a record for some years. Now entry qualifications restrict numbers but have raised quality. However at the Golden Retriever Club's annual championship breed show, records have continued to be broken for the last seven years. The 1969 Club show had a staggering total and all-time world record of 666 entries made by 446 dogs.

Noranby Jeptha, one of the best early dogs, was both an English field and bench champion.

Speedwell Rosie, Wilderness Noel, Ch. Wilderness Maud, Wilderness Tangerine and Wilderness Jade.

## British Goldens Today

For a number of years now Goldens have been third most popular gundog breed in England. In 1963 they were thirteenth in the registration order of over a hundred recognized by the Kennel Club with 3045 registrations, a record, but for 1968 they stood eleventh with a new record of 4025 registrations.

I think it can be said that they stand very high among the gundogs for dual-purpose. Many show dogs are first-rate workers at home, some excellent workers get shown occasionally. It would be impossible to mention these, but a fair illustration of the breed's dual-purpose is that besides three dual champions (holding both bench and field titles) made, fourteen champions actually won at trials out of eighty-two made up in the years 1947-1961. Of eleven field trial champions made, during that period three have won at shows.

In England at present there are 27 challenge certificates for each sex in Goldens a year. Three under different judges have to be won to become a show champion. To gain the full champion title a gundog must also either win a field trial award, or be entered for, and get, a "qualifying certificate" at a field trial meeting. For this—very briefly—a retriever must not be gunshy, show he will hunt and retrieve tenderly, and enter water, but need not be steady. There are usually from 12 to 18 (27 at Crufts) classes for the breed at general championship shows with the average entry per class between 10 and 20. Three clubs hold specialist championship shows every year.

## Contemporary British Field Trials

About 40 field trial stakes in which the breed can compete are run from October to January. Except for the seven or eight held by three breed clubs all these are for any variety retrievers. To become a field trial champion a dog must win two firsts in all-aged open stakes of championship status, one of which must be an A.V. (any variety) stake. At the end of the season the retriever championship is held by the Int. Gundog League, for which qualification is now on a points system. Usually over 30 dogs compete in this stake, Labradors (which have three times the registrations of Goldens) being in the ratio of about 6 to 1 over Goldens in numbers.

## Post War Champions

Since the war a few particularly noteworthy dogs have been: Mr. W. Hickmott's Ch. and F.T. Ch. Stubblesdown Golden Lass, dam of two field trial champions, Mrs. Charlesworth's Ch. and F.T. Ch. Noranby Destiny, Miss Ross' Int. Ch. and Int. F.T. Ch. David of Westley (the only Int. Dual Ch. ever). Mr. and Mrs. Atkinson's F.T. Ch. Musicmaker of Yeo, and her son F.T. Ch. Mazurka of Wynford, unique winner of the Retriever Ch. Stake 1954 and runner-up 1955, his son F.T. Ch. Holway Zest runner-up

FC Stubblesdown Larry (left), Dual Ch. Stubblesdown Golden Lass (center) and Stubblesdown Riot were all owned by the late W. E. Hickmott.

English and Irish Dual Ch. David of Westley, owned by Miss Lucy Ross.

1959, and Mazurka's sister Holway Melodymaker of Wynford, dam of two field trial champions. Mrs. Lumsden's F.T. Ch. Treunair Cala, winner of the Retriever Ch. stake 1952. On the bench, Mrs. Pilkington's Ch. Alresford Advertiser (also field trial winner) with 35 challenge certificates, Mrs. R. Harrison's Ch. Boltby Skylon with 29 and Miss Gill's Ch. Simon of Westley with 21 and five times best field trial winner at Crufts. These totals all beat all previous records. Mrs. J. Harrison's Sh. Ch. Janville Renown and Mr. J. Raymond's Sh. Ch. Gainspa Florette of Shiremoor hold the bitch post-war record with 14 challenge certificates each. Curiously enough this score is exactly the same as that of the pre-war bitch record holder, Mrs. Parsons' Ch. Torrdale Betty. Mrs. Stonex's Ch. Dorcas Glorious of Slat was leading sire for three years, and one of only two Goldens ever to sire more than one field trial champion. Miss R. Clark's Ch. Colin of Rosecott sired six champions, a post-war record, Mrs. Stonex's Dorcas Timberscombe Topper was leading sire for two years, and sire of five champions, and his son, Mrs. Tudor's Ch. Camrose Fantango, was leading sire six times and sire of five champions, Miss Gill's Westley Frolic of Yelme was leading brood bitch for four years.

The breed in England has never before achieved such all-through good type, nor A.V. trial standard, as it is generally recognized as holding today, in spite of much increased numbers, which reflects great credit on breeders. It is of tremendous importance that all-through soundness, power in limb and action, and activity, so essential to retriever make-up, are never lost. The Golden's glamorous looks as a companion and show dog could otherwise be its undoing. I feel that the word "pretty" should never be applied to a Golden! Appearance must, and can, be combined with the great intelligence, biddability, activity, and faithfulness which make the Golden the best of all in every way.

### The Golden Worldwide

Comparatively little can be said about the past history of the breed in other countries as unfortunately not many details have come to hand.

Probably the first Golden to go overseas was Lady during her visit to Canada in 1894, referred to at the beginning of this chapter. Mrs. Maclaren's imported Foxbury Peter, by Dual Ch. Balcombe Boy ex Wonham Duchess, became the first Canadian champion in 1928, the year after the Canadian Kennel Club officially recognized the breed. The famous pioneer kennels were Mr. Armstrong's Gilnockie in Winnipeg, and Col. Samuel Magoffin's Rockhaven in Vancouver. The latter's imported Speedwell Pluto (litter brother to Ch. Speedwell Brandy) was the fourth Canadian champion in 1932. The first field trial champion was Mr. Snell's Stalingrad Express in 1947. Since the 1939-45 war Mr. Kenneth Chant, Dr. Noble, Mr. Drysdale, and others have made imports from English kennels, including Pennard, Elsiville, Dorcas, Beauchasse, Janville, and Camrose.

Int. Show Ch. Ambassador of Yeo, owned by Clarence Newton of Flen, Sweden. "Toby" has won in field trial and conformation competition. This photo, taken by his owner, appeared in the Winter, 1982 issue of *Retriever International*.

FC Musicmaker of Yeo (foreground) with some of her winning progeny: (l. to r.) National FC Masurka of Wynford (1954-National Champion, 1955-Second in National, Winner of Rank-Routledge Cup, 1956-most field trial points of any variety); Holway Leo (winner of an Open stake at twenty months); Melodymaker of Wynford (field trial winner and the dam of two field champions). *Courtesy June Atkinson and Carma Futhey.*

In 1956 Mr. Seguin imported the field-trialler Karl of Felsberg from Ireland, and later Irish F.T. Ch. Stubblesdown Vanda, in whelp to Karl's sire Int. Dual Ch. David of Westley. The first breed club, the Golden Retriever Club of Ontario was formed in 1959, and ran its first trials in 1960 with 75 entries.

One of the earliest countries to import the breed was India. About 1927 the English trial winner Ch. Flight of Kentford, bought by the Maharajah of Patiala, became an Indian dual champion. Woolley and Hersham imports also did well in trials. In the early 1920's Sir William and Lady Ibbotson used two English-bred Goldens to retrieve chukar (a kind of partridge) and pea fowl from the backs of elephants in the Himalayan foothills. They climbed back on to the elephants by means of stuffed sacks suspended from the howdahs. Quite a number of champions have been made by various breeders since then, but distances are the difficulty with only eight championship shows a year. The working side is very much to the fore, and the breed in demand for it. Since the war Mr. and Mrs. Lawrence imported Alresford Countryman (a brother to Ch. Alresford Advertiser) who became an Indian champion, and one of his sons won best of all breeds at a championship show. There have also been good variety wins by other breeders. It was very interesting to hear that a fully police-trained, six-year-old Golden, MADHU (Honey), guarded the late Prime Minister, Mr. Nehru's house and grounds night and day. He was trained by Raja Bajrang Bahadur Singh of Badri, president of the newly-formed Retriever Club there. Mrs. Indira Gandhi, the present Prime Minister ultimately owned Madhu and two other Golden companions.

By 1931 Goldens are recorded as having been exported to the U.S.A., Canada, Uruguay, Kenya, France, Belgium, South America, Holland and the Argentine.

The breed was first shown in Holland in 1933, an open class of ten being won by Mr. J. W. Wilson's (Bloemendaal) dog. I believe the first Dutch champion was Miss Jacob's (later Mrs. Van Schelle) Pennard Golden Garland, imported from Mrs. Thompson about 1947. Now there are quite a few enthusiastic breeders particularly keen on work of which much is wild-fowling, and English imports from the Ulvin kennel have done extremely well in the annual A.V. retriever trial there. Thirty-two dogs, then a record number which has since been well exceeded, were shown under me at the 1961 Amsterdam "Winners" show, many up to English championship show form, best going to the almost unbeaten veteran Dutch Ch. Bosco Brit imported by Mevrouw van Crevel, founder in 1956 of the Golden Retriever Club of the Netherlands, who has done much to further the breed there, and is now chairman of the Club. The Crown Princess of Holland has a Golden companion dog, Dutch-bred from English imported parents.

The win of the Ulster Gundog League's open stake by Mrs. Charlesworth's Ch. Noranby Jeptha in 1928 was probably the first time the

Ch. Camrose Cabus Christopher, owned and bred by Joan Tudor of Surrey, England. A true breed great, this dog won 41 C.C.s and was one of England's top all-time sires.

*Pearce*

Party Piece of Yeo (Gladiator of Brackengold ex Mystic Charm of Yeo), owned by Lucille Sawtell of Yeovil, England.

Ch. Deremar Rosemary, owned by Elsie Price Harding of Kent, England, photographed when she was five years old. Rosemary counts field triumphs as well as show honors in her record and is a true, dual purpose retriever.

breed came to notice in Ireland. Several of the best field trial dogs have started their careers there, Miss Ross' Int. Dual Ch. David of Westley, and Irish F.T. Ch. Stubblesdown Vanda, Mrs. Barron's Irish F.T. Ch. Moonbeam of Anbria, and also Karl of Felsberg, all trained by Mr. Jim Cranston, and Mr. Dobb's Irish F.T. Ch. Holway Legato. Vanda and Karl were subsequently exported to Mr. Seguin in Ontario. Entries at Irish shows are not as good as might be hoped. The first Irish champions were Mrs. Metcalfe's Tullynore Linda and Mrs. Twist's Pennard Golden David about 1954. Mrs. Twist has done excellent work to encourage the breed, which was virtually unknown in the country before the war. A new triumph for the breed was Mr. N. Blossom's David of Corrieverne's win of the first-ever Irish Retriever Championship field trial stake in December, 1963. There is now a flourishing breed club in Ireland, running a breed show and several trials annually.

Goldens are making great strides now in New Zealand. Lately a number of English imports have been made, and there have been quite a lot of champions. The first I think was Pennard Golden Grania imported from Mrs. Thompson in 1948. Mr. and Mrs. Tucker, Canterbury, have two or three pure English lines in their Lakenheath kennel, and have had considerable success in group placings with their 1959 import N.Z. Ch. Johathan of Cleavers. They have won in obedience, and Dr. Jensen has won an A.V. trial with a Lakenheath-bred youngster.

Increasing interest is being shown in Australia, where I believe there is a good deal of American blood. Boltby, Halsham, Alresford, Beauchasse, and Golconda are among many English bloodlines imported in the last fifteen years, several becoming champions. A few years ago an English champion bitch Iris of Essendene (later an Australian Ch. and F.T. Ch.) and a Holway puppy from field trial champion parents, were imported to build up the working side. There is however great enthusiasm for show stock and showing at the present time, and I believe more than one breed club.

Other countries importing a good many from England lately are Sweden and Denmark (where to become a champion a field trial first is necessary). Goldens have also gone to the West Indies, South Africa, Finland, Germany, Belgium, France, Switzerland, Ceylon and Italy. A few years ago in a motoring magazine there was a photograph of a Russian sportsman with gun and smallish dark-colored Golden leaving a motor-cycle and sidecar for a day's shooting in the snow. So there is yet another country to find the best breed of all!

## THE GOLDEN WORLDWIDE—1970-1983

(Since Elma Stonex was ill and unable to update this chapter at this time, I have summarized some of the information. It was my pleasure not only to contact Jann Trout but to learn that Cheryle Stonex is a distant

Australian Ch. Balandra Delta Darius, CD, owned by J.R.E. and J.L. Trout and bred by Mrs. J. Bridges. This dog is a pacesetter in Australia and was BIS at the 1981 Sydney Royal over 5175 dogs under R. James of England. He has made other outstanding wins under such international authorities as Catherine Sutton of England and Anne Rogers Clark of the United States.

Balandra Chenka Chief (Ch. Karrell Beau Brockwell, CDX ex Brygolden Sharisma), owned by Mrs. B. Abbott and bred by Mrs. J. Bridges. This dog is typical of the Goldens being used in training and field work in Australia at the present time.

These 3½ month old littermates grew up and made good in Australia. The puppy at the left became Ch. Balandra Deerflight and her brother is now the celebrated Ch. Balandra Delta Darius, CD. Deerflight is owned by Alison Trout.

Australian Ch. Brygolden Madonna Mist, CD, owned, bred, trained and handled by Messrs. B.J. Westbury and K. Bright.

relative of Elma Stonex. I am also indebted both to Mrs. Trout and Mrs. Stonex for the information on Goldens in Australia and New Zealand that appears in this section. The material on Swedish dogs and dogs in Switzerland and in England came from other sources as well as my own friends in England.

Australia has many large cities and attractive wilderness areas, and the Australians are interested in animals and their welfare. In New Zealand, the countryside is beautiful and lends itself to many dog activities including show, obedience and field competition. In both countries people enjoy the outdoors and working with animals, particularly dogs. The high standard of living in these countries enables residents to enjoy the luxury of many and varying activities.)

In recent years, Golden Retrievers have increased in popularity in many countries. In Europe, the Golden has experienced the greatest gains in popularity in Switzerland and Sweden. Overall, however, the most notable increases have been in Australia and New Zealand. In both these countries, the original stock and recent arrivals have, for the most part, come from England. These dogs are brought by immigrants or sent to residents. One of the reasons for the predominance of English lines in these two countries is that the dogs can be imported without long quarantine. American dogs cannot be sent to England or other countries without six months quarantine. In both countries, the dogs compete in shows, obedience and field trials. Dog shows in Australia are somewhat more formal than in New Zealand and are often family affairs.

Among the breeders in Australia, Mrs. Jann L. Trout, of Kathy Close, Pymble, N.S.W., has had some of the most impressive successes in furthering the breed. Her Australian-born Darius, Ch. Balandra Delta Darius, CD, won Best in Show at the Sydney Royal Easter show in 1981. Sydney Royal is Australia's "Crufts," and Darius was Best in Show at two years, four months of age, over 5,175 entries. Mr. R. James from the United Kingdom had just judged Crufts, and he felt that Darius could win Best in Show in England and elsewhere. Darius had also won a gundog class when only a year old.

Among the dogs in Australia that have won obedience awards are: Australian Ch. Karrell Be Lucky, AOC, by English and New Zealand Ch. Happy Chance of Stolford (imported to New Zealand from the United Kingdom) and Ch. Karrell Beau Brockwell, CDX. Brock has the distinction of being the only Golden Retriever in Australia to hold the Jack Goldstein Gold Medal for excellence in breed and obedience. Both "passes" must be achieved at the Royal. Brock accomplished this triumph by winning the intermediate class breed section under Mrs. James E. Clark, (U.S.A.) and going on to Reserve Challenge and qualifying for open obedience.

Photographs of the winners and handlers are usually taken with the appropriate ribbon draped over the dog's back. The top winners are always photographed with the judge and owner-handler.

Stolford Sherriff, an English import, owned by Mrs. C. Stonex and Mrs. J. Agar.

Australian Ch. Karrell Harmony Girl (Ch. Wildheart Caviare, CDX, ex Ch. Balandra Deerflight), owned and bred by Mrs. J.L. Trout.

New Zealand Ch. Charterhall Anzac, QC, CDX, owned by Mr. and Mrs. C. Robinson.                    *Judy Webby*

Goldens are also becoming very popular in Australia's eastern neighbor, New Zealand. In the nation's Kennel Club Registry, Goldens have jumped from the 13th most popular breed in 1977 to 7th in 1980. The first imports arrived in the 1940's and 1950's. These Goldens were mostly from the British kennels of Roundwood, Pennard, Alresford, Beauchasse, Chelsea, and Stubblesdown, and it was from these stocks that the first champions and dual champions came. Ch. Pytcheley Annabelle, CDX (Chelsea Sandy Mac ex Mistair Rustic, CDX), bred by Mrs. D. Randall, was the leading bitch in the breed's background in New Zealand.

In the 1960's, Mrs. M. Evans (Vanrose) and Mrs. W. Reed (Penkori) came to New Zealand, bringing with them nine Golden Retrievers. Three of these, Vanrose Victoria, Vanrose Vittorio, and Vanrose Vanity Fayre, won their New Zealand titles. One year later, Mrs. Evans imported Chieftain of Greatropers, who became a New Zealand champion. This flow of new blood influenced the breed greatly and is seen in the pedigrees of the 1970's and 1980's.

Others imported dogs during the 1970's and 1980's. In the top of the North Island, Mrs. Reed and Mrs. J. Marden (Markwell) imported FiddleDee of Glennessa Penkorki from England. This dog gained his New Zealand title and sired three litters before he was accidentally killed. Some believe that his three litters improved the breed in New Zealand.

Other New Zealanders, including Mrs. Cheryle Stonex, Summertime Kennels, have imported dogs as well. Mrs. Stonex's Ch. Carousel of Yeo arrived from England in 1976 and won Best in Show at the Golden Retriever Show in 1977. Carousel also won the Bitch Challenge at the National dog show the following year.

Obedience is important in both Australia and New Zealand. Field trials are held but differ from those held in the United States and the United Kingdom as dead birds alone can be used in training.

In Switzerland and some other countries, Goldens must meet a certain standard before they can be registered with the kennel clubs in those countries. This will no doubt help maintain the breed at a high standard. The United States requires only that the sire and the dam of a litter of puppies be registered for the puppies to qualify for registration. This does not discriminate among high quality, mediocre or less attractive puppies. However, in any country, puppies with seriously faulty markings would not be registered. Owners like to be proud of the puppies that represent their breeding.

It is interesting to note that in the 1920's and 1930's in England people had their dogs checked by medical people before transferring to another owner. A short note by a member of the Royal College of Surgeons follows:

"Munro E. White,  THE LAURELS
M.R.C.V.S.  72 STATION ROAD
Telephone 73.  PETERSFIELD
March 1, 1937

New Zealand Ch. Vanrose Velvet Sparkle (Eng. Sh. Ch. & N.Z. Ch. Happy Chance of Stolford ex N.Z. Ch. Vanrose Velvet), owned by Mrs. J. Mann.

New Zealand Ch. Moorfield Ambrose, QC, owned by Mrs. M. Dobson.

*Bill Gamble*

New Zealand Ch. Vanrose Velvet at ten years of age. She is owned by Mrs. M. Evans.

New Zealand Ch. Calico of Summertime, owned by Cheryle Stonex. In New Zealand, as in most countries of the world, retrievers are trained to fur as well as feather.

I hereby certify that I have this day examined a golden retriever bitch, aged about nine months, answers to the name OF "Gillian." The property of the sons of the late Colonel the Hon. Douglas Carnegie of Fair Oak Royale West Sussex. I find the said animal free from disease and sound.

Munro E. White M.R.C.V.S.
Inspector for Petersfield Division
    Haubs County"

An example of an English Kennel Club registration of Heydown Gillian is shown.

Kennel Club (England) registration certificate for Heydown Gillian.

# 3

# The Golden Retriever in the United States and Canada

---

### The First Goldens in North America

IN THE HISTORICAL FILES of The Golden Retriever Club of America there is a photograph believed to be the earliest picture of a Golden Retriever taken in the United States. The dog looks very much like our Goldens of today. The picture was taken at the Rocking Chair Ranch in Collingsworth County, Texas; the man in the picture was the ranch owner-manager, the Hon. Archie Marjoribanks, youngest son of Lord Tweedmouth; the picture was taken between the years of 1891 and 1894.

In the early part of this century, a good deal of British money was invested in both land and industry in the United States and Canada. Travel was mainly by train in either Pullman or private car. Trips extended to several weeks or months. The travelers often combined business with pleasure, so investors and travelers of the day were able to take with them their personal or hunting dogs. As game was plentiful, and hunting was a part of the social life before television, radio, and the common use of the automobile, a favorite dog added to their pleasure.

This historic photograph shows the Hon. Archie Marjoribanks (youngest son of Lord Tweedmouth) at the Rocking Chair Ranch near Collingsworth, Texas. With him is "Lady." The picture was taken sometime during the early 1890's.

A closer view of Lady with Archie Marjoribanks. Lady was the ancestress of Lord Harcourt's first brace of yellow retrievers (thought to be Culham Brass and Culham Rossa).

In GRCA history files, there are two pictures taken in Ottawa, Canada, in 1894. One shows the Marchioness of Aberdeen (Ishbel Marjoribanks), youngest daughter of the first Lord Tweedmouth, with her children and her brother, the Hon. Archie Marjoribanks. Her husband was Governor General of Canada from 1891 to 1894. At the feet of the Marchioness, and leaning against one of her children, is a Golden Retriever with a beautiful head and ear set.

The second picture is that of the Hon. Archie Marjoribanks with Lady, ancestress of Lord Harcourt's first brace of yellow retrievers, thought to be Cullham Brass and Cullham Rossa.

Due to distances and other reasons, there was no appreciable impact or promotion of the breed during the 1910's and early 20's, although some Goldens may have been brought to the East or West Coast from Great Britain or Canada. The late Mr. William J. Harvey, Sr., owner of Twin Hill Kennels, Beverly Farms, Massachusetts, had Golden Retrievers in 1925. He continued to own them through the 1930's and 40's.

According to David Elliott, in an article written for the August, 1937 issue of *Sporting Dogs Afield,* the very first Golden Retriever kennel in North America was established by Bart Armstrong in Canada. He founded Gilnockie Kennels in 1918, at Winnipeg, and his line went on to have a strong influence on American Goldens.

Colonel S. S. Magoffin, who in 1928 founded Rockhaven Kennels in British Columbia, acquired the Gilnockie Kennels when Armstrong died. While still retaining his Rockhaven Kennels in British Columbia, he established the Gilnockie Kennels at Inglewood, Colorado, where he and his brother had homes. Both Gilnockie and Rockhaven had an important influence in the early development of the breed in the United States.

**Breed Growth in North America**

It was the interest generated by Colonel Samuel Magoffin's excellent import, Speedwell Pluto, in 1930 and the development of the Rockhaven Kennels that gave impetus to the breed in the United States and Canada. The first Golden Retriever to become a bench champion in the United States, Speedwell Pluto, was Best in Show at Puget Sound, Washington in 1933. He also achieved a Canadian championship. In 1934, Wilderness Tangerine won both a Canadian and an American championship. She was owned by Col. Magoffin.

In Canada, the Golden was recognized as a separate breed and so registered in the Canadian Kennel Club in 1927. Previously, the breed was registered with other retrievers.

The first Golden Retriever registered in the United States with the American Kennel Club was in November, 1925. The dog was Lomberdale Blondin 490685. His owner was Robert Appleton. Blondin was whelped in England, August 14, 1922. His sire was Lomberdale Duke and his dam, Brandy. Captain C. Waterhouse was the breeder.

Dr. Charles H. Large of New York imported several Golden Retrievers and started Frantell Kennels in 1931. Later, Michael Clemens acquired the stock from these kennels. He used the prefix for some time, but in the 1940's changed the name to Indian Fields. Also in the early 1930's, Peter Jackson of Santa Barbara, California, brought the English Dual Champion Marine of Woolley, and Trace of Wooley to Santa Barbara.

In Pennsylvania in 1938 Shelia Clark imported some Golden Retrievers from Noranby Kennels. Among these was Noranby Deirdre who was in whelp at the time she was shipped. Some of the correspondence of the transaction, as well as the registration follows. Mrs. Charlesworth's book is mentioned in the letter. Some of the dogs mentioned are pictured in Chapter 1.

GOLDEN RETRIEVER CLUB
The Chequers Hotel
Newbury, Berks.

26.7.38

My dear Miss Clark,
    Thank you so much for your letter. You are very flattering in your remarks about my book, it is a great pleasure to hear that it is a help to owners.
    Now about Deirdre, will you tell me quite frankly what you could give for her? I would rather come down in price for her to have a home such as you would give her, than to stick out for more and not know where she was going. She is the most awful pet, and of course is house, car and train trained. Would you like her to be mated to F.T. Champion Anningsley Stingo, before she goes, if you do take her? That would make you a real good start, unless you think that both she and Stingo being by Ch. Heydown Grip, is too close? They are otherwise *not* connected.
    Let me know as soon as you can; and I hope you will join the Club, I enclose all details in the Year Book.
    I have to apologise for this hurried note, but I am in the throes of the last two days before our Club show, so you will know what that entails in the way of work?

                    Yours very sincerely,

                    M.M. Charlesworth"

Mrs. Clark bought Deirdre as this letter suggested and registered her with the American Kennel Club, as testified by this registration form, on November 10, 1938. At this time many dogs were shipped by sea rather than by air and some of the great liners had special accommodations for shipping dogs who were traveling with their owners or en route from England to new owners in the United States. Occasionally dogs were transferred from ship to train to get to their ew owner. Shipping today is much different. Now a dog can be shipped by plane in a few hours in special kennels designed for air shipping. Veterinarian inspections are required

# KENNEL CLUB,

84 PICCADILLY,

LONDON, W.1.

## CERTIFICATE OF TRANSFER

(This Certificate should be preserved and handed over with the Dog on change of ownership.)

*24 August* 1938

*I hereby certify* that the ownership of the *Retriever (Golden)*
*Noranby Deirdre (ch) (b)*
has this day been transferred from *Mrs. W. M. Charlesworth*
to *Mrs. S. Clark*, *and that the fee of 5/- has
been paid.*

H. T. W. BOWELL, *Secretary.*

Notice of Transfer will be published in No. *702* of the " Kennel Gazette,"
which will be issued on the third Saturday in *Sept' 1938*

(Price 1/2, post free.)

---

### REGISTRATION CERTIFICATE

(AKC)

## AMERICAN KENNEL CLUB STUD BOOK

AMERICAN KENNEL CLUB
NEW YORK, N.Y.

REGISTERED November 10, 1938
ASSIGNED No A 284863

| | |
|---|---|
| NAME OF DOG | Noranby Deirdre |
| BREED | Golden Retriever  SEX Female  VOLUME 56 |
| SIRE | Heydown Grip  January ISSUE |
| DAM | Noranby Diana |
| WHELPED | January 4, 1933 |
| COLOR | Golden |
| BREEDER | Mrs. W. M. Charlesworth (England) |
| REGISTERED BY | Sheila Clark |

*Perry B. Rice*
SECRETARY
GK

SEE TRANSFER RECORD ON BACK OF THIS CERTIFICATE.

Kennel Club certificate of transfer and AKC registration certificate for Noranby Dierdre, bred in England by Mrs. W. M. Charlesworth and imported and owned by Sheila Clark.

today, just as they were then. In some states and countries, special medical information is required from one agricultural department to another.

## Prominent American Breeders and Dogs

There was a great interest in the central United States through the Stilrovin Kennels owned by Ralph Boalt, a brother-in-law of Col. Magoffin. Mr. Boalt's kennels were at Winona, Minnesota, and over a period of many years, have been a unique, outstanding producer of top field and bench winners, though the emphasis has been upon field workers. Here is Mr. Boalt's account of the Goldens, written for this book:

> During the late 1930's and early 1940's it was my pleasure and privilege to see and to know most of the early great Golden Retrievers in this country, as there was an early concentration of Goldens in the Twin Cities, Milwaukee, and St. Louis areas—the Woodend, Goldwood, Roedare, Stilrovin, Chateau d'Or, Golden Valley, Giltway, Willow Loch, Tonkahof, Beavertail, Gunnerman, Kingdale, Bushaway, Beautywood, and Whitebridge strains.
>
> All were backed by the Rockhaven blood lines, and back of Rockhaven, as sire, was Speedwell Pluto.
>
> As there was an abundance of game during those years, all the Goldens in the Middle West might be classified as tri-purpose retrievers, as all were bought as hunting dogs and were hunted hard. To improve their hunting ability, all were field trial trained and competed in field trials. To satisfy one's ego, the owners even competed on the bench, and won.
>
> The "foundation sire" of the Goldens in this country might be considered Speedwell Pluto, with a Best in Show and two Best Sporting wins to his credit; and what a magnificent animal he was—big, powerful, handsome, and courageous. Fortunately, he did reproduce himself in his offspring.
>
> Pluto was hunted hard, and I watched him retrieve by the hour off of twenty- and thirty-foot-high rocks into the icy waters of Vancouver Bay. He was never run in field trials, as anything alive was crunched by him so that it never would have to be shot again.
>
> Nero of Roedare and Rip, both Gilnockie Challenge Cup winners, began placing in licensed trials in the late 1930's—trials that had been dominated by the Labradors and Chesapeakes up to then.
>
> Nero was a good-looking, big-mouthed, leggy Golden that had been hunted hard from the Pas to Southwestern Minnesota and into Arkansas. That was the reason that Nero was the only real contender at that 1942 National trial at Madison, Wisconsin. In ten-degree-below-zero weather, he took off from the ice into freezing water courageously, willingly, and happily. Nero was shown successfully and qualified for a CD in obedience.
>
> As regards Rip, there was a dog—a real field trial contender and a great showman. He looked somewhat like a "camel"—big, long-legged, with a big white blaze on his forehead. He could sure pick up and put down those long legs so that he could outrun the best, and his marking ability was uncanny, but he would look for help when needed and would handle perfectly—a real champion.

Gilnockie Coquette, owned by Ralph Boalt, was the dam of several dual champions and an influential producer in the breed.

Dual Ch. Stilrovin Nitro Express, a member of the Golden
Retriever Field Dog Hall of Fame.

```
                              Ch. Speedwell Pluto
                    Ch. Rockhaven Rory
                              Can. Ch. Rockhaven Amber
          Sire: Stilrovin Bullet***
                              Cecil's Pride
                    Patience of Yelme
                              Ch. Biltonpru
DUAL CH. STILROVIN NITRO EXPRESS
                              Beppo of Yelme
                    Eng. & Am. Ch. Bingo of Yelme***
                              Alveley Biddy
          Dam: Gilnockie Coquette
                              Ch. Speedwell Pluto
                    Can. Ch. Rockhaven Russet
                              Eng. Ch. Saffron Chipmonk
```

FC Stilrovin Katherine, one of the outstanding dams of the breed.

```
                    Am. & Can. Ch. Speedwell Pluto
            Ch. Rockhaven Rory
                    Can. Ch. Rockhaven Amber
    Sire: Stilrovin Bullet***
                    Cecil's Pride
            Patience of Yelme
                    Eng. Ch. Biltonpru
FC STILROVIN KATHERINE
                    Beppo of Yelme
            Eng. & Am. Ch. Bingo of Yelme***
                    Alveley Biddy
    Dam: Gilnockie Coquette
                    Am. & Can. Ch. Speedwell Pluto
            Can. Ch. Rockhaven Russett
                    Saffron Chipmonk
```

Champion Toby of Willow Loch, with a Best in Show and a Best Sporting win, was a hard-headed, hard-mouthed, and hard-driving Golden that retrieved more than his share of game on his owner's farms in southwestern Minnesota and on famous Heron Lake.

Unbeknownst to the judges, Toby ran and placed in field trials with a rubber band under his tongue and around his lower jaw. In some way, when he crunched the retrieve, he bit his tongue. Never could he be trusted to run without the rubber band.

The first National Field Trial champion was King Midas of Woodend. King Midas won the champitnship in 1941, but it was at the Midwest trial that year where he proved what a small dog with a courageous heart could do when he went through those ten-foot-high Lake Michigan breakers for a water retrieve, after the best of the Labradors and Chesapeakes had quit.

Because she was unique, Gilnockie Coquette should probably qualify for the Golden Hall of Fame, as it was obvious she could never win on the bench. During the heyday of the pheasants in South Dakota, she showed no interest in hunting, and as regards field trials—that was for the birds.

Yet, by three different sires, Coquette produced two dual champions, two field champions, and four bench show champions. Her progeny produced nineteen bench champions, one CDX, and four CD's, including Czar of Wildwood, with six Bests in Show, and Golden Knoll's Shur Shot, CD, with 14 Bests in Show. The celebrated Golden Knoll's King Alphonzo, 24 times a Best in Show winner, was a great-grandson of Coquette.

Probably the best known of Coquette's get was that famous trio—Dual Ch. Stilrovin Nitro Express, FC Stilrovin Super Speed, and FC Stilrovin Katherine—all out of the same litter—and to date this has not been duplicated by any retriever bitch.

Nitro Express was a big, handsome animal who partially won his bench championship the hard way, as Winners Dog at the 1945 Specialty. He was the gallery's delight at field trials, as it was difficult to keep him from breaking and the gallery was there to watch the fun. He was hunted hard for ducks in the Mississippi bottoms and Heron Lake. In South Dakota, he was hunted ahead of the guns like a Spaniel, and that was when pheasants were there by the thousands.

At field trials, Super Speed literally flew, and he had style that few trial dogs could equal. At the 1943 National Championship trial, Speed was runner-up, a distinction for Speed only, and he was hunted during the winter months on his owner's southern plantation.

After Derby year, Katherine ran mostly in the East, where she did well.

All three were amateur trained—Nitro by a teenage high school girl, from a pup until after he won the *Country Life* Trophy against the best of the professionals; Speed by a garage mechanic—his first dog; and Katherine by a printer—his first trial dog.

Then there were the Golden Valley Goldens, with Pirate, the youngest, at two and one-half, ever to qualify for the National Championship trial.

Goldwood, too, had an enviable record on the bench and in the field. Ch. Goldwood Pluto was a flashy, stylish field trial dog, and FC Goldwood Tuck would do anything asked of him in the field—willingly and gladly.

58

FC Shelter Cove Beauty, owned by Dr. L. M. Evans. *Percy T. Jones.*

```
                        Eng. Ch. Cubbington Diver
            Eng. Ch. Marine of Woolley
                        Balcombe Pride
     Sire: Rockhaven Ben Bolt
                        Am. & Can. Ch. Speedwell Pluto
            Rockhaven Lassie
                        Am. & Can. Ch. Wilderness Tangerine
NATIONAL FC SHELTER COVE BEAUTY
                        Ch. Rockhaven Rory
            Ch. Toby of Willow Loch***
                        Rusty Heger
     Dam: Happy of Willow Loch
                        Stilrovin Terrence
            Belle of Willow Lake
                        Rusty Heger
```

Goldwood Toby, UD (Ch. Toby of Willow Loch ex Goldwood Ditt), owned by Mrs. Mark D. Elliott. Toby is the first Golden Retriever to hold the utility degree in obedience.

Dual Ch. Tonkahof Esther Belle, owned by Kingswere Kennels, photographed at the National Retriever Trials, Herrin, Illinois, December 1946.

Out of this bench-field trial combination came the first of the famous obedience Goldens—Goldwood Michael, CDX and Goldwood Toby, CDX.

Tonkahof Kennels contributed greatly to the breed on the bench and in the field, with Dual Ch. Tonkahof Esther Belle and Ch. Tonkahof Bang, a Best in Show winner, to mention just two.

Whitebridge contributed Rip, as already mentioned, and FC Whitebridge Wally, a consistent trial dog.

Sheltercove Beauty, sired by a Rockhaven dog, as was King Midas and a *Country Life* winner, was the second Golden to win the National Championship trial. Beauty was a willing worker and could not do enough for her handler. At all times she wanted to please.

Any names of those early greats that have been overlooked, forgotten, or not mentioned are engraved for all posterity on the Challenge Trophies of the Golden Retriever Club of America.

The early bench show winners of the Rockhaven Speedwell Pluto Challenge Cup almost all had placed in trials or were hunted hard. The Gilnockie Challenge Cup winners, with the exception of Rip, had been shown successfully on the bench. The same is true of the Rip Trophy winners. I am sure, with that Goldwood bench-field trial background, those two early obedience Goldens—Michael, CDX and Toby, CDX—could have qualified for something else with other owners.

As regards the early members of the Golden Retriever Club, all were vitally interested in improving the breed, whether on the bench or at field trials, as all this was incidental to owning the finest non-slip retrievers in a country that abounded with game.

Another kennel of this period was Carlton Grassle's Pirates Den Kennels in Rochester, Minnesota. The star of this kennel was FC Pirate of Golden Valley. In North Dakota, Mr. and Mrs. C. H. Overvold used the prefix Krystolida; the star of this kennel was FC Royal Peter Golden Boy. Kingswere Kennels, at Winona, Minn., owned Dual Ch. Tonkahof Esther Belle and Dual Ch. Stilrovin Rip's Pride. Gunnerman Kennels, earlier known as Beavertail Kennels, and owned by Mr. and Mrs. Ben L. Boalt, Random Lake, Wisconsin was the home of the outstanding field worker, Dual Ch. Stilrovin Nitro Express. This dog was featured in *Life* magazine, December 30, 1946. Other great kennels in the Midwest were Golden Valley Kennels owned by Richard Ryan of Rochester, Minnesota, and F. W. Noonan of Minneapolis. The stars of this kennel were three field champions— Golden Beauty of Roedare, Patricia of Roedare, and Pirate of Golden Valley. From these bloodlines came several bench champions— Ch. Highland Chief and Dual Ch. Tonkahof Esther Belle.

In 1933, Mr. and Mrs. Henry B. Christian established Goldwood Kennels at Dellwood, White Bear Lake, Minnesota. From their kennels came Ch. Goldwood Pluto, FC Goldwood Tuck, Ch. Goldwood Sonia, and two outstanding stars in obedience—Goldwood Michael and Goldwood Toby. Other kennels of this period were Tonkahof Kennels, owned by Henry Norton of Minneapolis. Mr. Norton contributed to the

From Charles Morgan's book on retrievers, page 7, he says:

"In 1950 I won the National Field Trial with FC Beautywood's Tamarack owned by Dr. L. M. Evans." Dr. Evans is possibly the only individual to breed and own and run a National Open All-Age winner.

Dual Ch. Stilrovin Rip's Pride, owned by Kingswere Kennels.

American Kennel Gazette in the late 1940's and 50's. Tuckluck Kennels of Long Lake, Minnesota, owned by George D. Alt and F. Robert Noonan, were devoted exclusively to the training of retrievers for field trial competition.

Dr. L. M. Evans of Sauk Rapids, Minnesota, owned two national field trial winners. One was FC Shelter Cove Beauty. Beauty was the 1944 national champion; in 1943 she was a national finalist; and in 1942 she was the national derby champion—an excellent record for a four-year old. FC Beautywood Tamarack was also a national winner. Bred by his owner, Dr. Evans at Beautywood, he won a National Championship stake. Dr. Evans believes that this is the only Golden Retriever to make this record for a kennel. Both dogs were trained and handled by the late great Charles Morgan.

On the East Coast, Taramar Kennels imported some excellent stock and furthered the breed on the bench, although theirs were good working dogs as well. Taramar was owned by the late Mr. Theodore A. and Mrs. Rehm.

Another kennel on the East Coast still active today is Featherquest, owned by Dr. and Mrs. Mark D. Elliott of River Road Farm, Carlisle, Massachusetts. Mrs. Elliott has done much research on Goldens and is especially interested in gait and soundness. She collaborated with AKC in producing the 1974 landmark film *Gait: Observing Dogs in Motion,* and wrote the classic gait studies *Dogsteps* (1973) and *The New Dogsteps* (1983), both published by Howell Book House.

Ch. Czar of Wildwood was owned by Eric S. Johnson of Woodland Hills, California, and twice became Best in Show at Golden Gate in San Francisco. The first year, he was the only Golden in the show. He skipped a year and returned to win the BIS honors again. Among other dogs in the Wildwood kennels was Ch. Winnie of Wildwood, a bitch which had been acquired from the Squawkie Hill Kennels of Mt. Morris, New York. Mr. and Mrs. D. Eugene Parks owned these kennels. Mrs. Parks both imported and bred Goldens. Among the stars of Squawkie Hill were Ch. Early Autumn Sunshine, Ch. Princess of Many Trails, Etta Zoloto, an outstanding dam, Ch. Culzean Flower, and Dual Champion Squawkie Hill Dapper Dexter.

Golden Knolls Kennels of Waterloo, Iowa, later Mountain Home, Idaho, owned by Mr. and Mrs. Russell Peterson, produced some fine bench champions and show winners—the star being Ch. Golden Knoll's Shur Shot, a large, but sound dog. An excellent producing matron of this kennel was Ch. DesLacs Goldie, CD, which Mrs. Peterson had obtained from Bartlett Foster who owned the DesLacs Kennels at Winona, Minnesota. Int. Ch. DesLacs Lassie was the first bitch to win a Best in Show, and was the dam of a litter of nine. Six bitches of this litter became champions in different parts of the United States. The DesLacs dogs were all working dogs.

Ch. Chee-Chee of Sprucewood, owned by Mrs. M. C. Zwang, was in every way a breed immortal. Among her wins are three all-breed Bests in Show and two National Specialty Bests of Breed. She was the dam of 16 champions including three Specialty winners and two all-breed Best in Show dogs. *Frasie Studio.*

Ch. Tonkahof Bang***
Ch. Highland Royal Flush
Golden Treasure
*Sire:* Highland March Echo
Ch. Beavertail Butch
Lanenberg's Princess Pat
Chee-Chee
**AM. & CAN. CH. CHEE-CHEE OF SPRUCEWOOD**
Ch. Beavertail Butch
Butch's Buff
Kingdale's Sunshine
*Dam:* Tomboy Toby of Sprucewood
Beautywood's Buckshot
Co-Co of Hillaire
Cheyenne of Vox Pop

Breeding was done by Bud and Maurine Zwang

Stilrovin Bullet
Ch. Stilrovin Shur Shot
Gilnockie Coquette
*Sire:* Ch. Golden Knoll's Shur Shot
Tonkahof Admiral
Kingdale's Toast
Amber Lass
**CH. GOLDEN KNOLL'S KING ALPHONZO**
Donald of Great Cove
Sir Gay Roxie
Ch. Early Autumn Sunsh
*Dam:* Sunnyshine of Sans Souci
Rick Rooney of Roo Roi
Sally of Sans Souci
Ch. Princess of Many Tra

The pedigrees of King Alphonzo and Chee-Chee produced a record number of 16 champions in two litters: from a litter of 8—7 champions, from a litter of 6—5 champions.

In the 1940's and early 50's Oakcreek Kennels in Hillsboro, Oregon, produced some outstanding field trial dogs. One of these was Can. National Field Champion, FC-AFC Oakcreek's Van Cleve, owned first and trained by Charles Bunker of Canada, then by Alfred Schmidt of Portland, Oregon. Van Cleve was a very happy working dog and made many friends for the breed because of his accurate and joyful work. Van had 125 field points (78½—Open, 46½ Amateur) and had a first placement in the Open Stake at 10 years of age. Another dog with the Oakcreek prefix which contributed to the breed as a fine field performer was FC-AFC Oakcreek's Sir Dorchester, owned and run by James Stilwell of Klamath Falls, Oregon. Sir Dorchester (Ty) sired FC-AFC Oakcreek's Fremont, FC-AFC Red Ruff, FC-AFC Tyson Rowdy, and FC-AFC Rocky Mack. Red Ruff and Fremont were not bred to any extent, but did sire some good working dogs.

Mr. and Mrs. M. C. Zwang produced a bitch puppy which they named Chee-Chee of Sprucewood, who became the foundation for the Sprucewood Kennels. Chee-Chee won several Bests in Show and became both a Canadian and American bench champion. She was bred but twice, to Ch. Golden Knoll's King Alphonzo. In the first litter of twelve puppies, nine became champions. In the second litter, though smaller, there were seven bench champions, totalling sixteen in the two litters. Chee-Chee was prepotent in transferring her qualities to her offspring, both to her own puppies and her grandchildren. The Sprucewood Kennels never at any one time contained a large number of dogs, but quality, care, and planning were ever in the minds of the owners. The kennels have not been active since the death of Mr. Zwang. Mrs. Zwang has since had a Golden from time to time.

Mrs. George H. Flinn, Jr., of Greenwich, Connecticut, owns the Tigathoe Kennels. She has exhibited her Goldens in the show ring successfully, but her interest is primarily in field dogs. She has bred her own, bought selected stock, and has ever had a most constructive breeding program.

Mrs. Flinn owned and trained seven field champions, including one Labrador. She has bred eight field champions including one dual champion, Dual Ch.-AFC Tigathoe's Funky Farquar.

The dogs she has owned and trained include:
FC-AFC, Can. Dual Ch. Rockhaven Raynard of Fo-Go-Ta
AFC Golden Star of Oakridge
AFC Sunshine Cake
FC-AFC, Can. FC Stilrovin Tuppee Tee
FC-AFC, Can. FC Bonnie Brooks Elmer
FC-AFC Chips of Sands
FC-AFC Mainliner Mike II (Labrador Retriever).
The dogs Mrs. Flinn has bred includes:
Dual Ch., AFC Tigathoe's Funky Farquar

Mrs. George H. Flinn, Jr., veteran Golden field trial enthusiast with her FC-AFC and Canadian FC Bonnie Brooks Elmer. "Torch" Flinn has made a long, distinguished record as an owner, breeder, trainer and amateur handler of many of America's top field trial Goldens. "Elmer," in addition to achieving field trial success on his own, has sired one Dual Ch.-AFC, three FC-AFCs, one AFC and one Canadian FC-AFC.

FC-AFC Tigathoe's Magic Marker (all-time High-point Golden bitch)

FC-AFC Tigathoe's Tonga

FC-AFC Tigathoe's Kiowa II

AFC Tigathoe's Choptank Child

Can. FC Tigathoe's Pekoe Tea

Can. FC Tigathoe's Pious Pete

FC-AFC Tigathoe's Mainliner Mariah (for several years all-time high-point Labrador bitch).

Mrs. Flinn continues actively and is training and running two Golden Retrievers at this writing. These are Cranwood's Chill Factor, which was the top Derby Dog in 1982. She co-owns this dog with Ben Lewis, and co-owns another, Handjem's Quicksand, with the breeder, Henry Lardy. Quicksand had 30 Derby points in 1980, a qualifying first in 1981 and has Open and Amateur points. These two dogs continued to run well in 1983. More recently, Mrs. Flinn was occasionally working with Michael Lardy, a young professional trainer.

The highest title to which Golden owners aspire for their dogs is that of a dual champion. This assumes a bench championship and a field trial championship. Such titles would be won in competition with other Goldens for the bench championship and competition with all breeds of retrievers for the field trial championship. The runner-up to these titles would be a combination of bench championship, amateur field championship, and obedience titles.

Some owners begin with an activity, such as obedience, then go on to show or field. There is no set competitive sequence. The owner's particular interests and the available facilities determine the activity at the time. Interested, dedicated owners with talented dogs, who enjoy working in all three areas, also enjoy their Goldens as personal companions.

Susan Brown-Leger gave a Golden to her husband for Christmas a few years ago. He named the dog Friday, though its registered name became Ch. Toryglen Idling Jerome, UD***. Susan and Ed Brown-Leger claim that Friday learned quickly and was almost always a step ahead. In fact, he raised their goals for training. Initially, Ed worked his Golden only in obedience and then was encouraged to show him, where Friday quickly finished his championship. The obedience training continued and Ed also used Friday as his hunting dog.

They saw their first field trial when Friday was just under two years old. This seemed to be Friday's first love. He received a JAM in his first licensed trial. There were few field trial people in their area. Friday actually began competing in all-age stakes and eventually became a qualified all-age dog, entitled to add the Golden Retriever Club's three stars (***) to his Ch. and UD titles.

Some bitches had acquired similar titles before. These were Ch. and AFC Riverview's Chickasaw Thistle, UDT, and Ch. Lady Butterscotch, UDT***.

Then there is Ch. Cimaron's Dusty Dawn, UD, TDX*** (TDX, March, 1983). Tara, as she is called, was first owned by Paul Owens of Cleveland, Ohio and won one High in Trial award from the Novice class. She then became Connie Drobac's Golden, who continued to train her while in high school. Tara has her Canadian CD and CDX titles, and is also the winner of a *Dog World* award. Connie did have some help in showing this bitch to her champimnship, as Jerome Hand piloted her in the show ring. Connie, however, did all of the training.

The UD, TD and TDX are difficult titles to achieve. As mentioned before, it takes a talented dog, time and dedication from the owner and money for travel expenses and entry fees.

There have been several dual champion Golden Retrievers. Two of them, bred by Ralph Boalt, were the offspring of Gilnockie Coquette: Dual Ch. Stilrovin Nitro Express and Dual Ch. Stilrovin Rip's Pride. Nitro Express, or Nite as he was called, won the *Country Life* Trophy in 1941 and was a national championship trial contender from 1942 through 1947. He accumulated a total of 54 field championship points, won the Field Trial Champion Rip Trophy in 1942, and the Kingswere Challenge Cup in 1947. Dual Ch. Stilrovin's Rip's Pride was a national champion trial contender in 1945, qualified for the national open in 1945, and was the Kingswere Challenge Cup winner in 1946.

Dual Ch. Esther Belle was bred by Tonkahof Kennels which were owned by Henry Norton of Minneapolis, Minnesota. Both Esther Belle and Ch. Tonkahof Bang were two of several outstanding Goldens bred or owned by Mr. Norton.

Dual Ch. Squawkie Hill Dapper Dexter was bred by Squawkie Hill Kennels owned by Mrs. Jeanne Parks. Deck was bought, trained, and run in trials by Dr. Gerald Howe, who enjoyed his first retriever as a personal companion and in field and bench competition.

Dual Champion Craigmar Dustrack was bred at the Craigmar Kennels, owned by Dr. O. Charles Olson. Dr. Forrest Flashman, who owned and campaigned Dustrack, worked closely with Dr. Olson in breeding programs. Dustrack had among his ancestors National FC Beautywood Tamarack. Dustrack was the first to win the Western region's William Lester Award for success in both field and show in the same calendar year. Dustrack also won the Kingswere Challenge Cup. Later, Ch. Craigmar Tule Topper, bred and owned by Dr. Flashman, received the William Lester Award. Dr. Flashman could have retired this award which his dogs had won, but preferred to rededicate it. The award was later won by Tish the II, owned by the Humphreys, and AFC Ronakers Novato Cain owned by Desmond Mactavish. Bow, as Novato Cain was called, won the award in 1970.

Dual Ch. Cresta Gold Rip was field-trained and handled by Wayne Mahan of Laurel, Montana. Friends of Mr. Mahan, Mr. and Mrs. James

Ch. Cimaron's Dusty Dawn, UD, TDX*** (Ch. Laurell's Especial Jason, UDT, ex Ch. Duckdown's Voodoo Charm, UD), shown here with her owner-handler, trainer Connie Drobac.

Dual Ch. Craigmar's Dustrack, shown with his owner, Dr. Forrest Flashman. Dustrack was a two-time winner of the Bill Lester Memorial Award. *Lewis Roberts*

The National Field Champion of 1951 Ready Always of Marianhill, owned by Mr. Mahlon B. Wallace, was a famous field trial winner with one of the most outstanding records in the breed. *Evelyn M. Shafer*

```
                          Ch. Rockhaven Rory
              Ch. Goldwood Pluto***
                          Ch. Sprite of Aldgrove**
          Sire: Bushaway Rocket
                          Rockhaven Tuck**
              FC Banty of Woodend
                          Rockhaven Judy**
NATIONAL FC READY ALWAYS OF MARIANHILL
                          Rockhaven Tuck**
              Nippletop of Woodend
                          Rockhaven Judy**
          Dam: Lady Hance
                          Rockhaven Ben Bolt***
              Victoria of Willow Loch
                          Belle of Willow Lake
```

70

Humphrey of Soquel, California, saw Cresta Gold Rip and liked him. As there were few major show possibilities in Montana at that time, the Humphreys offered to take Rip to California, where he finished his bench championship in five shows. Cresta Gold Rip won the Western region William Lester Dual Award and the GRCA Kingswere Challenge Cup. He was a delightful personal dog. Cresta Gold Rip's award followed that of Dustrack. The Humphreys had Goldens of their own breeding as well as imports at their Golden Anno Nuevo Kennels. These kennels are now no longer active.

While the dual championship (a combination of bench champion and field trial champion) is considered the highest achievement, the combination of amateur field, bench, and obedience titles is difficult to achieve, and indicates a fine dog and an interested owner. Two examples are Lorelei's Golden Rockbottom and Riverview's Chickasaw Thistle.

Ch. and AFC Lorelei's Golden Rockbottom, UD, bred by Lorelei Hills Kennels and owned by Reinhard Bischoff, was prominent in the 1950's. He was named among the 10 best retrievers in an issue of *Sports Afield* in 1955. The name, Lorelei, was important in Goldens for more than 25 years. Mr. Bischoff, a distinguished architect, continued to show in the 1960's. Lorelei is no longer active in the United States.

James and Sally Venerable owned and trained Ch., AFC Riverview's Chickasaw Thistle, UDT. Thistle earned her tracking title in 1969 and placed in a field trial the same weekend. Though Riverview Goldens and their descendants continue to be active in the field, the kennels are no longer active due to a change in family responsibilities.

Earlier, C. A. Frank used the prefix Duckerbird for some outstanding obedience dogs. Ch. Duckerbird Atomic, UD, had in his background National FC Midas of Woodend, English and Am. Ch. Bingo of Yelme, Am.-Can. Ch. Speedwell Pluto, and Gilnockie Coquette. There were several Atomics, some of which were said to have been able at nine months to retrieve ducks among 50 decoys on Lake Erie.

In Rockwood, Michigan, Gayhaven Kennels, owned by Betty and Sam Gay, have had a constructive breeding program for some time. Mrs. Gay was for several years the editor of *Golden Retriever News* and the GRCA yearbooks.

Casa Audlon Kennels, owned by Mr. and Mrs. M. B. Wallace, Jr., of Clayton, Missouri, was the home of FC Whitebridge Wally. Later, the Wallaces owned the 1952 National Field Trial winner, Am.-Can. FC Ready Always of Marianhill, one of the high point retrievers in history and an outstanding working dog whose bloodlines have contributed to some of the later field trial dogs. He won the Field Champion Rip Trophy twice, in 1950 and in 1952. Mr. Paul Bakewell III, had donated this trophy in memory of his great winner, FC Rip.

Valerie Fisher, now Valerie Fisher Walker, trained her FC-AFC Misty's Sungold Lad through the CDX when she was in high school. At the same time she became interested in field competition and field trials. At sixteen she ran the dog in a National stake. She followed this with continued interest in field work and qualified the dog for six National Open stakes, ran in three, and was a finalist in one. Lad also qualified for eight National Amateurs and was a finalist in three. He qualified for four Canadian Nationals but did not run. Lad was the first Golden to complete a double header. He completed two: one at the Samish field trial, in March 1969, and at Spokane in September 1969. Lad's total points were 88½ Open points, 124 Amateur points, with a total 212½. This is a distinguished record for any dog and any owner. He was also a beloved personal companion.

For those not familiar with field trials, the term "double-header" means a first place win in the Amateur All-Age stake, and a first place win in the Open All-Age stake on the same weekend. This would mean a first place win on two different days of a three-day trial.

Every field trialer hopes to win a double header. A few have done so:

| *Double Headers and Where They Won* | *Total Overall Points* |
|---|---|
| FC-AFC Misty's Sungold Lad, CDX<br>  Samish — March 1969<br>  Spokane — September 1969 | Open: 88½<br>Amateur: 124 |
| Dual Ch. Clickety Click<br>  Helena — September 1970 | Open: 20½<br>Amateur: 11¼ |
| AFC Wild Fire of Riverview CDX***<br>  Buckeye — April 1982 | Open: 9<br>Amateur: 25 |
| FC-AFC Tigathoe's Magic Marker<br>  Golden Retriever Specialty — October 1975.<br>  (Does not count because it was a Specialty show.) | Open: 39<br>Amateur: 78 |

FC-AFC Nicholas of Logan's End, who was owned by the late Hugh Adams of California and Arizona, had 123½ amateur points and 50 Open, totalling 173½ points. There were other field trial winners—FC-AFC Oakcreek's Fremond, FC-AFC Oakcreek's Red Ruff and FC-AFC Brandy Snifter.

Mrs. F. H. Strawbridge, Jr. of Wynnewood, Pennsylvania, owned the Ballytore Kennels. Many of her dogs had distinguished records in obedience; some of them used the Sun Dance prefix.

In the early 1960's Am., Can., Mex., Ber. Ch. Beckwith's Cooper Coin became one of the outstanding bench winners. Mr. and Mrs. R. E. Beckwith own the Beckwith Kennels, then in Duluth, Minnesota, and now located in Snohomish, Washington.

FC-AFC Misty's Sungold Lad, CDX, owned by Valerie Fisher Walker with whom he is shown, was the oldest finalist in the 1974 National Amateur Stake. Lad had the highest number of combined points of any Golden Retriever; 212½, 88½ of which were Open points. He qualified for seven straight National Opens and eight straight National Amateurs, plus four Canadian Nationals. This dog was the first Golden to win a double header, and he won two in 1969. He was handled either by Valerie, her father, or her husband; all amateurs.

FC Commanche Cayenne (Rick of Sun-N-Aire ex Evergold Amber), owned by Sheldon Coleman and handled by D. L. Walters.

Ch. Amberac's Asterling Aruba (Ch. Gold Coast Here Comes The Sun, CD, ex Ch. Sunhaven's Amberac's Aruba), owned by Mary Wuestenberg and bred by E. Manke. A BIS winner, she is the dam of the multiple BIS bitch Ch. Asterling's Tahiti Sweetie. This is believed to be the only BIS mother and daughter in breed history.

Am. Can. Ch. Golden Pine's Courvoisier, Am. Can. CDX, Am. Can. WC, Am. WCX (Ch. Misty Morn's Sunset, CD, TD, WC, ex Ch. Golden Pine's Punkin Pi, CD), owned by Nancy and Dean Belsaas. A popular West Coast winner, "Cognac" is also the sire of a number of champions and obedience title holders. *Richard Oshiro*

## Contributions of the Small Breeder

Some excellent Goldens have been produced by small and occasional breeders. These people often take a great deal of time, and do much research as to what they want, and often obtain very fine results in their dogs for show, obedience, or field. Their interests are not primarily in making money but in obtaining the dogs they want for themselves or friends and in furthering the breed.

In the 1970's and 80's many new kennels have contributed to the breed. Terry and Julie Hubbs' Chaparral Kennels is a small, select California establishment. The Ronakers Kennels, also located in California, has won both in the show ring and obedience trials. It has bred one dual champion and some excellent field dogs. In the State of Washington, John and Roberta Anderson have Bonnie Island Kennels. Their Goldens compete in conformation, have many obedience titles and some working certificates.

Nancy and Dean Belsaas, of California, use the prefix Golden Pines, granted them by a long-time, successful East Coast breeder—Mary Luise Seamans. Nancy and Dean encourage their puppy buyers to work with their dogs in conformation, obedience and field competition.

In the Midwest, Asterling Golden Retrievers, owned by Mary Wuestenberg, has produced two Best in Show winners—mother and daughter in 1983. This may be the first time in history a mother and daughter have each won a BIS. Silvia Donahey is co-owner of Ch. Asterling's Tahiti Sweetie. Another Midwestern kennel that has had considerable success is Cherrie Berger's Meadowpond Kennel. Several of the Meadowpond dogs have done outstanding work in obedience as well as in conformation. Betty Drobac is another accomplished owner and breeder; her Goldens have achieved success in many activities. Jackie and Joseph Mertens with their Topbrass prefix and Phil Uehling with his talented field-bred dogs also loom large in the Midwest.

On the East Coast there are many successful small and large kennels. Two names to review are Marjorie Trowbridge in Connecticut and E. J. Brown-Leger of Wood's Hole, Massachusetts.

Mrs. Mark Elliott, mentioned earlier, has the well-known and long successful Featherquest Kennels in Massachusetts. She breeds selectively and her dogs always reflect high quality. The Pepperhill Kennels of New York, owned by Jeff and Barbara Pepper, have enjoyed success in the show ring. The Seneca Kennels, owned by John and Sandy Kelly, in Germantown, Maryland, have bred a Best in Show winner.

Carolee Kennels, owned by Mrs. Shirley Goodman of Don Mills, Ontario, Canada, have bred one dual champion, as well as a number of top show dogs.

The prefix, a part of the dog's name, tells which kennel the dog or bitch came from. It would be impossible to list all kennels located throughout the United States and Canada. Some breed an all-around Golden Retriever;

some favor show, field or obedience depending on the preferences of the owner(s).

The size of a kennel or the number of breedings per year do not necessarily mean this is where you'll find your special dog. Quality and mediocrity may be found in many places. The dedicated small breeder has contributed much, and is quite in contrast to the breeder who is interested only in pin money or thinking of puppies as just fun—sometimes known as a "backyard breeder."

For those wishing to research further prospective puppies or breeders, contact the GRCA and review information in the *GRCA News*.

### Goldens in Early Field Trials

The early promotion of the Golden in field trials and the success of the dogs had much to do with their advancement and increasing popularity. In the August, 1937 issue of *The Sportsman,* David D. Elliott had an article on the Minnesota Field Trial Club. He wrote,

> On looking over the program, I was very much surprised to find such a large entry of Golden Retrievers, for this is a breed we never see at our Eastern trials, and although by no means a new breed, they are comparatively unknown in this country. In England they have been a recognized breed almost, if not equally, as long as the Labrador.

He goes on to discuss the trial. In the same issue, a photograph shows H. R. Ward with Rockhaven Tuck which took second in the Open All-Age and the Novice stakes at the Minnesota Association's trial. Mr. Ward owned the Woodend Kennels. Also pictured is Sprite of Aldgrove retrieving to his owner, H. B. Christian, to win third in the Novice stake at Mound, Minnesota, and Richard Ryan and his Novice stake winner, Nero of Roedare, also at Mound. Women had a place in the trials too. A picture in the same issue shows Mrs. Gordon P. Kelly with Czar of Nicholas, third in the Puppy stake in the Midwest trial at Barrington, Illinois.

Reported in *The Milwaukee Journal* of May 19, 1940, is a story of The Golden Retriever Club of America which held its first licensed trials near the Ozaukee Country Club. Among the dogs was Rockhaven Ben Bolt. He was owned by Ralph G. Boalt of Winona. On Friday, October 23, 1942, *The Milwaukee Sentinel* showed the picture of Stilrovin Nitro Express who won the Open All-Age stake in Omaha, Nebraska. The description states that Stilrovin Nitro Express, a big rangy Golden Retriever, became the first dog to win top honors in his first year of open competition, and also had the outstanding distinction of bringing Wisconsin its first field trial championship. Nite, a high-scoring derby dog, was owned by Ben Boalt of Milwaukee, and was handled by Roy Wallace, professional trainer.

In the September 1941 issue of *Point and Fetch,* a magazine then published in interest of field trial dogs, conservation and better hunting, Ben L. Boalt wrote an article entitled "Rip—in Memory." He tells the story

FC Stilrovin Super Speed, 1945 Field Dog Hall of Fame. This dog, owned by Paul Bakewell, was a standout in the early days of the breed in America and one of the greatest field dogs of all time.

of how Goldens began to appear in retriever trials in the Middle West and how much promise they showed. Rip was trained and handled by his owner, Paul Bakewell III, of St. Louis. The article said, in part:

Rip, while well-bred as a specimen, was not what the Golden fancier was looking for, but who could tell what was in that young head of his? Early in his running, Paul seemed to know—at least he campaigned him with the utmost confidence of his future success . . . This continued through the spring of 1939. It was a favorite alibi with all except Paul and Rip that because of the newness of the breed, the judges wouldn't put him up. That fall, Paul and Rip were determined. Paul, an amateur handler, and Rip, a Golden, competed with the best professionals . . .

At the Wisconsin trial, Paul and Rip were back for the water against one of the top handlers and two of the best black Labradors from the East. A shot well out on the left, and a blind retrieve well out on the right at the end of a peninsula. Each of the professionals had two dogs back, handling to perfection . . . I stood with Bakewell as the four blacks were handled, either diagonally through the water to the blind bird, or around the back, far in back. The work of the handlers with each of the four dogs was spectacular, and having given the judges the two obvious methods of recovering perfectly, it seemed that Rip could show little. Bakewell was of the same opinion, unless? . . . Paul was sure of Rip, so he gave him a straight line out across the pond. To the gallery, Rip was out for a swim and Bakewell couldn't show where the blind duck had been placed. Rip never faltered, swimming strong until a toot from the whistle, with a look around and a perfectly-timed signal, Rip turned sharp, and in a straight line went directly to the end of the point and the bird. Rip's wins were all the hard way.

Rip continued to place in many of the trials . . . On the day Rip won his first Open, Mr. Bakewell had forgotten his whistle, but the judge made the statement that this was the most natural retriever he had ever seen run . . . Rip was the only retriever to win the *Field & Stream* trophy twice (as of 1941) and the only amateur-trained one ever to win it. There was a very complete understanding between Rip and his owner, Paul Bakewell. It seemed that Rip understood his master first and sensed what was expected of him.

Mr. Bakewell also owned the outstanding FC Stilrovin Super Speed.

In 1945, the dogs seemed to know that the war was over, and the Golden Retriever Club of America held its Specialty at Winona, Minnesota. *The Minneapolis Sunday Tribune* in 1945 had a picture of the Best in Show winner, Ch. Highland Chief, with Henry W. Norton of Maplewoods, Minnesota. Many other Golden Retriever fanciers from other states were also at that specialty.

National Specialty shows are held each year, usually in September. They alternate in location between the Eastern, Central and Western United States, and include conformation judging, field trials, and obedience trials. In recent years, Tracking (TD) and Tracking Dog Excellent (TDX) trials have been included. Both Working Certificate tests (WC) and Working Certificate Excellent (WCX) tests are held for those owners who wish their dogs to compete in hunting stakes, but who do not have the time or interest to pursue field trials.

This is the only breed which holds an annual three-way event to encourage breeding for working qualities as well as beauty and temperament, to keep the Golden Retriever an all-round sporting breed.

## The Golden Retriever in Canada

Many people who live near the Canadian border, or even greater distances, travel to Canada—and Canadian exhibitors cross to the United States for dog shows and field trials. For this reason, there is a continuous exchange of breeding and ideas regarding Goldens bred in the United States and in Canada. Field trialers particularly like to travel. More and more people interested in obedience and show competition enjoy the pleasure of the activities in both countries. This is especially true around the Great Lakes and Middle Western areas and in the Washington-British Columbia areas.

Mr. Christopher Burton knew Golden Retrievers in England, and it was through him that Col. Samuel S. Magoffin got his first Golden Retriever which was the basis for the famous Rockhaven Kennels. Col. Magoffin had the time, talent, and interest to encourage the development of the breed in Canada and later in Colorado. Mr. Randolph Hall who loved and appreciated Goldens was the highly respected manager of Rockhaven Kennels.

Mr. Charles Bunker was a trainer in British Columbia, and particularly successful with field trial dogs. He trained some of the Rockhaven dogs. This combination of talent and interest, and the knowledge of where to go for foundation stock made possible many of the great dogs in Canada and the United States. Rather than summarize the material which I have in my files, the reader should have the pleasure of reading the personal material written by Mr. Burton. Mr. Burton still owns a direct descendant of Speedwell Pluto. Some of his correspondence follows.

The Canadian Kennel Club very kindly informed me some years ago that without a great deal of research they would be unable to positively state when the Canadian Kennel Club recognized the Golden Retriever; even if that research were conducted, there would still be some doubt. The first reference they can find to the Golden Retriever as such in their stud books was in the year 1927. In checking the same stud books previous to 1927, they say that all retrievers were grouped simply as retrievers, without any indication of the particular variety of the breed. They say that they have no doubt, however, that they did register Golden Retrievers previous to 1927, but in order to establish the first such registration, it would be necessary to take all of the registrations previous to that year and check them back in the hope that they could ultimately identify each by the breed as we would know it today. On checking the list of breeds about 1915, the Canadian Kennel

An historic picture of some pioneers of the breed in North America: (l. to r.) Randolph Hall, manager of Rockhaven Kennels; Samuel S. Magoffin, the owner of Rockhaven; Charles Bunker, Mr. Magoffin's trainer, about 1946-47 and Christopher Burton.

Rockhaven Beau Brummel (Ch. Speedwell Pluto ex Saffron Chipmonk), owned by Christopher R. Burton and bred by S. S. Magoffin. This dog traces back to Ch. Michael of Moreton through his sire and Chs. Dame Daphne and Haulstone Dan through his dam.

80

Club says they included Retrievers (wavy coated), Retrievers (curly coated), but whether the reference to wavy coated Retrievers meant the Golden Retriever is hard to say.

In the American Kennel Club's *The Complete Dog Book,* I am told that *Yellow* Retrievers were classified as Wavy or Flat-Coats until 1913, at which time they received recognition from the British Kennel Club as a separate variety and were called Yellow or Golden Retrievers. In 1920, the name Yellow was dropped altogether.

As I said above, the Golden Retriever as such was recognized by the Canadian Kennel Club in 1927, and the first Canadian bench champion, I believe, was Ch. Foxbury Peter, imported September 18, 1927, by Mrs. Alex MacLaren of Buckingham, Quebec, presumably from the breeder, E. Mackintosh of England. Foxbury Peter was by Champion Balcombe Boy ex Wonder Duchess, the sire going back to Culham Tip and Culham Amber II, and the dam to Worram Peter ex Peterkins, and back to Culham Copper.

Long before Foxbury Peter, however, and about the years 1890-1895, the Honourable Archie Marjoribanks, who was, I believe, the assistant manager of the Rocking Chair Ranch in Texas, came up to Canada to the Coldstream Ranch at Vernon, British Columbia, which was owned by the Marquis of Aberdeen, the Marchioness of Aberdeen being the sister of Marjoribanks. The Marquis of Aberdeen was Governor General of Canada, 1893-1898. Archie Marjoribanks is reported to have taken his Yellow Retriever, Lady, and possibly others, to the Coldstream Ranch in British Columbia. When I visited the Coldstream Ranch a few years ago, I saw on the office wall a photo taken in 1909 of a group of people belonging to the ranch, including, I believe, Marjoribanks and a dog which I feel sure was a Golden. Unfortunately, the dog's back was to the camera, but I will bet it was a Golden.

From the above one might say with some assurance that the first Yellow Retrievers in Canada were brought from the ranch in Texas to the Coldstream Ranch in British Columbia by the Hon. Archie Marjoribanks, or by the Marquis of Aberdeen. However, there are stories about some Yellow Retrievers being brought to British Columbia by retired officers of the Indian Army or from Hong Kong, but no direct evidence has been found to actually substantiate this.

In the year 1922, Mr. B. M. Armstrong of Winnipeg, Manitoba, registered the kennel name, Gilnockie, and in the kennel were a number of Golden Retrievers. When Mr. Armstrong, whom I knew, died about 1932, the kennel name was transferred by the executors of the estate to Col. S. S. Magoffin of West Vancouver, British Columbia, who had then started the Rockhaven Kennels in North Vancouver, under the management of Randolph Hall. Mr. Magoffin also had a kennel of Goldens in Denver, Colorado, and named it Gilnockie. And so, the Golden Retriever age in Canada and the U.S.A. really started. I believe there were only a few Goldens in New York State and California at that time.

The late Sam Magoffin was a great friend of mine—we were talking one day at his lovely West Vancouver home, Rockhaven, about shooting and gun dogs, and he asked me which breed I liked best, and having seen and shot over Goldens in England, before I came to Canada, I suggested a Golden. He got up and walked to his study and came back with a cable form and asked me to send a cable to my brother-in-law, as I had already told him that he had Goldens and knew about them. A copy of my original cable is now in possession of the Golden Retriever Club of America, and I had the honour to present it to the Club's most able historian, Mrs. Mark D. Elliott, at the Golden Retriever Club of America's Specialty Banquet at Horicon, Wisconsin, in 1964.

My brother-in-law replied that he could obtain a young Golden with a placing in a field trial and a third at a show, which he thought would be suitable. As a result, out came Speedwell Pluto from the Speedwell Kennels at Saffron Walden, England. I mention all these things because Speedwell Pluto was destined to be, after obtaining his Canadian and U.S. show championships and several bests-in-show, one of the greatest sires of the breed on the North American continent. Speedwell Pluto was sired by Eng. Ch. Michael of Moreton ex English Show Champion Speedwell Emerald. Speedwell Pluto's name, or the names of his get appears in the pedigrees of four winners of the U.S. National Retriever Championship, and in one winner of the Canadian National Retriever Championship. And so Rockhaven Kennels was started.

Soon after the arrival of Speedwell Pluto, Col. Magoffin acquired two Golden bitches, Saffron Chipmonk and Saffron Penelope. These two sisters were born April 28, 1930; they were bred in England and imported 'in dam' by Mr. E. N. M. Vernon of Kaleden, British Columbia. Mr. Vernon imported the dam, Dame Daphne, sire Ch. Haulstone Dan. The bitches were named with the use of the word Saffron by Mr. Vernon.

These two bitches were truly to make history for the Rockhaven Kennels and the result of it all was the interest in Golden Retrievers proceeded to grow at a rapid pace with Col. Magoffin's Gilnockie Kennels in Denver, and Rockhaven Kennels in North Vancouver. At one time, the Rockhaven Kennels had 98 Goldens in residence. Additional bitches were later imported to Rockhaven Kennels.

You will now know from all I have told you that Goldens and Yellow Retrievers were probably known in Canada from about 1895.

The information I have given you in this letter is not guaranteed, but comes from resources believed to be reliable.

Will you please give acknowledgments to:

1. Golden Retriever Club (Canada)
2. Canadian Kennel Club
3. Canadian National Livestock Records
4. Golden Retriever Club of America Year Book (1964)
5. Dogs in Canada

With best wishes to you for a best seller.

Yours sincerely,
/s/   Christopher R. Burton     E & O.E.

Canadian and American Ch. Speedwell Pluto, owned by S. S. Magoffin, was one of the great pillars of the breed in North America. He was the first Golden Retriever to win a Best in Show. His record also included two Sporting Group Firsts.

(PRINTED IN CANADA)

FORM T. D. 2D

# CANADIAN PACIFIC RAILWAY COMPANY'S TELEGRAPH

## DAY LETTER

### CABLE CONNECTIONS TO ALL PARTS OF THE WORLD

TIME FILED

CHECK

J. McMILLAN, General Manager of Telegraphs, Montreal.

Send the following Day Letter, subject to the terms printed on the back hereof which are hereby agreed to.

Deferred Rate.

September 5th, 1930.

Bickersteth,
   Lymphe,

L.C.O.          Kent (England)

Want large well broken Golden Retriever male not over age three points according to Kennell Club regulations stop Cabl immediately price and availability.

Burton,
Branson, Brown& Co. Ltd.

This is a replica of the historic cable sent by Mr. Christopher Burton that resulted in the arrival of Ch. Speedwell Pluto to Rockhaven.

I would say that the Golden Retriever Standard in Canada leans more to the British Standard than it does to the American Standard.

The C.K.C. informs me that they do not maintain records in a way that would enable them to provide any reliable statistics of the approximate number of Golden Retrievers in Canada; the number of field trial champions or the number of bench champions.

Canada is a very large country and the Golden Retriever is spread out from the Atlantic to the Pacific, with I would say, the largest concentration in the Provinces of Ontario, British Columbia, Quebec, and Nova Scotia.

One Golden Retriever has won the Can. National Championship (1952). As a guess, I would say that there have been approximately 25 Canadian field trial champions since 1940, approximately six dual champions, and an unknown number of show champions, tracking dog degrees, and companion dog degrees.

Of the field trial champions, I think one stands out above all others— Oakcreek's Van Cleve (July 12, 1946 to December 25, 1961), sire, Victorious of Roedare, dam, Oakcreek's Celestial Queen. Van was owned by Charles Bunker, one of Canada's outstanding owners and trainers of Goldens. Charlie trained Van in his early career and later Jack Smyth took over. Van was eventually sold for a very large sum of money in the U.S., and finally was purchased by Alfred H. Schmidt of Portland, Oregon. Van, handled by Jack Smyth, won his Canadian field championship and the Canadian National Championship (1952) and then went on to amass the highest number of field trial points, up to the time of his death, ever won by any Golden Retriever in the U.S. or Canada. He won his American field championship, American amateur field championship, and qualified for the U.S. National Championship each year from 1951 through 1955. His full title was Canadian National Champion (1952), Canadian FTC, American Field Champion, American Amateur Field Champion. He died on Christmas Day, 1961, and few will attain the heights that Oakcreek's Van Cleve reached. Unfortunately, Van was reported to be sterile.

In the show champions, Canadian and American Champion Speedwell Pluto must take the first spot. Sired by Eng. Ch. Michael of Moreton, dam, Eng. Ch. Speedwell Emerald. He not only won his Canadian and American championships, but was best in show on several occasions in Canada and the U.S. He proved to be one of the greatest sires of the breed on the North American continent and was first stud dog for Col. S. S. Magoffin when he started Rockhaven Kennels. In the dual champions, Rockhaven Raynard of Fo-Go-Ta and Stonegate's Golden Tamarack must be mentioned as outstanding all-round Goldens. Rockhaven Raynard, sired by Rockhaven Rastus, dam, Judye of Dewstraw, was owned by Col. S. S. Magoffin and later by Mrs. George H. Flinn, Jr., of Greenwich, Conn. His full title—U.S. Field Ch., U.S. Amateur Field Ch., Canadian Dual Champion. Stonegate's Golden Tamarack, believed to be one of the most all-round qualified dogs on the American continent, was owned by Dr. and Mrs. Duncan Croll of Winnipeg, Manitoba. His full title: Cdn. Dual Ch., Cdn. Amateur FTC, CD (Canada & U.S.A.).

In the companion dog and tracking section, one should mention Mrs. James A. Smith, 4304 Torquay Drive, Victoria, B.C., and her two Goldens,

FC-AFC, Canadian Dual Ch. Rockhaven Raynard of Fo-Go-Ta retrieving to his trainer, Charles Bunker. Raynard was originally owned by Samuel S. Magoffin and then passed to Mrs. George H. Flinn, Jr. He was a dog of considerable accomplishments and made great contributions to the growth of his breed.

      Am. & Can. Ch. Rockhaven Harold
    Rockhaven Rawdon
      Rockhaven Niobe
  *Sire:* Rockhaven Rastus
      Can. Ch. Rockhaven Punch
    Rockhaven Lady
      Can. Ch. Gilnockie Patience
  **FC-AFC, CAN. DUAL CH. ROCKHAVEN RAYNARD OF FO-GO-TA**
      Stubbings Golden Dandylyon
    Trooper of Matsonhouse
      Saffron of Haydown
  *Dam:* Judye of Dewstraw
      Prince of Dewstraw
    Tythe Lassie
      Golden Bounty of Dewstraw

Canadian Dual Ch., AFC Stonegate's Golden Tamarack (1956-1970), owned by Dr. Duncan Croll.

Canadian Dual Ch., Can. AFC Carolee's Something Special 2nd, Can. Am. CD, Can. Am. WC (Ch. HGL's Golden Pine Gibson Solo, Am. Can. CD, Am. Can. WC, ex Ch. Carolee's Cafe au Lait, Am. Can. CD, Am. Can. WC), owned by George Stewart and bred by Shirley Goodman. This is the first Dual Champion Golden Retriever in Canada in twenty years.

Ch. Mossbanks Golden Honey, CD, CDX, UD, TD. Honey has all the degrees she can obtain except Fld. Ch. Mrs. Smith's other Golden, Quamorlys Golden Sasha, CD, CDX, TD, American CD, is Honey's daughter.

The obedience degrees in Canada are:

CD   Companion Dog degree
CDX  Companion Dog Excellent degree
UD   Utility degree
TD   Tracking Dog degree[1]

The UD is the highest obedience degree obtainable in Canada and carries the right to Obedience Trial Champion.

A few of the principal breeders of Goldens in Canada:

| | |
|---|---|
| Goldrange | R. Jack Reid<br>20167—72nd Avenue<br>R.R. 4<br>Langley, B.C. |
| Anjamar | Douglas & Marion McKenzie<br>1024 Talbot Street<br>St. Thomas, Ontario |
| Mel-Bach | George N. Mehlenbacher<br>Fisherville, Ontario |
| Shadywell | Clifford Macdonald<br>R.R. 2<br>Schonberg, Ontario |
| Skylon | Judy & Brian Taylor<br>R.R. 1<br>Wainflect, Ontario |
| Rojan | Ross & Janet Randale<br>Box 277<br>Petrolia, Ontario |
| Falcon Lake | Mrs. Vivienne Muller<br>R.R. 1<br>Freelton, Ontario |
| Forget-Me-Not | Mr. & Mrs. Schlotzer<br>Forget-Me-Not Kennels<br>Locust Hill, Ontario |

---

[1]Since this was written, the Canadian Kennel Club has added two additional obedience degrees. One is an advanced tracking degree known as TDX or Tracking Dog Excellent. The other is O.T. Ch. or Obedience Trial Champion and is automatically given when a dog has acquired a UD (Utility Dog) degree.

E. & O.E.

/s/   Christopher R. Burton

Through the 1950's, 60's and 1970, there continued to be an exchange of showing Goldens in both the United States and Canada. Sometimes, residents of the United States exhibited in Canada, and Canadians exhibited in the United States. There continued to be an exchange in field trials. People became more interested in obedience in Canada than they had been before; there have been several examples of dogs receiving obedience titles on both sides of the border.

One outstanding example of a fine field trial dog was Can. Dual Ch. Stonegate's Golden Tamarack, CD, owned by Dr. L. Duncan Croll of Winnipeg. The dog was whelped in 1956, and was bred at Stonegate Kennels by John H. Hall in Moorhead, Minnesota. Dr. Croll wrote that he had enjoyed training and handling "Barry," as this dog was called. Some people considered Barry the best-handling retriever in North America for two or three of his prime years. At the time of winning his field championship in July, 1960, he won over a field of 17, including the dog that was to be the 1960 national champion. A professional, who saw the trial, said that this dog ran the best trial he had ever seen a dog run. The judges showed his lowest mark as a 9-, 10 being a perfect score. Barry went on to his final sleep in October, 1970, at 14 years and four months.

At the present time, there are several large groups of Goldens in Canada, centered mainly in British Columbia, Manitoba (Winnipeg), and Ontario (mainly Toronto). In 1968 and 1969, there were approximately 50 bench champions in Canada, two tracking dogs, no UD dogs and no new field champions. A list of Canadian dual champions, and field champions from 1953-1960 follows (Courtesy Golden Retriever Yearbook 1938-1963, published 1964):

### Canadian Dual Champions

| 1953 | Rockhaven Raynard of Fo-Go-Ta | Dog | Samuel S. Magoffin then Mrs. George H. Flinn, Jr. |
|------|-------------------------------|------|------------------|
| 1957 | Byrcober Sir Alexander | Dog | Frank Morley |
| 1958 | Lady Bess | Bitch | Alex G. Wilson |
| 1961 | Stonegate's Golden Tamarack (also Can. Amateur Fld. Ch.) | Dog | Dr. L. Duncan Croll |
| 1980 | AFC Carolee's Something Special 2nd | Dog | George Stewart |

### Canadian Field Champions

| 1947 | Stalingrad Express | Bitch | Charles E. Snell |
|------|--------------------|-------|------------------|
| 1949 | Oakcreek's Van Cleve | Dog | C. F. Bunker |
|      | Ready Always of Marianhill | Dog | M. B. Wallace, Jr. |

| 1952 | Rockhaven Raynard of Fo-Go-Ta | Dog | Samuel S. Magoffin |
|------|-------------------------------|-------|--------------------|
|      |                               |       | then |
|      |                               |       | Mrs. George H. Flinn, Jr. |
| 1954 | Lady Ricki of Hillhaven | Bitch | George Walker |
|      | Walker's Rhett | Dog | George Walker |
| 1955 | Walker's Kim | Dog | Austin C. Taylor |
| 1956 | Royal's Tuck of Stonegate | Dog | Ross L. Gabriel |
| 1957 | Byrcober Sir Alexander | Dog | Frank Morley |
|      | King's Ransom II | Dog | R. A. Laidlaw & |
|      |                  |     | H. V. P. Lewis |
| 1958 | Lady Bess | Bitch | Alex G. Wilson |
|      | Shadywell Hi-Speed | Dog | Gordon G. Rolph |
| 1960 | Stonegate's Golden Tamarack | Dog | Dr. L. Duncan Croll |

Additional Field Champions 1960-1984 not listed.

Goldens in the United States and Canada started from quality and were furthered by dedicated men and women who were interested in high standards of appearance and performance. The fanciers in the 1930's and 40's were truly dedicated and furthered the high potential of the breed. This start from high quality helped overcome some of the problems that have beset many other breeds. Undoubtedly, this dedication has had much to do with the popularity of the breed today.

## Color Preferences

The question has been asked, how has the Golden Retriever changed in the last 50 or 60 years? In face and character, the dogs are much the same as in the earlier pictures. The breed has sometimes been influenced by a popular winner; for example, Ch. Czar of Wildwood was dark and was a delightful Best in Show winner. The public, who saw him and liked him, became partial to the rich, deep gold color. FC-AFC Oakcreek's Sir Dorchester was dark, though his sire was lighter, and as "Ty" was a great field worker, and people liked him, many who admired these two preferred the darker color. Many hunters and field trial enthusiasts seem to prefer the darker color.

On the West Coast, people grew to like Ch. Oakwin, Jr., a medium-colored English import, and through this dog, became interested in a lighter golden shade. Oakwin, Jr. had a broken coat, i.e., the deeper coat on top and the lighter feathering as pictured in *Hutchinson's Encyclopedia,* and as his offspring were good in both field and show, people began to enjoy both the lighter and darker gold colors.

This was also true on the East Coast where there were more imports than on the West. Mrs. Patricia Corey, who owned Goldendoor Kennels, had imported some Goldens as had Taramar earlier. Ch. Alstone Sutter Creek Charade, UD*, was imported by Susan Breakell and Ch. Footprint of Yeo by Betty Hoggard. Others who preferred the lighter-colored dogs from England were Mr. and Mrs. John B. Bissett and Dr. and Mrs. Geoffrey Bewley.

Whether light or dark, a successful show dog will have its following. Some kennels may have both shades since they are more interested in sound, alert dogs of quality than in a particular color. Although the medium, true gold has been the most popular shade for the show ring, good structure, gait, alertness, and personality are favored over color.

## The Golden into the Present

Perhaps no other breed made such an advancement in the lifetime of one individual as has the Golden Retriever. In 1930, Speedwell Pluto was one of the two dogs that were sent from England from the Speedwell Kennel owned by Mrs. Evers-Swindell and her husband. Speedwell Pluto, later to become both an American and Canadian champion, was acquired by Colonel Magoffin. Other Goldens from this kennel were also shipped to the United States. Mrs. Evers-Swindell's first dog, Cornelius, had a very important dual influence on the entire breed. Until her death in 1970, Mrs. Evers-Swindell was always willing to start other fanciers with quality, as well as retaining quality animals for herself. This dedication was an advantage to the breed, not only in England, but also in the United States and Canada.

The general soundness of the dogs has improved as breeders have become more aware of the importance of this in a personal or a field dog. Many breeders are concerned, and do use more medical checks in their breeding program. There are fewer dogs born with physical defects in proportion to the number bred. All of this has influenced the breed. The informed public is more aware of what to ask for because of the educational free materials published by such organizations as the American Dog Owners Association, Inc., the Golden Retriever Club of America, Inc., and local Golden Retriever clubs. The Badger Golden Retriever Club of Wisconsin and the San Diego Golden Retriever Club are particularly active regarding education.

The more direct route from breeder to buyer, in puppy buying, is more satisfactory for the new owner, the Golden, and the breeder. The wise new owner prefers making his selection by seeing the whole litter, the dam, and perhaps the sire. In this way he can judge how the litter is cared for, what the adult animals may become so that he knows what type of companion he may have for 10 or 15 years. Second and third steps between breeder and new puppy owner, regardless of promises, may be disadvantageous in both quality of animals and price. Dogs are not commodities such as grain, or animals used for food.

There are two exceptions to this. One, a more costly exception, might be the selection by a knowledgeable professional handler who might be looking for a prospective show or field trial winner for a customer, and who

Ch. Oakwin Junior, imported from England and owned by the author and her husband. This dog enjoyed a successful show career and exerted a strong positive influence over the breeding program for Guide Dogs for the Blind. He is shown here with his handler, Harry Sangster.

Ch. Misty Morn's Sunset (Ch. Sunset's Happy Duke ex Amber Lady of Tercor Farms), owned by Mrs. Peter Lewesky, is a holder of the working certificate and has sired over 100 champions, including many outstanding winners. *William Gilbert*

Ch. Czar of Wildwood (FC Ch. Stilrovin Super Speed ex Beavertail Rock Ripple), owned by Eric S. Johnson, was BIS from the classes at the 1946 Golden Gate KC. Two years later, he returned to the same show to repeat his outstanding triumph. The puppy shown with Czar is his son and also grew up to become a BIS winner.

Ch. Rockhaven Rory

Stilrovin Bullett***

Patience of Yelme

Sire: FC Stilrovin Super Speed

Eng.-Am. Ch. Bingo of Yelme***

Gilnockie Coquette

Can. Ch. Rockhaven Russet

**CH. CZAR OF WILDWOOD**

Speedwell Reuben

FC Rip

Ch. Speedwell Tango

Dam: Beavertail Rock Ripple

Can. Ch. Rockhaven Rust

Ch. Rockhaven Glory**

Can. Ch. Rockhaven Carole

would, through his choice, be laying both his reputation and future business on the line. The other exception would be selection with the help of a dedicated fancier interested in the breed. Such an individual would have had considerable experience and success with the breed and would be interested only in placing a good dog in a good home.

The more concerned and dedicated breeders and an informed public have influenced the breed. Thoughtless purchasers and breeders can seriously harm this, or any breed.

The first Goldens, as explained by Ralph Boalt, were thought of first as hunting dogs, then as show dogs. As the breed became increasingly popular, there appeared to be more interest in exhibiting in shows, enjoying the dogs as personal companions or family dogs, and participating in obedience trials, though many of these dogs were also distinguished field trial winners. Recently, people have again become more aware of the trial potential of their dogs and participate in various training groups in both the United States and Canada to further their dogs in the field.

A working certificate is prized by the owner of a pet, show champion, or obedience trial dog. A working certificate is automatically awarded, upon application to GRCA, for a Golden which has placed in any stake in a licensed field trial; for example, a JAM (Judge's Award of Merit) or places one through four. Such a placement may be more difficult to achieve.

Wider interest in conservation has encouraged the use of the Golden in the field, and has encouraged the training of the family dog as a hunter. In some states, game laws require the use of a dog for any two or three hunters hunting together. This, it is felt, may prevent leaving downed birds in the field.

The versatility of the Golden, as well as its beauty, has made it a popular breed for television commercials. One Golden took his turn going down a slide at Disneyland; others have appeared in advertisements in sailing magazines, fashion magazines, and at least one, "Flare," participated in a fashion show at the St. Francis Hotel in San Francisco, where she wore a diamond necklace and carried a rhinestone purse.

The emphasis is upon an all-round, trainable dog, sometimes spoken of as a dual or tri-purpose dog. This is sound development.

Many people reviewing pedigrees of field dogs will find several dogs appearing frequently in the background of notably outstanding workers. Golden fanciers particularly interested in the genealogy of top field dogs will find the following survey of interest. Those whose bitches trace back to one or more of these Goldens should seek common ancestors in the background of males they select for breeding.

*FC-AFC Bonnie Brooks Elmer* was a great sire. Among his get were three FC-AFCs, one dual champion, one Canadian FC-AFC, one O.T. Ch., and other qualified Open All-Age dogs. He was owned by Mrs. George H. Flinn, Jr.

*FC-AFC Misty's Sungold Lad, CDX,* was the first Golden to receive a double-header, actually two double-headers, and went on to sire some excellent offspring. He was owned by Valerie Fisher Walker.

*FC-AFC Chief Sands* had an excellent field record. Owned by Richard Sampson, he sired three FCs or AFCs, one UD dog with O.T. Ch. points, and at least 15 qualified Open All-Age Goldens.

*AFC Coin of Copper* had an interesting record himself, and his name appears in many pedigrees of quality field dogs. Bred by Ben Boalt he was owned and run by Vernon Weber.

*Shenandoah of Stilrovin, CD***,* was the dam of many of the great dogs. She was owned by Phil Uehling.

*Poika of Handjem* sired four FCs, two O.T. Chs., two champions, and six or more qualified Open All-Age dogs. He was bred by Dr. Henry Lardy and sold to a neighbor as a pet. He proved such an outstanding working dog and was so easy to train that Dr. Lardy suggested he be used as a sire. When a breeder of champion field dogs came to see Poika and saw the style with which the dog worked, he bred his bitch to Poika. Poika was prepotent and sired many excellent field dogs. He was owned by Carl Toby Potter.

*FC-AFC Tigathoe's Magic Marker* was the first Golden bitch to receive a double-header at a National Specialty field trial. She had 117 points (Open and Amateur), was an excellent Derby dog, and was the mother of one AFC and some qualified Open All-Age dogs. Owned by Joseph Wattleworth, she had great style and was a pleasure to watch.

*AFC Holway Barty* was an English import who was a fine sire. He was imported and owned by Barbara Howard. Barty not only produced fine field dogs, but he was the grandsire of six from a litter of seven that graduated as service dogs for *Canine Companions for Independence.*

*FC-AFC Right-On Dynamite John* currently has 41½ Open points and 45½ Amateur points. He is descended from Dual Ch. Cresta Gold Rip and other talented hunting, show, and field dogs. He is owned by Elaine Klicker.

*FC-AFC Tigatohe's Kiowa II,* owned by Pat Sadler, a fine working dog, has many accomplished offspring, including one AFC, one champion, five UDs, 10 Open All-Age dogs, and one guide dog. There may be more to follow.

*Dual Ch.-AFC Tigathoe's Funky Farquar,* was a top Derby dog in 1973. He later won both his field championship and AFC and qualified for the National Open and the National Amateur. His sons and daughters have done well in the field and one has been successfully trained as a disaster dog. Quar is owned by Dorothy Ramsay Mikeska.

*AFC Wildfire of Riverview, CDX,* was the third Golden to win a double-header. He is owned by Lewis and Kathleen Daniels.

*Cranwood's Chill Factor* was a top Derby Golden in 1982 with 34 Derby points. He was fifth on the National Derby list. He also won a

FC-AFC Right-On Dynamite John, owned by Elaine Klicker. This photo appeared in *Field Trial News*.

FC-AFC Tigathoe's Magic Marker shown with her owner Joseph Wattleworth and her breeder Mrs. George H. Flinn, Jr. An outstanding field trial competitor and producer, she is one of four field champions produced by the pairing of Bonnie Brooks Elmer and Tigathoe's Chickasaw. *Kevin Fitzgerald*

qualifying stake at 17 months of age. He is co-owned by Mrs. George H. Flinn, Jr., and Ben Lewis.

Two other dogs are important among the currently (1984) running dogs. Handjem's Quick Sand had 30 Derby points in 1980 and he has Open and Amateur points. Bred by Michael Lardy, he is owned by Mrs. George H. Flinn, Jr. and Henry Lardy. Handjem's Midas Touch is also among current qualifying dogs. He was bred by Michael and Henry Lardy.

In the 1950's and early 60's those interested in show dogs would probably have sought lines which included Am. Can. Ch. Chee-Chee of Sprucewood or her get in the pedigrees of their show prospects. Chee-Chee was prepotent in the two litters she had by Ch. King Alphonso (see pedigree in the appendix) and later Harvest Sugar was the dam of several excellent dogs. In the 1960's and early 70's Ch. Misty Morn's Sunset was the outstanding sire. He sired more than 100 champions and utility dogs. Of course, these were from various bitches to which he was bred.

A line of three, Misty Morn's Sunset; his son Ch. Wochica's Okeechobee Jake; and Jake's son, Ch. Camelot's Noble Fella, CDX, all were BIS winners. Another prepotent show line was that of Ch. Cummings' Gold-Rush Charlie followed by Ch. Gold-Rush's Great Teddy Bear, who won the 1978 National Specialty, and his son Ch. Goldwing True Bear who was also a BIS winner.

Other examples of prepotent lines might be cited. For example, in the early 1950's on the West Coast, field people sought lines from FC-AFC Oakcreek's Sir Dorchester, and show people liked Ch. Czar of Wildwood and Ch. Prince Copper of Malibu. They also respected and sought the lines that William and Phyllis Shiners had, such as from Ch. Czargold Lassie, who in turn came from Bart Foster's Best-in-Show winner Ch. Des Lac's Lassie—both a show dog and an excellent hunter. She helped Mr. Foster retrieve baby ducks from the marshes to be banded and returned to the nest. Boats would have disturbed the flora and fauna in the sloughs and marshes.

The person looking for the special dog should familiarize himself with the Goldens exhibited in dog shows, obedience and field trials and review pedigrees of the producing families.

Goldens have also distinguished themselves in police and rescue operations. They have been used in drug detection, especially at airports, and in other types of investigations. However, due to the breed's typical, kindly disposition, Goldens are not generally used as attack dogs.

Goldens have participated in various types of rescue work. They have seen service in the High Sierras with other dog breeds in the WOOF team, and have been successful in avalanche rescue operations. They have also worked well in tracing people and animals lost in snow and wilderness areas, and are successful in other forms of rescue work such as K.H. (*Katastrophenhund* or disaster dog).

Ch. Almaden Sundowners Sequoia, UD, WC, KH, ("Digger")

Ch. Wochica's Okeechobee Jake (Ch. Misty Morn's Sunset, CD, ex Ch. Little Dawn of Chickasaw), owned by Susan Taylor and bred by Janet Bunce. Jake was a top winner among Sporting dogs and has made numerous good wins including Best at the Golden Retriever Club of America Specialty in three different years. Jake also was a top sire and his influence on the breed is both strong and durable. He is handled by Robert J. Stebbins with whom he is pictured. *John Ashbey.*

performed well at Love Creek in the Santa Cruz Mountains during the disastrous floods in 1982 when so many people died and so many homes were lost. His picture shows him as he appeared with his owner, trainer, and handler, searching for people who had been lost in this disaster. Pluis Davern, his owner, writes as follows:

> When Digger started his search and rescue training at almost five years of age, he had already obtained his AKC titles, his working certificate, and was trained to "qualifying" level in his field work. It was, therefore, a relatively simple matter to switch him to this new area of endeavors where an air-scenting dog, able to be handled at a distance, was a prime requisite. Within one year he was at "mission ready" status when, in general, a dog could not hope to attain that level before at least two years of training.
>
> Of the three branches of canine search and rescue: avalanche, wilderness, and disaster, I chose the last due to ready availability of training facilities in my area.
>
> Digger was taught to move comfortably, but with care, over obstacles of all kinds—simulating real rubble left after a major disaster such as an earthquake, fire, or mudslide. The need to have a confident dog, unconcerned about terrain, is imperative because a dog worried about his footing will not use his nose to search for victims.
>
> This was an interesting switch for Digger and me as I had always taught him to jump over obstacles, as in obedience rings. To have a dog leap through the rubble, however, could cause him injury and even death, so quiet, steady movement was of prime importance.
>
> Probably the most difficult and critical skill that a search and rescue dog must master is to "alert" or indicate to his handler that he has found a missing person.
>
> In disaster this means digging at the location of maximum scent and barking. This enables the handler to pinpoint the area which crews and heavy equipment must clear to reach the victim.
>
> Avalanche dogs also indicate by furiously digging in the place where the human scent is strongest.
>
> A dog sent out to search in the wilderness indicates its find by flipping a small leather cylinder (*bringsel*) attached to its collar into its mouth and then delivering this to the handler. On the command "show me" the dog will then lead its owner back to the victim.
>
> Digger lived up to the potential necessary for a reliable search and rescue dog—trainable, confident, and with a tremendous search drive. As a Golden Retriever he exemplified the standards of his breed—a wonderfully enthusiastic member of our human and dog family and a talented gun and rescue dog.

Digger was the son of Dual Ch. and AFC Tigathoe's Funky Farquar. "Quar's" sons and daughters have been successful in many areas of Golden activities. He was bred by Nancy Reader, who then lived in San Jose, California.

Recently, Golden Retrievers have played an important role as service dogs for the handicapped.

Ch. Almaden Sundowner's Sequoia, UD, WC, KH (Dual Ch. Tigathoe's Funky Farquar ex Sundowner's Bronze Sherry, CDX, WC), owned and trained by Pluis Davern and bred by Nancy Reader. The initials KH stand for the German word *Katastrophenhund* or Disaster Dog. "Digger" has had a number of occasions to put his valuable training to vital use. He is shown here at the site of the 1982 Love Creek mudslide near Santa Cruz, California.

*Canine Companions for Independence* is a new organization located in Santa Rosa, California. It trains dogs for three specific purposes—signal, social and service. The signal dog assists the hard-of-hearing and the deaf. For example, the dog, upon hearing the door bell or the telephone, alerts the owner.

The social dog is often used in a convalescent home. It visits the patients and offers an affectionate response; in turn, the residents enjoy petting and talking to the animal as it makes its rounds. The dog thus becomes an interesting topic of conversation among the patients.

The service dog is unique, used primarily by wheel chair patients. It learns to perform tasks which a person in a wheel chair cannot. For example, the dog can stand up and push an elevator button or light switch with its paws. It can deliver a package to a counter, or take a package up a stairway and return with another. In addition, the service dog is trained to pull wheel chairs up a ramp, or to free the chair if it becomes stuck in grass or gravel. It may wear a back-pack or knap-sack to carry a book or needed items, as it walks beside its owner.

Many breeds are used by Canine Companions. The dogs are carefully matched to the personality and needs of the owner. Among Sporting breeds field-bred dogs are preferred because of their high energy level. Goldens have particularly distinguished themselves as service and social dogs; smaller breeds are often used as signal dogs.

Recently, Joan Pollack gave Canine Companions a Golden Retriever stud dog, Sunclad Culynwood Would He, by AFC Holway Barty ex Culynwoods Sunclad Hellion. He sired a litter of seven, six of which graduated as service dogs in the summer of 1983. Joan was fortunate enough to be invited to the graduation of these six dogs sired by her gift.

Dedicated breeders are promoting better qualities in the Golden Retriever today through field, show and obedience activities. They are interested in a sound, healthy dog. Because of its quality, temperament, and trainability as an all-around dog, as well as a hunting, show, and obedience dog, the Golden Retriever has gained considerably in numbers and in popularity. Numbers have not, however, reduced the quality of the Golden. The Golden Retriever Club of America and other breed clubs sponsor clinics to provide information on all phases of dog keeping to breeders and to the public. Though Golden Retrievers have few hereditary shortcomings, officers of the Golden Retriever Club of America were the first to initiate a registry for hip dysplasia. They established an Advisory Council which later became a part of the Orthopedic Foundation for Animals (OFA). The chief sponsor of the OFA was John Olin of Illinois. A field trial sportsman and a Labrador breeder, he felt that all dog owners should have the opportunity to submit x-rays to a research group similar to that of the GRCA's Advisory Council. Thus, the OFA was formed, thanks in large part to Mr. Olin's prestige and financial support. The OFA is a consulting medical referral, advisory and registry for hip dysplasia. Its services are available to any dog owner and his veterinarian who wishes to send properly identified x-ray plates on a dog of any breed. A nominal fee is charged for services. The organization is now located at the School of Veterinary Medicine at the University of Missouri, Columbia. Through the efforts of the late Mrs. Verneca Bower of Indiana, chairman of the Hip Dysplasia Committee of the Golden Retriever Club of America, the OFA has become a registry for all breeds. The late Josiah Seaman of New York, a former GRCA president, and his wife, Mary Luise Seaman, deserve credit for the appointment of Mrs. Bower to the OFA. Her objectivity and fairness were helpful to everyone. Now in Maryland, Mrs. Seaman continues her activities in Golden Retrievers.

In addition, the Golden Retriever Club of America has fostered research in other fields through financial contributions, interest, and the dedication of breeders and owners. The club's efforts have included contributions to cancer research at the University of California, Davis, and at other research institutions. The Yankee Golden Retriever Club, for example, sponsors eye research. In this manner, genetic or hereditary problems are discouraged through better breeding practices.

Ch. Cummings' Gold Rush Charlie, owned by Mrs. Robert V. Clark, Jr. and Larry C. Johnson, was the top-winning Golden Retriever of all time. A multiple Specialty and Best in Show winner, he was the leading Sporting dog of 1974. Charlie is shown with his handler William J. Trainor making a Best in Show win under judge Kurt W. Mueller, Sr. at the Old Dominion KC of Northern Virginia.     *John L. Ashbey*

EARS rather short, flat against head

Broad in SKULL

Good STOP, FOREFACE deep and wide, nearly as long as skull

EYES set well apart, medium large with dark rims. Color preferably dark brown.

NOSE black or dark brown

TEETH scissors bite with lower incisors touching inside upper incisors

MUZZLE (viewed in profile) slightly deeper at stop than at tip. No heaviness in flews.

SHOULDER blades wide, long and muscular showing angulation with upper arm of approximately 90 degrees

CHEST at least as wide as a man's hand, including thumb

LEGS straight with good bone

PASTERN short and strong, sloping slightly forward with no suggestion of weakness

NECK medium long, sloping well back into shoulders

LOIN short, muscular, wide and deep with very little tuck-up

CROUP slopes gently

TAIL well set on, neither too high nor too low, following natural line of croup. Length extends to hock

HOCKS well let down

FEET medium size, round and compact with thick pads

BRISKET extends to elbows

STIFLE well bent

BODY well balanced, short coupled, deep through the heart. Ribs long and well sprung but not barrel shaped, extending well to rear of body.

The most constructive judging in the show ring takes into account that a Golden Retriever should be first of all a field dog. Minor variations from the Standard—such as too long ears, a few white hairs other than on the chest, lighter or darker color than the ideal—do not affect the dog's work in the field. The more serious variations from the Standard which have to do with anatomical or skeletal structure—such as loose shoulders, a weak rear, slack loin or broken down pasterns— may weaken or cause the dog to break down under serious working conditions.

*Text - R. Elliott & G. Fischer*

# 4

# The Golden Retriever Breed Standard—An Analytical Discussion

*by Rachel P. Elliott (Drawings by Marjorie B. Perry)*

---

**W**HEN the Golden Retriever Club of America was incorporated in 1939, the English Standard of points for Golden Retrievers was adopted with little change. The wording was brief, and a rating scale placed a numerical value on various qualifications. About ten years later the American club began an in-depth study of its Standard in an effort to encourage more uniformity in size and to caution breeders against faults which were beginning to appear with greater frequency as the breed gained popularity. The latest revision was approved by the American Kennel Club effective January, 1982. This breed Standard is a guide for breeders and judges, describing type and conformation in the ideal Golden and pointing out numerous deviations called faults. It is a goal to aim for, whatever one's connection with the breed.

## Type

Type and conformation are closely related, yet each has distinct meaning and importance in the over-all picture. Type, in a broad sense, is what separates one breed from another in shape, size, use, performance, and temperament. For example, Dachshunds are badger dogs designed to dig into and slide out of burrows; Greyhounds are coursers bred for speed;

Siberian Huskies are sled dogs built to pull; Golden Retrievers are primarily swimming dogs used by hunters to recover game in water and upland fields. In a more limited sense, type applies to the specific traits which lend individuality to a dog as an example of his own breed, in features such as expression, character, coat-texture, or color. Conformation has to do with actual body structure, i.e., how the bones, muscles, and ligaments fit together to best accomplish a specific function—this subject will be discussed more fully later on.

To be really outstanding, a purebred dog must possess good type as well as sound conformation. Most have a moderate degree of both, but occasionally a specimen is seen that is strong in the one quality and weak in the other. A Golden might display good type, for instance, through a beautiful head and expression, a lustrous coat, and an outgoing personality, but in conformation he could be a disaster—his elbows might fly in the wind, his hocks rub together, and his feet be badly splayed. Another Golden, sound in conformation, heavy in bone, and a good mover, could in type be just a common brown dog with a hard expression and a long silky tail curled high over his back.

Luckily, such extreme departures from the breed standard do not occur very often; however, these examples serve to illustrate why type and conformation have always been topics for lively discussion among dog people, regardless of the breed. Human nature being what it is, interpretations and opinions are bound to vary somewhat, and new friends of the Golden should realize this. One judge might look first at head and expression; another, gait. Each has his preference, but in the show ring the good judge will place exhibits only after considering all aspects. An exhibitor who knows the worth of his Golden should not be discouraged by an occasional loss, nor should a novice become overly confident with a single win. Success depends much on the competition of the day, the condition of the dog, and the way he is presented. Win or lose, one should always try to evaluate one's own dog when vying with others, as this is the best way to compare his relative virtues and shortcomings. Also, it is wise to keep in mind that the improvement or impairment of a breed is directly influenced by the ability of exhibitors and breeders to recognize and promote good quality.

## Temperament

The supporters of every kind of dog tend to eulogize their favorites, Golden enthusiasts being no exception, and praiseworthy characteristics such as intelligence, courage, loyalty, friendliness, trustworthiness, devotion and responsiveness have a common ring. These qualities, plus others that seem unique to Golden Retrievers, have won for the breed an ever-growing following.

Typical is the Golden that lives for his family, befriends the cats and neighborhood dogs, plays with the children, and waits for the arrival of the school bus with uncanny punctuality; that welcomes guests with paw shake, yet stands his ground with discriminating detachment at the arrival of questionable strangers; that goes to the door asking to go out, when actually all he wants is to have the door opened for some four-legged friend who wants to come in; that offers gifts—a leaf, a ball, a slipper, or possibly an unharmed baby duck which has wandered from its nest by the pond. Typical is the Golden that relaxes in a favorite spot in the house, but springs to attention at the click of a gun or the sound of hunting boots on the stairs; that takes treatment in the veterinarian's office with unquestioning tolerance; that patiently and proudly allows visitors to view newly born pups. Typical is the Golden that actually reasons how to turn a clumsy stick the long way for pulling through a narrow opening, or "coils" a rope for easier carrying, and the Golden that captures high honors in obedience tests, where learning and pleasing are his greatest desires. Typical, too, is the Golden that guides his blind owner—steadfast and dutiful—in assignments where initiative and common sense are prime requisites.

As a breed, Goldens are not intended to be watch dogs, but they do possess a keen awareness of the unusual, and most of them will alert their owners by barking or showing signs of uneasiness when things seem amiss. Signs of aggressiveness, sullenness, or viciousness, however, should not be tolerated, and any tendency to growl at other dogs should be disciplined on the spot. Restraining is not training. Antipathies among stud dogs may seem natural, but very often Golden Retriever studs are kenneled together with no problem. Shyness should be avoided. A dog that is gun shy may be the victim of an unfortunate introduction to firearms, and perhaps can be cured; but if the tendency ties in with a temperament that is unstable attempts at correction will probably prove futile.

Thunder shyness in many dogs has long been a perplexing problem and seems quite unrelated to other characteristics. Occasionally the most stalwart hunting dog is terrified of thunder and the only solution is the use of tranquilizers or confinement where he cannot injure himself. It is believed by many that dogs feel sudden drops in barometric pressure, something they fail to understand, and therefore fear.

## Head and Expression (Plate I)

A good head is essential for true type. It should be well proportioned, with a strong muzzle, not wedge shaped, or weak in any way. The step between the eyes, called the stop, should not be as abrupt as in the Cocker Spaniel, but sufficiently elevated to lend definition to the sculpture around the eyes, setting them well apart and on the front of the skull, not slanting out sideways. The eyes should be of medium size, preferably dark, with an expression of kindness, gentility and trustworthiness. The very light eye is apt to have an untrustworthy, hard look. Though there is little evidence to support their claim, some sportsmen insist that the light-eyed dog is better sighted. Such a characteristic probably never made or failed a field trial dog, but there is little doubt that a majority of breeders and judges prefer the eye that is dark, and outlined with dark pigmentation. Small pig eyes are unattractive, also those rimmed with very loose eyelids. Eyes that are too prominent have a wild expression and are subject to injury in rough cover.

Some Goldens show a slight occiput on the top of the head (occasionally referred to as the "bump of knowledge"), which should not be faulted unless it is accentuated by a narrow skull that falls away on either side above the eyes. Capt. H. F. H. Hardy, author of *Good Gun Dogs* (one of the first to enter Golden Retrievers in English field trials), had this to say about the occiput:

> For the rest, if I had the pick of a litter I would pick the dog who showed the bone on top of his head prominently. It is an unfailing sign of a good worker, and it is a sign of this in other breeds as well. A sheepdog-trial expert has told me that in sheep-dogs it is very rare—but if one of the litter had this prominent bone no money would buy that puppy from the breeder.[1]

Of all the sporting dogs in his experience, Captain Hardy liked Goldens best, because he found them "easy to train and to manage, good trackers of wounded game, and excellent at water work."[2]

The breed standard says nothing about reverse ridges of hair growing up the nose. This feature, seen occasionally, is an oddity that detracts from the beauty of an otherwise good head. The furrowed brow with its worried look also detracts from an expression that is supposed to convey calm and nobility—particularly if the furrows are deep and the skin loose and heavy. Neither of these traits is desirable.

The ears should be attached "well behind and just above the eye with the rear edge slightly below." To gain correct perspective of this position, the head should be in profile with the muzzle horizontal. Ears hanging too low tend to accentuate the faultiness of a skull that may be narrow or apple-headed. Correct ear-set contributes to good expression and has the practical advantage of helping to keep the ear canal above water level while the dog is swimming. Ears of medium length have an advantage, too, for they have better ventilation than ears that are long and heavy. Swimming dogs naturally get water in their ears, most of which they shake out, but if the ear passages have a chance to dry quickly they are far less subject to fungus infection. According to some sportsmen, long ears act as funnels for ground scent—which helps to explain this feature in setters, spaniels and some of the hound breeds.

Pigmentation of the nose should be dark, preferably black. Quite

---

[1]Hardy, Captain H. F. H., *Good Gun Dogs;* Charles Scribner's pages 55, 56
[2]*Ibid;* page 55

A

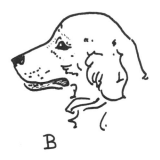

B

C

D

E

F

**Plate I: Studies in Head Type**

A. Well Shaped, Good Expression
B. Domey Skull, Ear Set Too Low
C. Roman Nose, Ear Set Too High
D. Level Foreface, Lacking Stop, Small, Slanting Eyes
E. Coarse, Ears Too Long and Heavy, Pronounced Occiput
F. Weak Snipey Muzzle, Dish Face, No Stop

often a black nose will turn brown temporarily in winter, or during gestation, but if it is black without pink pigmentation it will remain jet black at all times. Really pink noses and eyelids on mature Goldens should be faulted. The pads and feet of newborn puppies are often pink at birth but turn black within a few days. If a pad under a toe remains pink, and there is white hair above it, the white is likely there to stay; however, it will become less noticeable as the darker hair grows down over it. Physical faults are far more serious than odd white markings, but the true character of the Golden could quickly become impaired if the white factor is not carefully weighed in breeding programs.

## Teeth (Plate II)

A Golden's teeth should fit together snugly in a scissors bite, the front surfaces of the lower incisors just touching the inside surfaces of the uppers. The expression "even bite," which appears in some of the old standards, has often been misconstrued to mean a bite in which teeth meet end to end. This is not correct, as the end-to-end bite causes rapid wearing. So when a standard calls for an "even bite," the term can be interpreted as meaning "scissors bite." Misaligned teeth cause crowding, often resulting in gum troubles and in the loosening or loss of incisors with old age. Normally, the long, pointed lower canine teeth, located beside the incisors, should fit snugly in front of the long upper canines. A bite that is severely undershot discloses considerable space between the canines, in addition to the lower incisors jutting ahead of the uppers. When the bite is overshot, the upper incisors protrude well ahead of, and do not touch, the lowers. A very bad bite can throw an entire jaw out of alignment, but fortunately, this condition is rarely encountered in Goldens. The occurrence of missing premolars, however, is becoming more frequent and should be dealt with as a hereditary defect of some concern.

## Coat and Color

Always popular is the coat that is medium gold in color; but each fancier has his own preference, and this flexible range from light to dark is one of the interesting features of the breed. Less favored in America are the two extremes, cream and mahogany red. The ears or face color of young puppies are a reliable indication of the color their coats will become in maturity. Most Goldens darken a bit with each shedding until they are three or four years old, yet many retain feathering of a lighter shade on the back of the legs, belly, buttocks, and under the tail—which is quite legitimate and, in the opinion of many fanciers, very attractive. When the coat is in full prime there should be a thick undercoat to give body warmth in cold weather and to help repel moisture. Variation in the length of the outer coat is not uncommon. A very long coat has the disadvantage of retaining a burdensome amount of water, particularly if it is soft and silky

108

**Bites**

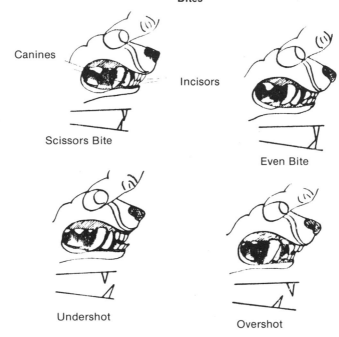

Canines

Incisors

Scissors Bite

Even Bite

Undershot

Overshot

**Forefeet**

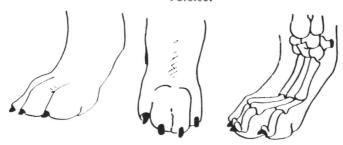

Three views of a well-constructed forefoot

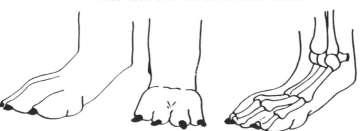

Three views of a splayed forefoot

in texture. All long-coated dogs are subject to the hazards and nuisance of burrs, and the longer and softer the coat, the more troublesome this can be. The ideal Golden coat is of medium length, firm but not coarse, and either flat or wavy. Rather curly or rough coats are seen now and then—no doubt a throwback to the Golden's spaniel ancestry. This sort of coat is harder to cope with, but it can be controlled by grooming and toweling if the dog is to be shown.

## Tail

The tail should follow the line of the croup, its tip reaching no further than the hock. This rule of thumb applies to the bony tip at the end, not the hair. Extra long hair on the tail may give the illusion of too much length to a dog that is already stretching the limit. In such instance, a small amount of careful trimming will help to tidy it up for show purposes and improve the dog's symmetry. The tail is highly expressive of personality, even to the wiggle of its very tip in response to a familiar voice during deep slumber. It should be carried happily with a slight upward curve, but not curled over the back, as this tends to spoil the effect of a straight topline. However, when *making game* in the field, a Golden almost always carries his tail very high, conveniently signaling to his handler how well he is tending to business.

## General Conformation

Inasmuch as the Golden Retriever's most important function is to hunt and to retrieve, and since much of his work is recovering water fowl, he should have greater substance than either the spaniel or the setter, yet still be of a size which permits him to share a duck blind or a small boat. He should be rugged, firmly muscled, and possess courage, endurance and persistence under all sorts of hunting conditions, whether in thick upland cover, heavy reeds, icy water, or salt water marshlands.

Ruggedness and sturdiness should never be confused with coarseness. Good bone is strong bone, not necessarily bone that is over-large. Bone varies in density, and differences in weight in dogs of the same size may be due to the quality of bone structure. Males in good condition often weigh close to eighty pounds, bitches up to seventy.

In conformation, the body of a mature Golden should have more length than height to allow room for the ribs to extend well back and to provide free action. The short cobby body which some breeders mistakenly seek in their quest for perfection can be had only at the sacrifice of certain features which are needed for stamina and endurance. The stiff back and bouncing gait is not an efficient substitute for suppleness and smooth rhythmic movement.

Years ago, a friend commented about my first Golden, Goldwood

110

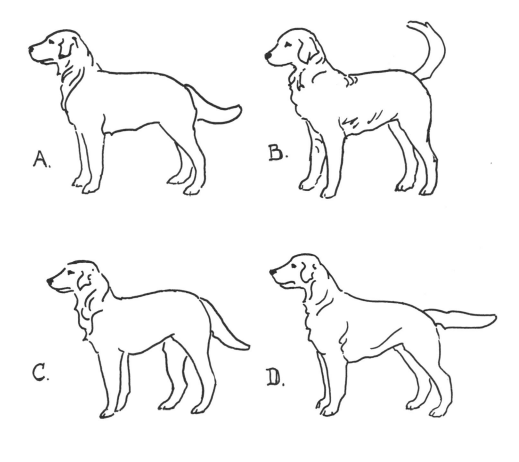

**Plate III: Balance and Imbalance**

A. Good balance and angulation with correct length of body for height which contributes to smooth and efficient action.

B. "Steep" front and rear quarters combined with too short a body, causing quick, choppy stride.

C. Imbalance of body, accentuated by high rear quarters. Left rear leg appears "sickle-hocked."

D. Imbalance due to falling off in the rear quarters with faulty topline.

Toby, UD, saying that a glass of water placed on his back would not spill as he trotted across the yard. The functional implications of this compliment to the dog's conformation meant but little at the time—I was just a lucky beginner with a good dog. A few years later I came into possession of McDowell Lyon's *The Dog In Action,* and the canine world took on new meaning. My interest in dog shows and field trials quickly went beyond just the ribbon winners, and even the mongrels roaming the streets became objects for study. Since then other written material has come to my attention, and the time and effort spent in perusing it has brought endless reward. Some people may have an instinctive eye for quality and proportion in animals, but for most of us a good eye is made, not born— achieved only through experience, observation and study.

It is interesting to watch retrievers running in a field test, especially along a path where their bodies are half eclipsed by a stand of tall grass, and to observe how the backs of some remain almost level with the horizontal while others seem to bob up and down. The differences, which at first glance may seem barely perceptible, become more noticeable—and significant—as the dogs return to line carrying game. Water tests also reveal interesting contrasts. Some retrievers seem to cut the water swiftly and easily on their way to a fall, while others paddle heavily and awkwardly with their shoulders chopping from side to side. Some, when picking up game, make a tight circle in the turn to pick up and return game. Others seem to need a wider circle and sweep to pick up the bird. These variations in movement are the result of differences in conformation which relate basically to angulation and balance.

Balance in the Golden has to do not only with the proportions of head-size, neck, depth of chest, and the ratio of body to legs, but to the angulation in both ends. If the front fails to match the rear, a Golden will not move properly, and gaiting defects will show up in the form of crabbing, over-reaching, hackneying, stiltedness, or other irregularities. Lack of balance also contributes to a dog's being higher in front or in the rear, perhaps creating the appearance of running uphill or downhill, even though he is moving on level ground. A dog with well angulated shoulders is off balance if the bones in his rear end are steeply set. Conversely, a dog with well bent hindquarters is off balance if his front is straight. It is all a matter of degree, but this is what the breed standard means when it says in the first paragraph, "over-all appearance, balance, gait and purpose should be given more emphasis than any of his component parts" (Plate III).

### Angulation (Plate IV)

Angulation refers to the bend in any or all of the joints and their influence on mechanical function and efficiency. In looking for balance, foremost consideration must be given to the two joints formed by the largest, strongest bones in the dog's body. One is the shoulder joint where

112

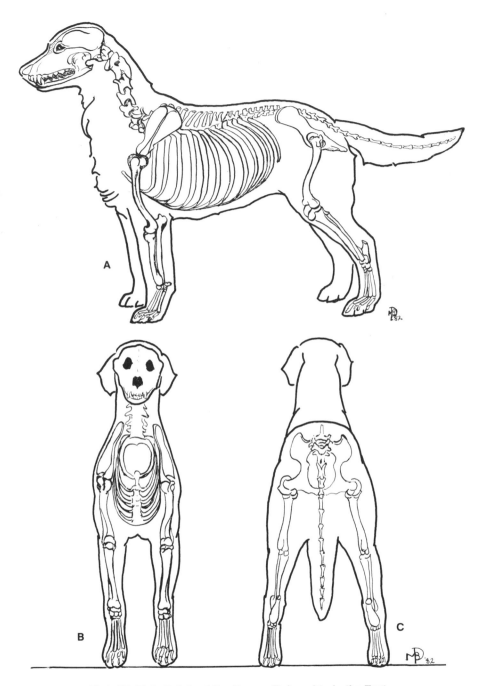

**Plate IV: Main Points of the Dog as Referred to in the Text**

Diagram A illustrates angulation in front and rear quarters. Length of a Golden from buttocks to forechest measures a bit longer than height from withers to pad in the ratio of 12:11. Diagrams B and C show the set of the bones from front and rear. These should remain relatively straight (from shoulder joint through the elbow and wrist to the pad and from the hip socket through the stifle and hock to pad, even when the legs tend to angle inward as speed increases).

the shoulder blade (scapula) meets the upper arm (humerus); the other is the hip socket where the thigh bone (femur) attaches to the pelvic girdle. The angles at these junctures should be approximately equal. The stifle and the hock should also have good bend, though not as acute as the aforementioned. Good angulation is largely responsible for freedom of motion and strongly influences the length of stride. To function as efficiently as possible, however, there must also be close interplay with a rib cage that is properly shaped, muscles that are firm, and ligaments that are strong.

### Front Quarters (Plate V)

In the ideal front, the shoulder blade should set moderately oblique with the ground and the upper arm should slope down and back at approximately the same angle. Correct positioning gives the scapula and humerus optimum bone length within the anatomical limitations established by the ribcage and muscles, and sets the elbow correctly against the chest wall. What we have failed to recognize is the great mobility of the shoulder blade as it pivots in elliptical fashion from its upper edge where it "lays in" against the foremost spinous processes (the withers). Nor have we recognized how the humerus serves as a powerful lever as it lifts the blade and helps transport the central body as smoothly as possible through the pectoral girdle. The assembly as a whole works like a shock-absorbing mechanism in cushioning impact with the ground. If the blades and upper arms are positioned too vertically, they become deprived of length and the shoulder joints assume a wider angle. As a result, the gait may be choppy, the body may roll from side to side and forelimb action may be restricted. An upright humerus, in combination with a well laid back shoulder, also restricts freedom of action and may cause padding.

It is important to understand what constitutes a good front. It is an easy matter to read about canine structure, quite another to apply what one reads to live dogs. A good first step is to find a knowledgeable judge or breeder who will show an example by which to set a standard. It may not be the ideal for a Golden, but will perhaps come close to it. Then one should observe a few classes of short-coated Sporting dogs at a show. There will be varying degrees of quality in almost any class—none of which can be disguised through clever grooming. On each entry, the observer should study the neck and backline. If the neck seems to have good length by reason of merging gradually into the withers, chances are the shoulder is correctly laid back. If the upper arm is also properly positioned (slanting back as well as down) there will be normal prominence of the manubrium breastbone—which means better attachment of the pectoral muscles that support the trunk and help stabilize movement. The dog has no fully developed collar bone to act as a supportive buttress or strut between the lower blade and breastbone, so optimum muscular control is vital to

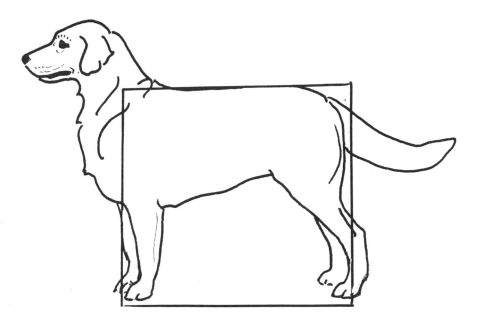

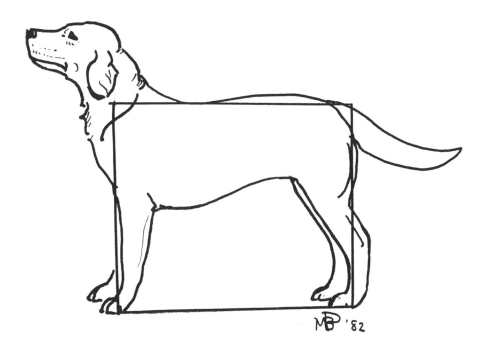

**Plate V**

One dog can appear longer than another even though both are equal in height and length of body. The desired short back of the dog in the top figure is due to properly set shoulders and pelvic bone.

correct gaiting. It must be remembered that there is a wide range from poor to perfect, and placements in the show ring can be based only on comparisons among the entries present. On one's own Golden, a carpenter's rule may be used to indicate *approximate* angulation, but there is no scientific accuracy in measuring the live dog, for the slightest shift in position, even a turn of the head, can change things. Muscles are never stable, and the various landmarks used in measuring angulation can result in widely different figures on the same dog. We should rely on the trained eye rather than on the measuring stick.

### Back, Rib Section, Coupling (Plates III, V)

A short back is desirable when it is the result of good shoulder lay-back and a well angulated rear, but shortness should not be mistaken for a virtue when it is due to a middle piece crowded together by steep shoulders, short rib cage and slack hindquarters. Short necks, steep shoulders, and short rib cages are often found as a trio. People differ in their understanding of back measurement; the length is usually determined by the distance from the upper tips of the scapula to the front edge of the pelvis. It is possible for a Golden of correct length and height to appear too long because he may lack angulation in one or both ends, leaving him with a comparatively long mid-section. If the brisket should lack depth he will look "spare" and "leggy." The coupling (flank) may also be too long—a fault that often combines with lack of muscling across the loin to make the back *soft*. Sometimes excess length in the coupling causes roaching which helps to relieve strain on spinal vertebrae, not supported by ribs. Any number of combinations can affect the total picture.

The rib cage should be oval in its cross section, gaining most of its spring from either side of the spinal column and narrowing gradually to the sternum, or forechest (Plate IV). Too round a rib cage interferes with front action and may cause the dog to move out at the elbows or toe in. Or the front may be so steeply positioned toward the forechest that the legs must swing in pendulum fashion, causing roll at the shoulders and restricting forward reach (Plate VI). The sternum base of the rib section should reach to the level of the elbows and extend well to the rear. This gives more room for shoulder layback and muscle attachment, making the dog well ribbed up. An ample rib section also increases staying power by supplying more space for heart and lungs, which of course contributes to a retriever's swimming ability, and at the same time lends strength and suppleness to the back. It is rare that a Golden's rib section is so narrow that the tips of the blades squeeze too tightly together when the dog lowers his head to pick up game, but it is possible. In Goldens the reverse condition is more usual, i.e., the shoulders tend to be widely spaced because of the prevalence of steep short blades. When fronts of this sort become heavily muscled, they give the appearance of being loaded in the shoulder.

116

## Forefeet

The front pasterns should be strong with only a bit of slope, the feet round, cat-like, and well knuckled, with thick pads. Not only are the pasterns and feet part of the shock-absorbing effectiveness of the forequarters, but good feet help to resist injury when the going is rough. Splayed feet are flat feet, a fault that encourages fatigue. Exercising helps to strengthen the muscles, but really good feet are born, not made.

## Rear Quarters (Plate VIII)

Retrievers need rear quarters that permit good extension of the limbs and easy flexion of all joints in order to provide strong thrust and follow-through in water as well as on land. Outline of the croup is influenced largely by the way the spine connects with the pelvis at the sacrum. When correct, the Golden's croup will show only a gentle slope toward the base of the tail. The pelvis itself has a normal slant of about thirty degrees off the horizontal.

When viewed from the side, a Golden that is properly angulated in the hind quarters will stand naturally with his rear pasterns perpendicular to the ground on a line just behind the point of the buttocks. If the second thighs are too long and spindly, the dog will be over-angulated and give the appearance of standing too far behind himself. If the second thighs are too short, the legs will set under the rear too much and the dog will be steep or straight.

Occasionally dogs are faulted for being "too long in the hock." The hock is the joint between the second thigh and the pastern, so should be correctly referred to in terms of strength or bend rather than length. On the Golden, the hock should set moderately low. A cat, a rabbit, or a deer depends upon initial spring for its get-away and therefore requires a high hock and long pastern. Moderately low hocks mean shorter rear pasterns and stronger second thighs—features which contribute to endurance in long distance running. A severe fault in hind action stems from lack of hock flexion, called sickle hocks, where movement is so restricted that the lower legs shuffle with little, if any, extension or contraction.

The sloping stance seen now and again in the show ring is sometimes a cover-up for a poorly angulated rear, as the unnatural crouch accentuates bend at the joints. Most exhibitors are quite critical of this sort of showmanship and prefer to present their Goldens in natural stance and to gait them on loose leads. Whether standing or trotting, the Golden should move with his back as level as possible. If he is balanced and well angulated, this should present no problem. Smooth rhythmic action is what judges look for when they watch entries from the side, for whether in the show ring, field, or home, sporting dogs should be constructed to cover the ground with as little effort as possible. Their ability to move well may be of no consequence to pet owners, but it makes a vast difference to hunters, and breeders should therefore be ever watchful for the qualities needed in working retrievers.

### Gait (Plates VI, VII)

The trot is generally considered the best gait at which to judge conformation, for it shows how the position and relative length of the bones influence over-all balance. At this gait, the diagonally opposite legs move back and forth simultaneously, each assuming an equal portion of stress, and the timing should be such that the front feet leave the ground just ahead of the oncoming hind feet—with no interference or over-reaching. As the dog moves faster, it becomes increasingly important that there be as little body sway as possible in order to minimize fatigue and facilitate efficient forward travel. To accomplish this, nature makes every effort to balance the bulk of weight over a single line of support as speed increases, just as a human being runs in a straight line with one foot in front of the other. Thus, when viewed from the front or the rear, the dog's legs should tend to angle inward toward a central line beneath his body, seeming almost to converge on one track as he trots faster. When the action is correct, the hind legs travel on the same planes as the front, with no excess twisting or turning in or out at the various joints. Variations in height, breadth of body and length of leg influence the extent to which movement is achieved according to this principle, but all dogs make the effort—even the low-stationed Basset Hounds and Bulldogs.

Occasionally a Golden prefers to pace rather than trot. Pacing is a rolling lateral gait in which both legs on the same side move forward and back at the same time, in contrast to the diagonal action of the trot (Plate VII). There are several reasons why dogs pace. It may be a compensating action to avoid leg interference when variances in body proportions are a factor. It may be caused by spinal injury, or discomfort in the hip or stifle joints. Often, however, it is caused by fatigue, because dogs that are weary sometimes rest their muscles by switching to the lateral movement. I have seen sledge dogs pacing as they neared the finish line of a race, some due to exhaustion, others because of strain which caused painful roaching in the backs. Still others, perhaps because of better physical condition, or better over-all balance, trotted across the line in tireless effort. Pacing is frowned upon in the show ring, and if a Golden resorts to it a quick jerk on the leash will usually make him break into a trot. Better still, his handler should start him off squarely and briskly so that he will have no chance at all to be pulled off balance, and thus run the risk of not moving as he should.

Rather common among Goldens is the fault known as crabbing, (Plate VII), where the rear legs track to one side to avoid interference with the front feet. The expression is taken from the sea crab which moves forward in a more or less sidewise position. This sort of action is caused by structural imbalance where there is less angulation in front than in the rear,

118

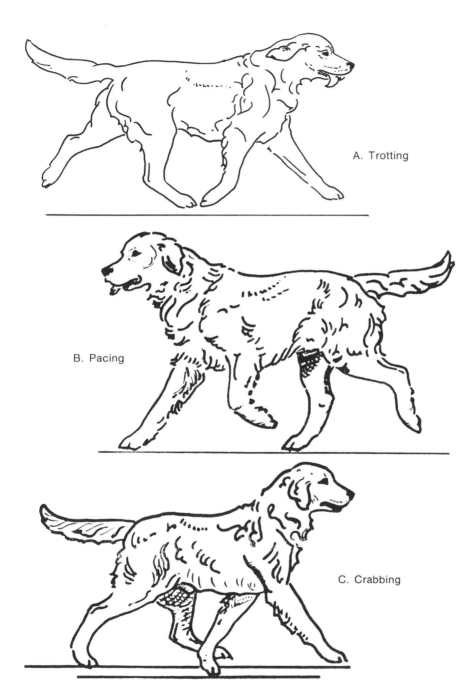

A. Trotting

B. Pacing

C. Crabbing

**Plate VI: Gaits**

in combination with a short back, or it may be due to spinal disorder. Over-reaching is a similar fault, but less serious because the line of the body remains fairly straight, whereas in crabbing the rear actually twists to one side.

Closely related is pounding where the steep front restricts reach and causes the feet to strike the ground hard before the rear drive is expended— almost like a person taking a quick step to keep from falling forward when pushed suddenly from behind. The jarring is transmitted directly upward through the shoulders and can be seen through jerking withers as the dog trots or gallops. To avoid pounding when trotting, a dog may pad by flipping and extending his front feet a bit just before they hit the ground, thus gaining a split second more to soften the thrust from the rear. Hackney gaiting serves the same purpose. This term is derived from the fashionable hackney driving horses where high knee and hock action is sought for flashiness and style. For the ground-covering Sporting dog, however, nothing could be a greater waste of energy. The Golden that is very steep both fore and aft will gait with short bouncy steps, like a terrier. Such action may seem lively and gay, but it must be remembered that short steps mean more of them to get where the dog is going, and bouncing action compromises with motion that should be smooth and straight ahead.

As a Golden approaches a spectator, his limbs should remain as straight as possible from shoulder to pad, even as they angle inward with increasing speed (Plate VI). The elbows should not turn outward, called out at the elbows, nor should they punch or twist with pressure. Inward bending of the front pasterns causes the dog to move close or to throw his feet outward. Weakness in the pasterns also contributes to toeing in. A foot that swings both in and out is winging. Occasionally a Golden is muscle-bound or has trouble in the shoulder or elbow joints. This restricts freedom in those areas and causes the legs to swing out and forward in paddling fashion. As a result, the foot-fall may be wider than normal and the body will roll from side to side.

On going away, the limbs should remain as straight as possible from hip to pad (Plate VIII). A common failing is hocks that turn in, called cowhocks. If the fault is only slight, the rear pasterns will set parallel to one another, causing the dog to move closer as he trots away. It is more serious if the hocks and pasterns actually brush or interfere as they pass each other. Severe cowhocks cause a turning out of the stifles as well as the feet. This weakens the propelling power of the hind quarters, for the leg bones are thrown out of line and the muscles and ligaments subjected to unnatural strain. Opposite in appearance to cowhocks are spread or barrel hocks, which make the feet toe in and may even cause interference or crossing (Plate VIII).

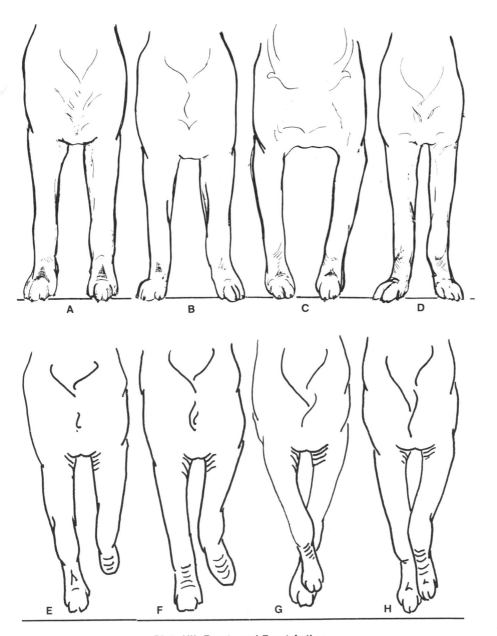

## Plate VII: Fronts and Front Action

A. Normal standing position. Notice that feet do not set "dead ahead," but position themselves naturally for better balance.

B. Faulty bend in left pastern joint.

C. Elbows out, causing dog to "toe-in."

D. Narrow front with feet turning "east and west" due to inward bending of wrists (carpal or pastern joints).

E. Normal action showing how limbs angle inward under center line of balance as speed increases.

F. Winging or twisting.

G. Crossing.

H. Moving close.

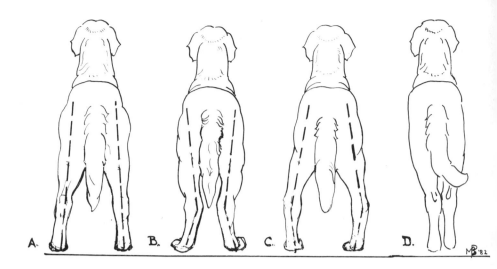

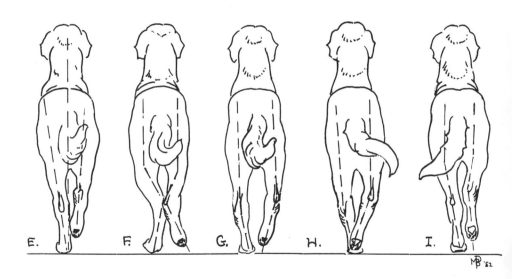

**Plate VIII: Hindquarters and Rear Action**

A. Normal Stance  B. Cowhocks  C. Spread Hocks  D. Standing Close
E. Normal action showing tendency of legs to angle inward as speed increases
F. Severe cowhocks with interference  G. Spread Hocks  H. Crossing  I. Moving Close

## Inherited Defects

There are innumerable combinations of merits and faults in both type and conformation, ranging from fair to excellent or from slight to severe. A few faults are listed as disqualifications and bar Goldens from the show ring. The maximum and minimum requirement for height helps to maintain uniformity of a size that is practical for hunting purposes. Eyelid deformities, which include entropion, distichiasis, and trichiasis, are inherited defects that cause irritation to the cornea due to abnormally positioned eyelashes. The condition causes considerable pain, and dogs have been known to lose their sight because of it. An operation is the only solution. Undershot and overshot bites are serious enough to cause early wearing, loosening and possibly premature loss of teeth. Malocclusions also encourage gingivitis (inflammation of the gums).

The American Kennel Club automatically rules against the showing of dogs that are blind, deaf, spayed or castrated, or which have undergone corrective surgery for congenital defects. Also, males must have two normal testicles normally located in the scrotum. The absence of one or both is known as monorchidism or cryptorchidism. The condition may affect fertility in males, often causing sterility, and dogs with retained testicles may be prone to cancer.

Among other inherited defects known to have occurred in Golden Retrievers are the eye diseases juvenile cataract and progressive retinal atrophy, both of which contribute to partial or total blindness. Hip dysplasia, a deformity of the hip socket, plagues many breeds and causes varying degrees of lameness. The wise breeder will endeavor to limit the occurrence of these abnormalities by having the sire and dam of proposed matings checked by a competent veterinarian ahead of time. A most serious aspect of this whole reference to inherited abnormalities is the effect that they may exercise on temperament, for dogs that are suffering from pain, or that are frightened of shadows or people because of partial vision, are apt to become irritable and shy, perhaps even vicious. If this occurs, the cause should be traced immediately. Bad temperament in the Golden should never, never be tolerated. His good nature is his greatest claim to fame, and it should be preserved above all else.

## OFFICIAL STANDARD FOR THE GOLDEN RETRIEVER

### Effective January 1, 1982

**General Appearance**—A symmetrical, powerful, active dog, sound and well put together, not clumsy nor long in the leg, displaying a kindly expression and possessing a personality that is eager, alert and self-confident. Primarily a hunting dog, he should be shown in hard working condition. Over-all appearance, balance, gait and purpose to be given more emphasis than any of his component parts.

**Head**—Broad in skull, slightly arched laterally and longitudinally without prominence of frontal bones (forehead) or occipital bones. Stop well defined but not abrupt. Foreface deep and wide, nearly as long as skull. Muzzle straight in profile, blending smoothly and strongly into skull; when viewed in profile or from above, slightly deeper and wider at stop than at tip. No heaviness in flews. Removal of whiskers is permitted but not preferred.

**Eyes**—Friendly and intelligent in expression, medium large with dark, close-fitting rims, set well apart and reasonably deep in sockets. Color preferably dark brown; medium brown acceptable. Slant eyes and narrow, triangular eyes detract from correct expression and are to be faulted. No white or haw visible when looking straight ahead. Dogs showing evidence of functional abnormality of eyelids or eyelashes (such as, but not limited to, trichiasis, entropion, ectropion, or distichiasis) are to be excused from the ring.

**Teeth**—Scissors bite, in which the outer side of the lower incisors touches the inner side of the upper incisors. Undershot or overshot bite is a disqualification. Misalignment of teeth (irregular placement of incisors) or a level bite (incisors meet each other edge to edge) is undesirable, but not to be confused with undershot or overshot. Full dentition. Obvious gaps are serious faults.

**Nose**—Black or brownish black, though fading to a lighter shade in cold weather not serious. Pink nose or one seriously lacking in pigmentation to be faulted.

**Ears**—Rather short with front edge attached well behind and just above the eye and falling close to cheek. When pulled forward, tip of ear should just cover the eye. Low, hound-like ear set to be faulted.

**Neck**—Medium long, merging gradually into well laid back shoulders, giving sturdy, muscular appearance. Untrimmed natural ruff. No throatiness.

**Body**—Well-balanced, short coupled, deep through the chest. Chest between forelegs at least as wide as a man's closed hand including thumb, with well-developed forechest.

Brisket extends to elbow. Ribs long and well sprung but not barrel shaped, extending well towards hindquarters. Loin short, muscular, wide and deep, with very little tuck-up. Back line strong and level from withers to slightly sloping croup, whether standing or moving. Slabsidedness, narrow chest, lack of depth in brisket, sloping back line, roach or sway back, excessive tuck-up, flat or steep croup to be faulted.

**Forequarters**—Muscular, well coordinated with hindquarters and capable of free movement. Shoulder blades long and well laid back with upper tips fairly close together at withers. Upper arms appear about the same length as the blades, setting the elbows back beneath the upper tip of the blades, close to the ribs without looseness. Legs, viewed from the front, straight with good bone, but not to the point of coarseness. Pasterns short and strong, sloping slightly with no suggestion of weakness.

**Hindquarters**—Broad and strongly muscled. Profile of croup slopes slightly; the pelvic bone slopes at a slightly greater angle (approximately 30 degrees from horizontal). In a natural stance, the femur joins the pelvis at approximately a 90 degree angle; stifles well bent; hocks well let down with short, strong rear pasterns. Legs straight when viewed from rear. Cow hocks, spread hocks, and sickle hocks to be faulted.

**Feet**—Medium size, round, compact, and well knuckled, with thick pads. Excess hair may be trimmed to show natural size and contour. Dewclaws on forelegs may be removed, but are normally left on. Splayed or hare feet to be faulted

**Tail**—Well set on, thick and muscular at the base, following the natural line of the croup. Tail bones extend to, but not below, the point of hock. Carried with merry action, level or with some moderate upward curve; never curled over back nor between legs.

**Coat**—Dense and water repellent with good undercoat. Outer coat firm and resilient, neither coarse nor silky, lying close to body; may be straight or wavy. Moderate feathering on back of forelegs and on underbody; heavier feathering on front of neck, back of thighs and underside of tail. Coat on head, paws, and front of legs is short and even. Excessive length, open coats, and limp, soft coats are very undesirable. Feet may be trimmed and stray hairs neatened, but the natural appearance of coat or outline should not be altered by cutting or clipping.

**Color**—Rich, lustrous golden of various shades. Feathering may be lighter than rest of coat. With the exception of greying or whitening of face or body due to age, any white marking, other than a few white hairs on the chest, should be penalized according to its extent. Allowable light shadings are not to be confused with white markings. Predominant body color which is either extremely pale or extremely dark is undesirable. Some latitude should be given to the light puppy whose coloring shows promise of deepening with maturity. Any noticeable area of black or other off-color hair is a serious fault.

**Gait**—When trotting, gait is free, smooth, powerful, and well coordinated, showing good reach. Viewed from any position, legs turn neither in nor out, nor do feet cross or interfere with each other. As speed increases, feet tend to converge toward center line of balance. It is recommended that dogs be shown on a loose lead to reflect true gait.

**Size**—Males 23-24 inches in height at withers; females 21½-22½ inches. Dogs up to one inch above or below standard size should be proportionately penalized. Deviation in height of more than one inch from the standard shall disqualify. Length from breastbone to point of buttocks slightly greater than height at withers in ratio of 12:11. Weight for dogs 65-75 pounds; bitches 55-65 pounds.

**Temperament**—Friendly, reliable, and trustworthy. Quarrelsomeness or hostility towards other dogs or people in normal situations, or an unwarranted show of timidity or nervousness, is not in keeping with Golden Retriever character.

Such actions should be penalized according to their significance.

**Faults**—Any departure from the described ideal shall be considered faulty to the degree to which it interferes with the breed's purpose or is contrary to breed character.

**Disqualifications**—1. Deviation in height of more than one inch from standard either way. 2. Undershot or overshot bite.

# 5

# Early Field Training

*by Forrest L. Flashman, M.D.*

---

**T**HE TRAINING OF DOGS for any purpose is quite similar to the training of children for their respective places in the world. I might say that there are two real basic differences: A puppy grows so fast that he covers, in one year, what most of our children cover in eight to ten years. Secondly, I am sure we all realize that the dog, while very willing to please and learn, has his handicaps in comparison to a child—to our way of thinking, at least by his limited intellect. In puppy training, and particularly retriever training for specialty field trials, we must outline clearly in our own minds a few basic habit patterns we wish to set up in the puppy, and then adhere closely to this training pattern, with a minimal number of commands.

I feel that the sooner a puppy can be brought to its new home (right after weaning, if possible) the better adjusted the animal will become, as far as our everyday human world is concerned. Close contact with humans at a very early age does much to give the puppy confidence, courage, and a knowledge of his master that he cannot gain if he is to stay in a kennel the first six or seven months of his life. The puppy should be allowed to come into the house and should be taught his place very early. Housebreaking should come naturally, and if it is necessary to kennel the puppy, he should be kennelled as close to the house as possible—part of the back porch, or some such arrangement, is ideal for the first few months.

FC-AFC Cherryhill's Rowdy Rascal (AFC Holway Barty ex Cherryhill Hawtdaugh***) owned and handled by Darlene Corona and bred by Cathy Shives, has a record of consistent placing in trials from Derby on up.

Skylab Belvedere's Baby Doll*** (AFC Holway Barty ex Skylab Gandy Dancer*), owned by Mercedes Hitchcock, is considered an excellent derby bitch.

Ben's Enchanted Budweiser (FC-AFC Benjamin Rajah Frisbee ex Pacapooche's Pollywog), owned by Darrell Frisbie. This is another example of a highly successful trial dog. In 1981 Buddy led all retriever breeds for the number of derby points with 66. He is a winner of the Charles Morgan Memorial Award and has numerous other impressive achievements in retriever trials.

**Obedience (sometimes called Yard-Training)**

A two- or three-month-old puppy should learn the basic commands of heel on and off leash, sitting, and staying. I have found my Golden puppies very apt pupils and capable of mastering these two or three simple commands within the first two or three days of their life at home. I usually use only two commands during the early life of the puppy; one is to heel, and that means no matter where the puppy may be in the yard when he hears the word "heel," he is to come directly to my left side and stay in position by the left knee. Secondly, once in this position and he gets the command to sit, he is to sit and stay there until he is commanded to leave this position. You must be consistent in correction and in commands to achieve this obedience early. In other words, once you start a series of commands, you should carry through with it. Don't attempt to train a puppy when you are playing with him. Avoid all the confusion possible. Very early, with a "sit" command, I introduce puppies to the whistle. The whistle command for "sit" is one sharp, short whistle. As you proceed through the months of retriever training, it is always advisable to use one short whistle to sit your dog, as it will make future handling-training so much easier. To heel early at the command "heel" and to stay heeled will avoid much future confusion, both in the hunting field and in actual field trials, as there is nothing more annoying than to have one's dog heeling 10 or 15 feet in front of you, and particularly when approaching the line under the ever-critical eyes of the judges. All dogs should come when called, and puppies should come as fast as their little legs will carry them. If the puppy is told to sit and stay as the handler walks away, he will be just "bustin'" to come when called, and it takes very little of this to set up a habit pattern of coming in rapidly when the dog gets his come-in whistles, a series of short, sharp toots. In fact, you usually have to brace yourself, as your puppy's small, inadequate brakes fail to hold as it approaches you. These little lessons should be repeated daily, and as a general rule five to 10 minutes at a time is sufficient to put your point across and still keep your puppy enthusiastic.

**Retrieving**

Early retrieving should be playing, as far as the puppy is concerned. An owner-handler and trainer of puppies can teach them quite a bit at this age. I usually use three very light training dummies, something that a puppy can snap up off the ground and bring in rapidly. These are small, cork-filled boat bumpers, rather soft. I always try to give the puppy at least two retrieves in succession, and preferably three, as I am firmly convinced that this alerts the puppy to the fact that there is usually more than one bird down, and it will help establish a habit pattern that will prevent him from becoming glued on any one downed bird at a time, so that he will fail to see other birds down that he must retrieve. The dummies for the puppies are thrown by me, and at 180° to each other. This serves two purposes: There is no difficulty in getting your puppy to bring the dummy back to you, as he has to come by you in order to retrieve the second. Secondly, there can be no question that the dummy he goes after is the one he brings back; in other words, there can be no attempt to change his mind and go from one dummy to the other, or switching birds, as retriever language dubs it. The third dummy is thrown after the puppy has retrieved his first and is on his way to the second, and this third dummy is thrown usually in the same position in which the first dummy was thrown, so that, as soon as the puppy delivers the second dummy, he is turned and sent for the third. I believe this teaches two things: one is the multiplicity of birds down, so that he does not get into the habit of retrieving one or two and quitting, and second, it establishes early the puppy's habit of going where you point. The ability to set a dog down (point the direction you want him to go and have him go in that direction) is a very basic part of his later retrieving training. After being exposed to this type of land work with multiple dummies, a four- or five-months-old puppy will have enough confidence in his handler to run out on a line some 30 to 50 feet and retrieve an unseen or hidden dummy.

## Introduction to Birds

A duck wing or a pheasant wing is a very natural feathered object for a puppy to retrieve; however, I would advise using such dummies for only a very limited time, as we are very anxious not to establish a retrieving pattern by which the dog picks up the pheasant or duck by a wing and drags it in, bumping the ground all the way back to the handler. I much prefer to use dead pigeons or small dead ducks, securing the wings to the body, so that there is nothing for the puppy to do except pick the bird up by the body and bring it in. Here, a word of caution: I think it is extremely inadvisable to introduce young retrievers (particularly Golden Retrievers) to crippled or live game. Golden Retrievers are soft-mouthed dogs to start with and will very rapidly develop annoying habits of rolling or mouthing the birds, if the bird is fluttering or struggling. Never give your puppy a chance to develop bad retrieving habits that you can avoid. There is plenty of time to learn to fight a wounded bird after the puppy has become big of bone, muscle and jaw.

## Introduction to Water

I do not believe that the average Golden Retriever has the same desire or liking for water that the Labrador or Chesapeake has, so that in introducing your Golden puppy to water it should be play and fun. I am sure you and I would both agree that we much prefer wading in warm, shallow water than we do being pushed off a bank into cold water over our heads. It helps to introduce puppies to water if they can go for walks with

It's not unusual for very young Golden puppies to exhibit behavior patterns for retrieving before any training is ever undertaken. This is 8-week-old "Clipper", owned by Nancy Corbin. He is linebred from FC-AFC Misty's Sungold Lad, CDX.

Culynwood's Sunclad Chloe (Ch. Ginger Rock Sam, CD** ex Ch. Tangelo's End of the Rainbow, CD, WC), owned by Joan Pollack and bred by Lynn Fletcher. Chloe commenced training early and at less than three months was doing well in the water. This was in part because she was taught to enjoy these sessions. Chloe later acquired a CD and a WCX.                    *Dorothy Carter*

131

Lucky indeed is the Golden breeder and trainer to have access to water for working with puppies. These six-week-old youngsters, owned by Claire Broderick, learn early to enjoy the water as they play in a gentle creek.

*Dorothy Carter*

As the puppies grow, their experience in water should become wider. While these nine-week-old puppies explore the lakeside, supervision is close by.

132

older dogs, play in and around puddles, streams, lake shores, etc., as a part of their daily outing, rather than as a necessary part of retrieving. This is particularly true early, and I feel that introduction to water, in the company of an older dog, will do much to help set up a good pattern of water entry, which is one of charging in, with a big bounce and splash, rather than running up and down the bank and finally tip-toeing out gingerly.

The Golden Retriever's return from a water retrieve has always been one of his weak points. There may be several reasons for this. 1: Many dogs are introduced to the water, at least part of it, by having to retrieve a live duck, which may be struggling, or which may be helping the dog (fastened onto the dog's ear). A youngster will often pick up rather a bad habit of placing his duck down at the water-land junction, in order to readjust a hold, when he should pick his head up and come bouncing in, with his bird. 2: Goldens, with their long hair, are probably very heavy when they first emerge from water and take their first few steps, and I am sure this further slows a dog that has any tendency to be slow. 3: I have seen very few trainers go into ecstacy and throw their arms around a very wet dog when he has brought back a duck, but we often see this on land when a puppy has returned with a dummy or bird. I am sure an intelligent, sensitive animal like the Golden very rapidly senses he is not quite as desirable when dripping wet as when dry, and I don't think it takes many retrieves in which the handler backs up and avoids his dog, to set up a habit pattern of slow return and delivery from a water retrieve.

There is no doubt in my mind that the Golden Retriever, out of the three popular retrieving breeds, usually has as good, or better, ability to absorb training, to seek out and find downed game with his eyes and nose, and to run as hard and fast as his black and brown contemporaries.

This can all be summed up in:

Be consistent
Keep it simple
Keep it fun

Mark's Mendota Luke (Sandstorm of Northbreak ex Mark's Mingo), owned by the Hon. Bruce F. Beilfuss, Chief Justice of the Wisconsin Supreme Court. This expressive photo, by Keith Buchert, was taken about eight miles north of LaCrosse on the Wisconsin side of the Mississippi. It was selected as the cover illustration for Volume 2, Number 2 of the popular magazine *Gun Dog*.

# 6

# Training for Retriever Field Trials

*by Ann F. Walters*

$F$IELD TRIAL COMPETITION is the ultimate goal of the retriever owner. Once struck by the desire to test his dog against the top retrievers of all breeds, the owner of a retriever may find field trials becoming an all-consuming interest.

## Introduction

There are many retriever field trials held in all parts of the United States. As of this writing, there are 136 trial-giving clubs in at least 42 different states, and many of these clubs give two licensed trials a year, as well as more frequent informal trials. These trials are open to all breeds of retrievers recognized by the AKC, as well as Irish Water Spaniels. In fact, only the three most popular breeds—the Labrador, Golden and Chesapeake—are regularly competing now, with an occasional Flat-Coated Retriever. Of these breeds, the Labrador is by far the most prevalent, since the average Labrador has the qualities that most field-trialers are looking for. But the top-working Goldens are second to none, and many is the number of retriever owners who would gladly sell their souls for a really good working Golden.

Goldens are often possessed of certain qualities that are a great asset in trial competition, and other qualities which can be a definite detriment. The average Golden of non-working background (i.e., his immediate

FC-AFC Stilrovin Savannah Gay, with her owner
Mrs. Ann Walters.

The Bill Lester Memorial Trophy is a rotating, perpetual award offered by the Golden
Retriever Club of America to the dog with the best record in the field and show ring for
the year. Open to dogs owned by Club members only. It was re-donated by Dr.
Forrest Flashman after he won it three times. *Harold Mack, Jr.*

ancestors have been bred for reasons other than real working ability) is generally a mediocre trial dog at best. On the other hand, he may well make a fine shooting dog, since he is inclined to be slow, but consistent. More and more conscientious breeders are trying hard to preserve the working ability in the breed, even though their main interest may be in bench show competition, or just raising nice family dogs. A few breeders are striving to breed Goldens of true trial caliber, and, by the record, it would seem they are succeeding.

Any prospective owner, who wishes to acquire a Golden for working competition, would do well to go to considerable effort to be sure his puppy is of proven working stock. If he can attend field trials and watch the dogs in actual competition, he will have a much clearer idea of what it is he is after. He should not hesitate to ask other retriever owners, even if they are not Golden owners. They will undoubtedly know with whom to get in touch in their area, or in other parts of the country. Retriever people are a clannish group, and know just what is going on in their field of interest all over the country.

Of prime importance, when looking for a puppy, is the breeding. Look for the trial record of both parents and grandparents. If it is possible to get an impartial criticism of the parents as workers, it can be even more helpful than the trial record, since not every top-grade worker gets to the trials.

Ideally, the future owner should see, not only his puppy and the parents, but as many close relatives as possible. He should watch them in action, looking for the characteristics that will make the type of dog suitable to his needs. If this is impossible, he will have to rely on the record. A puppy from a line that has consistently produced good workers is generally a safer bet than a puppy who has one spectacular parent, with the other ancestors unknown quantities.

The novice trainer-handler, who intends to make his dog a do-it-yourself project, can get great satisfaction from the calmer, more consistent type of dog. Many is the field-trialer who came into the game in this way, and great credit is due the dog who week after week can do the work while his inexperienced handler is learning the ropes. This characteristic of consistency and level-headedness is one of the Golden's fine attributes. When it can be combined with style, it is an unbeatable combination.

Style is a quality most desirable in a trial dog. It is made up of drive, speed, manner of moving, bird-handling, water-entry, etc. Every move the dog makes is done with style, or not, and, at a trial, will be judged accordingly. The really stylish dog is exciting to watch and exciting to handle, and will place over the dog without style as long as the quality of the work is the same. Sometimes, however, the great drive that makes a stylish dog can make this same dog highly excitable in a trial situation. A dog like this is harder to keep under control, and is more inclined to lose his wits and get into trouble. The great trial dogs must always combine brains and stability of temperament with the real desire and drive that create style.

Physical soundness is also an absolute must. A dog that is not properly constructed will break down under the hours of work necessary to train a dog for trials. An unsound dog is rarely a pleasing mover. It is usually wise to reject a puppy who is not soundly made as soon as the physical fault is apparent. It is heart-breaking to see a dog with the desire to work struggle against a physical handicap.

Therefore, the prospective owner of a field trial Golden is looking for a puppy from parents who have proved their working ability under actual trial competition, or are known to be excellent workers by competent authority. If these parents have proved their ability to produce good workers, it is even better. The qualities to look for in parents and offspring are: physical soundness, intelligence, a stable temperament, and the tremendous desire to retrieve, on both land and water, which results in a stylish worker.

## Field Trials

Retriever field trials are open to any purebred retriever or Irish Water Spaniel, registered or listed with the AKC, over six months of age. There are four stakes, or classes, in which a dog may be entered, but not all four are given at every trial.

The least advanced stake is the Derby, for dogs under two years of age. Derby entrants should be able to mark between one and three birds on land and water: handling ability is not required of Derby dogs. Judges are looking for promise—natural ability and style, rather than training. Derby dogs are required to be steady on line without a leash, that is, not break to retrieve until the judge gives permission, and they must deliver to hand. Recently, the quality of young dogs has improved to such a degree that Derby stakes can have marking tests as demanding as those in the more advanced stakes.

The next most advanced stake is the Qualifying, so called because the first and second place dogs in this stake become qualified for Limited and Special all-age stakes. This stake is open to retrievers of all ages, who have not had a judges' award of merit or better in an Open stake or placed in an Amateur stake or won two Qualifying stakes. This stake is a middle ground for dogs between the Derby work and the most advanced work. Marking tests may be somewhat harder than in the Derby, and some handling ability is necessary.

The top competition comes in the two championship stakes: the Open, or Limited and Special, all-age, which is open to all retrievers, and the Amateur all-age, which is open to all retrievers when handled by an amateur. Amateur and professional handlers can compete in the Open, but no professionals are allowed to compete in the Amateur. The four dogs that place in these stakes receive championship points, toward a field championship in the Amateur, or in the Open when handled by an

Ronakers Belvedere Firewater (Holway Gillie*** ex Skylab Belvedere's Baby Doll***), owned by Ronakers Kennels and bred by Mercedes Hitchcock. "Fire" is believed to be the youngest Golden ever to be awarded a working certificate. This remarkable youngster was just six months, six days old when he passed his tests.

amateur. The Limited and Special all-age stakes are limited to dogs who have been awarded judges' awards of merit or better in either championship stake, or who have placed first or second in the Qualifying.

More details concerning each of these stakes, and the rules and regulations of field trials in general, can be found in the booklet entitled, *Rules Applying to Registration and Field Trials,* which can be acquired from the American Kennel Club on request. A supplement to these rules is also available, giving more details on trial work. Anyone entering a licensed trial is expected to be familiar with these two publications.

In each stake four places are awarded. At the judges' discretion, dogs completing the trial with satisfactory work, but not placing, are awarded judges' awards of merit. Only dogs placing in the championship stakes receive points toward a field championship.

The placing dogs are decided by a process of elimination in each stake. The judges (there are two) start with a test on which each dog is tried, one by one. Those dogs who have not disqualified themselves, or whose work has not been considered unsatisfactory by the judges, are called back by the judges to a second test. This process is continued until the judges have seen enough work to make a decision. The dogs must be tested on both land and water.

Every effort is made to keep conditions equal for each dog. When a test is set up, the judges try to keep it the same for each dog running on that test. Generally ducks are used for the water retrieves, either shot or live-shackled (feet and wings tied). On land, pheasants are used, either flying and shot in the test, or thrown dead. In some parts of the country, pigeons are used in the minor (non-championship) stakes.

Many clubs give less formal trials, as well as the important licensed trials where championship stakes are held. At these the rigid rules of the AKC standards can be relaxed if the club so desires.

Retriever trial tests fall into two categories—marking tests and blinds. In a marking test, the dog can see the fall of the bird, and is expected to remember it, go to the area when commanded to do so, and hunt out the bird. In a blind retrieve, the dog has not seen the fall, the handler knows where the bird is, and the dog is directed, by hand signals and voice commands only, to the bird. Marking tests can have anywhere from one to three birds down, and occasionally even four. Blinds and marks often are combined in one test.

It is a good idea for anyone interested in competing at a trial to attend as many as possible before entering his dog. This way, he will have a good idea what is expected of him, and can prepare accordingly. It might seem that all the skill is needed on the dog's part, but this is not necessarily so. Even in the minor stakes, the handler can do much to help or hinder his dog. Also, if he is training his own dog, he will have some idea of the type of tests his dog will be required to do. It is a good plan to start out in the informal fun trials, if there are any nearby. The entry fee is considerably less

140

FC-AFC Topbrass Mandy, bred, owned and trained by Jacqueline Mertens, has established herself as an outstanding field trial bitch.

The Ralph Boalt-Stilrovin Memorial Trophy is a perpetual award made to the highest placing dog at the GRCA annual Specialty field trial. The winning dog must also be bred, owned and handled by a current member of the GRCA to qualify. First awarded in 1976, this magnificent bronze was executed by the celebrated artist Louise Shattuck.

than at the licensed trials, and there is usually more time to help along beginning dogs and handlers. Licensed trial competition is the big time. At these handlers are expected to know the rules and regulations, and mistakes cannot be forgiven.

Each year two National Championship stakes are held for retrievers. Dogs qualify for these stakes by winning a certain number of points in either Amateur or Open stakes during the year preceding the trial. These trials are held in different parts of the country each year. The necessary number of points in Amateur stakes qualifies a dog for the National Amateur Championship stake, held in the spring, and the winner of this trial becomes the National Amateur Champion of that year. Points in Open, or Limited stakes qualify a dog for the National Retriever Championship stake, held in the fall and open to both amateurs and professionals. The winner becomes the National Retriever Champion of that year, a goal worth striving for.

**Training**

There is lots of satisfaction when an owner can train and handle his dog himself. But it takes plenty of time, talent and training grounds. Also, a cooperative family and friends. Obviously, there are many owners who haven't the time, or who don't live in an area where it is possible to keep and train retrievers. There are excellent professional trainers in various parts of the country, who train retrievers for shooting work or for trial competition. Generally, when a dog is with a professional trainer, he is handled in the trials by the professional, but there are trainers who will do the training and turn the dog over to his amateur owner to run in the trials.

The owner who aspires to run his Golden in the trials should heed the advice already presented. His puppy should have been carefully selected from good working stock, and raised with the excellent advice of Dr. Flashman in mind. There is no question that early influences are the important ones, and the early training habits will stay with a dog. A puppy, like a child, can be raised with much loving kindness and a firm hand. The basic relationship between dog and master, and the dog's whole attitude toward work and training in general, is set in those early training periods.

When doing anything with a young dog, it is wise to keep in mind the questions, "What is this teaching him?", "Is this encouraging him in good habits?", "Is this discouraging him in bad habits?" The trainer has two tools at his command—praise and punishment—and should learn just what balance is most successful for his dog.

Obedience classes are an excellent place to start training the puppy. The work taught in novice obedience is all useful to the retriever, since it is basically control. Certainly, anyone who wants his retriever as a house dog, would want him to know and obey the obedience commands of come, heel, sit, stay, and down. For anyone who has never trained a dog, the obedience

FC-AFC Kate of Rocky Vue, owned and trained by Carma Futhey, photographed at the 1976 national Amateur. Carma has successfully trained several Goldens including Holway Joyful*** and FC-AFC Firebird of Rocky Vue.

FC-AFC Benjamin Rajah Frisbie (Rusty Rajah ex Puffer Belle Duchess), owned and handled by Darrell Frisbie, competed in the 1976 Amateur and sired the top derby dog, Ben's Enchanted Budweiser.

classes are also excellent training for the handler, since these classes teach the basic training methods. More advanced obedience work is not advisable for retrievers who are going on into field trial competition.

## House Dog vs. Kennel Dog

There is always argument and disagreement on the subject of keeping the working retriever as a house dog. There are advantages and disadvantages, and each owner had best work out the problem for himself. On the pro side is the close relationship between the dog and his master. Also, a dog brought up with people develops his personality, and probably his intelligence, to a greater degree than the dog raised in a kennel. A growing puppy must have contacts with all sorts of people and situations. Isolated in a kennel, a puppy is likely to become shy and unstable in temperament when faced with the world for the first time. On the other hand is the matter of physical condition. Especially in colder climates, a dog kept in an unheated kennel is certainly in better condition to face icy water and long days spent working in foul weather. Most owners manage to work out a compromise which avoids keeping the retriever in a heated house for long periods, but does afford frequent personal contacts.

There are some people who believe that their dogs are best kept in the kennel and taken out only to work, that any outside activities and social life will spoil the dog. This most certainly is not true of Goldens. The closer a Golden can be to his owner and trainer, the better he will work for him, and this intimate relationship is best established when the dog is a puppy. It is wise to keep in mind, however, that a dog who is weary from an active social life cannot be expected to do his utmost in the field. It is important to be sure that the working retriever, especially the young one, gets plenty of rest so that he has all his energy to put into his working periods.

## Working Condition

Top physical condition is an absolute must. This means not only good health, but plenty of hard exercise every day all year. A young Golden, in good condition, will naturally run as hard and fast as he can in his work, and look stylish. The same dog, overweight and in poor muscular condition, will move slowly and clumsily and look poorly. Dogs who are given a chance to swim whenever possible all year long take eagerly to the water, seeming not to feel the cold at all. Goldens can stand extreme cold, but wilt quickly in extreme heat. In the hot months of the year it is best to exercise the dogs in the early morning and late evening, and swim them as much as possible. As a retriever gets older, good fit condition becomes more and more important. The older a dog gets, the harder it is to get him back in condition once he has become soft.

Kinike Loki being sent out on a retrieve by her owner-trainer
Caroline Rogers.

Ken Gootee with AFC Kiowa's Holiday Joy.

AFC Holway Barty (Eng. FC Holway Westhyde Zeus ex Eng. FC Holway Flush of Yeo), owned and trained by Barbara Howard and bred by June Atkinson. An English import, Barty has had a strong, positive influence on the American field trial picture as a sire. At this writing he has sired 25 Open All-Age dogs, 3 FC-AFCs and a number of successful derby youngsters.

 

                                                 Eng. Nat'l. FC Mazurka of Wynford
            Eng. FC Holway Zest
                Holway Lyric
    *Sire:* Eng. FC Holway Westhyde Zeus
                Westhyde Merry Maker
            Westhyde Merry Lass
                Yarkhill Lady Luck

**AFC HOLWAY BARTY**
                Eng. FC Westhyde Stubblesdown Major
            Eng. Nat'l. FC Mazurka of Wynford
                Eng. FC Musicmaker of Yeo
    Dam: Eng. FC Holway Flush of Yeo
                Golden Arrow of Staverden
            Picture of Yeo
                Holway Klarinette of Yeo

## Introduction to Birds

Puppies are best introduced to birds and the conditions they will have to face in their work, such as water and cover, while still quite young. Learning to swim and hunt all come naturally to young retrievers in their play if given a chance. Care should be taken not to force a puppy into anything he does not take to willingly; puppies can be easily discouraged and frightened. Birds can be given to very young puppies to retrieve when dead ones are available. Most retrievers will show "birdiness" very young, and it is a good clue to future promise. The little puppy who will snatch up a pigeon eagerly is the one to watch. After dead birds, live, shackled pigeons can be tried, to get a puppy used to a flapping, moving bird. Finally, live shackled ducks can be used with care; ducks can bite, so the bill should be taped when puppies are around. It is best to get a puppy used to ducks on land before throwing a duck in the water, where its flapping and splashing can frighten a puppy. Do not let a small puppy retrieve a live or crippled pheasant, since pheasants can rake with their claws.

Puppies vary in their reaction to, and interest in, birds. Generally early encouragement to retrieve birds is helpful. Sometimes a little competition from an older dog will excite a puppy to retrieve a bird that he previously showed no interest in. Live birds should not be given to a puppy who is easily frightened. Never let a puppy take a bird off and play with it. Puppies naturally chew on anything in their mouths, and they should never be allowed to chew on birds. Once a puppy is used to birds, and handles them eagerly, they are not necessary for routine training. Training dummies (small boat fenders) are best for all early training, and for yard work.

## Training for Control

Dr. Flashman has covered very well the problems of early training for the field. A puppy of eight to nine months of age should know his basic obedience commands, sit, stay, come, heel, on and off leash. He should be letter perfect in his own yard, and reasonably well-controlled elsewhere. Heeling can be taught precisely at home, and allowed to become somewhat more relaxed in the field. Retrievers are bright dogs and learn these commands very quickly. Goldens, especially, take to this work, since they enjoy working close to their masters. They are also wildly energetic when young, and the trainer who has never worked with a retriever puppy before may not realize how rough and tough he can, and often should, be. A sharp yank on the leash that might be too much for other breeds is hardly felt by a little retriever.

The firmness of training methods must, of course, be set to meet the needs of each individual puppy. A wild young male, who thinks nothing of knocking over everything and eveyone in his way, needs a far stronger hand than a quiet little female, for whom a scolding voice is punishment enough. On the whole, most inexperienced trainers are too easy with a puppy, not realizing how much training they can take when young. It is far easier to set the correct behavior patterns while young, than to break bad habits later. The puppy who is going to make a promising field trial dog is likely to be a wild one at the start.

It is wise to have the young dog under good control before doing any formal training in the field. In this way bad habits can be avoided. The puppy should be delivering cheerfully to hand, but if he shows any tendency to run off and play, a good firm "heel" should take care of the situation. The first time a puppy is sent for a bird in the field, he may be so enchanted with it that he is reluctant to deliver it. Actual field work with guns and birds is so exciting that young dogs experiencing it for the first time can go out of control, and then all the early obedience training can really prove its worth. The same is likely to be true at the first field trials.

Firm control makes every step of the way easier. Good manners at all times are important in a field trial dog, especially in the more advanced stakes, and the dog with good obedience training has naturally good manners. The stay command is an important aid in steadying a dog. Control is the essence of handling. The dog who has been trained to sit at heel in any position is far easier to teach to take a line. The dog who is taught to sit to the whistle from puppyhood has taken a major step toward learning to handle.

## Working as a Team

Control must always be tempered with encouragement, however. Too much emphasis on control can discourage a young dog. The trainer must keep a careful balance all through a retriever's training years; on the one side is perfect control, on the other is realization of all a dog's natural abilities, including style. The wise trainer lets up on a dog who shows any signs of discouragement, boredom, reluctance or resentment.

This is especially important with Goldens. The team of Golden and trainer is just that—a team with two working elements, who must be cooperating with each other. A bright Golden, with good natural hunting ability, usually develops great strength of character as he grows older. The trainer who knows how to work with that character, and persuade it to work with him, also knows that force alone won't succeed. The sense of teamwork and achievement shared by both dog and owner is one of the great satisfactions of training a retriever.

## The Pick-up and Delivery

One of the major problems Goldens can have is in their pick-up and bird handling. Goldens are by nature very gentle-mouthed dogs, but speedy pick-up of a bird and a firm grip on the way back with it are desirable in a field trial. More and more Goldens are being bred with excellent mouths and a stylish pick-up. There is no question, however, that the extreme

FC-AFC Topbrass Cotton (AFC Holway Barty ex Ch. Sunstream Gypsy of Topbrass), owned by Jeff and Bev Finley and trained and handled by Jeff Finley, led all Goldens for the most All-Age points in 1982.

upiter's Golden Comet, owned by John Turkoitch and bred by Mrs. D. D. Fischer, was a qualifying stake winner. He also won a first in Amateur, qualified for the National Amateur, had two majors in conformation competition, 13½ Amateur points and some Open points before being retired at five years of age.

Kathleen and Lewis Daniels had good reason for their happy smiles at the Buckeye Retriever Club trial in April 1982. It was here that their Golden, AFC Wild Fire of Riverview, CDX*** (Riverview's Kinike Rocket*** ex Riverview's Nettles, CDX) joined the select circle of doubleheaders. Wild Fire was bred by James and Sally Venerable and was trained and handled by Mr. Daniels.

Smokehill's Copper Penny, UD, working at the Qualifying Stake GRCA national Specialty, Coto de Caza 1980. Penny is owned and handled by Major Tom Jones.

*Ince*

gentleness of mouth is an admirable quality in some situations other than field trials. Goldens are used by those who catch and band young ducks, since they can handle even a nestling without injuring it. It would be a shame to lose this quality completely.

The trainer should look for his dog to pick up a bird without lingering over it, or mouthing it in any way, and without dropping it on the way back. This problem can be worked on in the yard, using a heavy training dummy, and then heavy birds, both live and dead. The dog should be taught to obey promptly the command fetch it, meaning to pick up whatever object is indicated. He should be taught to hold it firmly in his mouth while heeling around the yard, while sitting and staying, and finally returning to heel. He should hold it for several minutes without letting it slip in any way. If he becomes butter-mouthed while working in the field, the commands fetch it and hold it should improve the pick-up and delivery.

Most Goldens deliver to hand naturally. Their joy in life is to bring everything they can lay their mouths on to their masters. By encouraging this pattern, delivery to hand is less of a problem.

**Working in Water**

Goldens can also have problems in the water. Actually, this is one of the great separators between the Goldens of true field trial caliber and those that don't quite "have it." The top working Goldens have no problems around water at all, they are just as stylish as the good retrievers of any breed in water-entry, swimming and return. But, lack of desire in the water, poor entry and slow return have been a frequent characteristic in the breed. Not much can be done to teach a dog to be stylish in the water if the desire isn't there, but plenty can be done to help a puppy gain confidence in the water, and to keep older dogs swimming eagerly. As much as possible, retrievers from puppyhood on should be given a chance to play and swim in the water, aside from their work, all year around. In icy weather it is generally better not to force them into the water while working, only short swims will keep a dog from becoming discouraged and reluctant to enter cold water. But plenty of voluntary swimming, not during training periods, will keep a positive attitude toward the water.

On the plus side for the breed, Goldens, without question, excel in scenting ability. They are also, generally, consistently good markers. This combination makes upland work one of their strong points. Most Goldens, being bright and tractable, learn to handle well, and can be counted on to turn in fine performances on the blind work in a trial.

**The Steady Retriever**

A retriever is required to be steady on line; that is, he sits at heel beside his handler, watching the fall of the birds, and does not make a move to retrieve before the judge calls the handler's number. In all championship

151

FC-AFC Firebird of Rocky Vue, bred, owned and trained by Carma Futhey.

FC Kinike's Rojo De Oro (Poika of Handjem ex Shenandoah of Stilrovin***), owned by James T. Venerable, is the brother of three FC-AFCs—Kinike Coquette, Chancellor and Sir Jim. He was handled to a first in the Open All-Age stake at the 1977 GRCA Specialty by Sally Venerable.

stakes, and some minor stakes, the retriever must also honor, that is, sit quietly at heel while another dog works. Teaching a dog to be steady is a gradual process. From puppyhood he should be held a moment before being sent to retrieve. As he grows older, the leash can be slack, so that, if he breaks, he can be stopped, corrected, made to wait, and then sent. By the time a dog is a year old, he should be steady without a leash. A young dog, who is steady as a rock on dummies in his yard, is more than likely to break on shot birds at a trial. It is a good idea to shoot birds for the dog in training, and control his breaking, before a trial.

The owner who uses his dog when hunting has an advantage, in that he can get his dog used to the excitement of birds. He should remember that it is harder to regain control over his dog if he has allowed him to break when hunting, than it is to control him properly at all times. There are some dogs, though, who quickly learn the difference between hunting and trial conditions. They may break constantly while hunting, but when put back into training for trials, they know the difference and remain steady.

## Refinements in Training

After a young dog has learned all his yard work, and is retrieving well to hand, it is best to have someone else do the throwing of dummies or birds for him to retrieve. If the handler continues to throw for himself, the dog will get into the habit of expecting falls no farther than the handler can throw. The falls should gradually become longer on both land and water. Hazards, such as ditches and hedgerows, should be introduced between the dog and the bird. Different types of cover should be used. At this stage, it is best to work with a group of people, and move to as many different areas as possible, so that the dog becomes used to working in all types of surroundings, with other dogs and people, and a certain amount of confusion.

The trainer who has learned to work with his own dog is the best judge as to what methods are most suitable for his dog. The dog is not a machine and cannot be worked by a rigid set of instructions. With subsequent dogs, the trainer may find quite different methods are successful. He should keep in mind his ultimate goal (for example, to teach his dog to handle), break it down into simple steps (stop on the whistle, line and cast), and decide how he can best teach his particular dog these steps with the facilities he has on hand.

There is much that can be done at each stage to prepare for following stages. The retriever still under two years, who is not required to handle in the Derby stake, can be learning lessons that will help him later. The so-called "baseball diamond," in which the dog learns the four casts commonly used in handling, can be taught at an early age. The dog is placed in the center of an imaginary baseball diamond, and dummies are put at 1st, 2nd and 3rd bases, with the handler at home plate. Arm signals to

Mrs. Ray Earnest and her FC-AFC Tigathoe's Tonga (FC-AFC Bonnie Brooks Elmer ex Tigathoe's Chickasaw***). In addition to being a fine field trial dog, Tonga is Ray's "fun" dog.

Bo Earnest with his AFC Tigathoe's Choptank Child. This picture was taken at the James River Retriever Club where "Chop" won the Amateur stake for two consecutive years.

Typical scene at an American retriever trial as the handler sends his dog under the scrutiny of the judge.

154

the right or left, with the command over, or an arm signal straight over the head with the command back, send the dog to the appropriate dummy. Later, a dummy is left at home plate, and the handler backs up, a recall whistle will bring the dog to the dummy to learn the fourth cast. Each cast is taught separately before more than one dummy is put out. The back cast is usually the hardest, and is best taught first. The two overs are easier. Most young dogs think this is a great game and learn it quickly. Even older dogs should be given practice on the baseball diamond frequently to keep them casting sharply.

Lining, also, can be taught at an early age. When a retriever is sent on a blind retrieve, ideally he should go in the exact direction his handler sends him, holding the direction without veering, until he comes across a bird or is stopped by a whistle. Young dogs are started down roads, or down rows in a plowed field, with the dummies at greater and greater distances, until they can run long distances without hesitating.

Each new step is taught under the most simplified conditions, with no distractions. When the dog has learned the lesson well, the conditions should be made more difficult until he is ready to try out the new skill under actual field conditions.

Too much emphasis cannot be put on the necessity of constant and frequent repetition. Dogs are creatures of habit and learn by repetition of a pattern until it is set in their minds. Only by hours and hours of drill in the simple steps can a reliable handling dog be made. These drills should be repeated routinely all through a retriever's working years. If they are not, a dog's work can become sloppy, careless, lacking in the precise responses that make a sharp, stylish job.

There are so many things for the starting dog and handler to learn, that it is impossible to discuss them thoroughly. The trainer will find that he is likely to learn more each day, with each different test. This is one of the joys of retriever training. No two tests are the same, every day's conditions vary. We really understand so little about the retriever's true capabilities, such as scenting and marking, that even the most experienced handlers are learning all the time.

## Aids for Dog and Trainer

Experienced amateur trainers are usually glad to have people to work with and enjoy helping others to learn the ropes. Many professionals welcome amateurs also. Some have a set fee for which the professional trainer will spend time with the amateur and his dog, helping them with their problems. Birds used are usually extra. It is well worth an amateur's time to spend a day now and then working with a professional trainer, even if it means going many miles. His dog will be worked with birds and guns and other dogs around, making conditions much like those of a field trial. Most professionals are glad to give what advice and help they can.

The man or woman who finds that keeping up with a retriever's training takes more time, effort, skill and strength than he or she cares to give may well wish to leave the dog with a professional. Then it is even more important to get together with the trainer as often as possible. The inexperienced handler will have much to learn before he is able to get the best possible work from his professionally trained dog.

The novice trainer will find that he can learn a great deal from working with and talking to as many people as possible, and from watching as many dogs work, under as varying conditions as possible. His motto might well be: Look, listen and learn.

There are a number of excellent books on retriever training, the best known being James Lamb Free's *Training Your Retriever.* This book covers early stages of training, with excellent illustrations. Another book which goes deeper into many training problems for the more experienced trainer is *Charles Morgan on Retrievers,* written by the late dean of retriever trainers. Charley Morgan won two Nationals with Goldens he had trained. For the trainer who wants to go on to more advanced training for blind retrieves, *Training Retrievers to Handle,* by D. L. and Ann Walters, gives a step by step program from starting a young dog to handle through advanced problems of the field trial retriever.

In the final analysis, trainer and dog will have to find out for themselves how best to get about the work of becoming a winning field trial team. And work it is—hours, days, months and years, in the yard and in the field, and many sleepless nights pondering on the problems. No one can give another trainer a strict set of rules; every dog, every situation varies, and the skillful trainer knows how and when to adapt. The greatest reward lies not so much in the blue ribbon and silver bowl, but in the tremendous sense of achievement when dog and handler can prove their ability in competition with the best.

Ch. Toryglen Idling Jerome, UD*** (Ch. Alstone Sutter Creek Charade, UD* ex Beckwith's Sparke Plenty, CD), owned and trained by E. J. Brown-Leger and bred by E. Verissimo. Jerome is one of the few champion UDs to become a limited all-age dog in licensed trials. It's a real achievement and calls for a talented dog and a dedicated trainer. *Bliss Glazebrook*

# 7

# Field Trials in the British Isles

*by Dora Gostyn*

---

THE atmosphere of a British field trial is like that of any good day in the shooting field, in the sense of anticipation of the unknown. Both dog and handler are in the lap of the gods, not knowing just what will be asked of them; for everything will depend on so many factors, such as what is shot, where it happens, whether it is a blind or a marked retrieve. One may even see, when one is not actually in the line, an opportunity where one's own dog (one thinks!) would have made a splendid job of the work in hand, but where one finds oneself at that moment with the spectators. This is all taken as part of the sport by the British field trial enthusiast. He knows before the first bird is downed that a good dog, the first and most essential factor, is not all; luck will also play a part, and all this adds to the enjoyment and good sportsmanship of the day.

Field trials are run under Kennel Club rules by many Societies. The Golden Retriever Clubs arrange their own trials, in which their own members usually have preference in the draw. As it is not very easy to run in the trials one would wish to compete in, for trialing in the British Isles is very popular, a draw has to take place for runners, if nominations exceed places.

The three main kinds of stakes are: Puppy or Non-Winner, Novice and Open. A Puppy is a dog or bitch over six months and under two years of

Eng. NFC (1982) Little Marston Chorus of Holway (Eng. FC Holway Chanter ex Belway Dove), owned, trained and handled by Robert Atkinson of Dorchester, Dorset, England, and bred by Mr. Dare. Mr. Atkinson is the son of June Atkinson, and together they have bred and owned a number of England's top performing field trial dogs for many years.

```
                    F.T. Ch. Palgrave Holway Folly
            Palgrave Enchanter
                    Panshanger Jesse
      Sire: F.T. Ch. Holway Chanter
            Holway Hunter
      Holway Sparkler
            Holway Zither
ENG. NFC ('82) LITTLE MARSTON CHORUS OF HOLWAY
                    F.T. Ch. Palgrave Holway Folly
            Glebespray Bracken
                    Palgrave Floss
      Dam: Belway Dove
                    F.T. Ch. Holway Westhyde Zeus
            Holway Glitter of Belway
                    F.T. Ch. Holway Gaiety
```

age; a Novice may not have won a first, second or third in any stake, but this handicap varies somewhat with different Societies. A Non-Winner is usually a dog which has not won a first, second or third in an Open stake or a first in any other stake. An Open stake is open to all. It is from the Open stakes that dogs qualify to run in the Retriever Championship stake at the end of the season. This is of course open to any variety of retriever duly qualified, and it is considered to be a great honor for the dog to represent his own retriever breed on that great occasion.

Field trial dogs are judged first and foremost on game-finding ability, but steadiness and a soft mouth are essential too. Good marking ability is also a great advantage, as a dog must not disturb game unnecessarily. With the exception of puppies a dog must retrieve fur as well as feather, and all dogs must enter water.

It is easy for those so interested to obtain a complete set of field and trial rules, but let me take you on an imaginary field trial and try and show you how the ordinary fellow and his dog can spend a wonderful day in good company, human and canine.

Two weeks ago the entries were posted, the hotel booked, and now your car speeds towards headquarters where you will meet many of your fellow competitors of tomorrow. It will be a happy evening and many trials will be run all over again, trials long gone except in the memory of the fellow and his dog who ran in them; and you will learn much from the old-timers if you quietly listen. But all too soon there is tomorrow to plan for, and before you know it the car is one in a long line of cars, moving towards the ground on which the trial is to be run.

Two alert eyes watch as your number band is tied to your arm. Between you there passes a look of understanding. He knows, this is IT! Our trial is a one day Open stake for 12 dogs, and there are quite a few well tried good dogs running; we know the standard of work could be top quality. The line is forming. The three judges, each with his or her own steward, take their places. The guns are now standing, two to each judge, and the dog steward sends one number to each judge. Now the dog steward comes towards us and calls into line numbers one, two, three, four, five and six. One and two go to the judge on the right, three and four to the center judge, five and six to the left-hand judge. Our very good host, who has invited our Society to hold the trial on his ground, is shooting; grateful indeed are the Field Trial Societies to these good friends.

The moment has come. The signal is given to move forward. The trial has begun. We walk up over a rise, the autumn sun filling the whole scene. The Golden at our side walks to heel, but we feel his anticipation. A shot rings clear, and the line stops. From the other end of the line over the brow of the hill you hear a call-up whistle, and you know the first bird of the day has been collected. All the dogs have been steady and we are ready to move on. But no! Number five has run in. A rabbit streaks across in front of the line closely followed by number five, and you feel a new, even greater

Dora Gostyn with Whamstead Kinsman, ready for a day in the field.

Marigold of the Wraes retrieving a pheasant. This picture shows the kind of cover retrievers in Great Britain usually encounter.

160

interest is taken in the proceedings by the dog at your side. Yes, number five is leaving the line, the judge has said those polite, but final words: "We shall not require you again, Sir," and the dog is out of the stake. The judge calls for a new dog, and number seven comes into the line. As we reach the end of the field a field of root crops is before us. Wonderful scents have an effect on the twitcing nose beside you. You hope that your gun will have cause to use his gun soon and the mounting tension beside you can be released in action. Two pheasants rise and one is shot in front of the line. But our judge passes it to the judge on his left, thus making it a more difficult retrieve for a dog out of sight. Your fellow competitor's dog is sent out; and you feel two dog eyes fix themselves on you as the other dog collects what your fellow thought to be his very own bird! But he sits rock steady, and when the seeking is over and the bird is in the judge's hands, we move on. A crack behind the line, a hare gets up, is shot. At the next moment out of the roots a pheasant rises and is shot too, marked well and truly by your dog; you realize he has marked both, but the one shot last was dropped with a thud but a few yards in front. As you know he must do in an Open stake, the judge says: "I want the hare." You wait for a second and then with clear direction send him out for the hare. Only for a split second does he hesitate. And as he goes out with joy you feel the wind on your face; you know it is in his favor, and with a strong hare scent he should have little trouble to find his game. He is at the fall, head hidden, nose down, the roots move and rustle, you can follow as the moving roots show his progress, you wait. A moment of stillness, then a head comes into view; holding the hare he gallops towards the line, then sees you and joyfully thrusts the hare into your waiting hands.

As the line waits the judges have met in the center to confer. Word is passed down that number eight has been put out of the stake for whining; the rule has been observed that a dog can not be discarded unless he has run under two judges. A new dog is called into the line. Still in roots we move on. An old cock pheasant is put up, a shot rings out and another, but he flies on, giving that call that is almost a laugh as he goes out of sight to live for another day, and we send him a salutation. A shot rings out at the other end of the line, we stop and we hear work going on for some time. We hear one dog called up and another being tried; tension mounts as yet another dog is sent out but also fails. Our number is called, we are to be tried. This is a moment when one can score if you can eye wipe two or more dogs, these are the chances we all hope for. At last we are told to send the dog. Out he goes in the direction we have been told to send him, we do not have to wait, down goes his head and back he comes with the bird. As we go out of the line to wait for our number to be required by a second judge all seems unreal and dreamlike. From a long way off we hear congratulations on our last effort. But we know it is early yet and a lot can still happen. Yet, a short rest from excitement is welcome. Now we have a chance to relax, put our dog on a lead and join the spectators, walking behind the spectators' steward.

A halt has been made at the edge of a wood, and the guns take their places for a drive. We can hear the beaters inside the wood coming towards the guns. The air is punctuated by the sound of driven birds. Shots begin to ring out and birds begin to fall thick and fast. At last the beaters are in view, the drive is over. The dogs are called to their judges and work begins to retrieve the birds. We do not have long to wait before we are called into the line once again. At the edge of the wood we go to our second judge. The bird, the gun tells us, is lying about fifteen yards inside the wood to our right; he is sure it was not a runner. That is our information. We are instructed to send. Over the wire fence he goes. For a long time there is quietness, then twigs break and we hear rustling in the undergrowth as he moves in his quest. These are the moments when one must trust one's dog. You cannot even see him to direct him. And even if you could, it would be very difficult to mark a bird down in the thick cover and to direct the dog to it. After what seems an eternity he is there, bird in mouth, a great leap over the wire, and another task done. He has collected the pigeon, and for the second time is out of the line and waiting for the call of judge number three.

This call soon comes. Our judge was on the other side of the wood, and as we round the corner spread before us is a pond, with the woods coming right down to the water's edge. We are told a duck has been shot and is in the reeds on the other side of the pond. We send out, a great splash, and off he goes; the wind ruffling the water towards us we realize luck is with us once again, for he swims towards the bank and has now marked the bird. Our second retrieve under our third judge is another bird in the wood; but more than that, another dog has failed on it, so once again we go out of the line in a rosy glow!

Lunchtime, and the judges have a working lunch. Some dogs, like numbers five and eight have eliminated themselves through breaking rules by running in or whining. Hard mouth too can put a dog out of a stake. But at lunch the judges confer to decide which of the dogs merit another chance to run. In a two-day, 24 dog stake this conference would possibly not take place until the end of the first day. So we sit and eat together with our fellow competitors and ask each other "how are you doing?", and the tales come thick and fast. In spite of feeling that one is doing fair work, not until your number is called can you be sure, for one or two others may be doing even better. It is with pleasure we hear our number called with that of six other dogs, and we know we are still in the running.

The walk up after lunch does not produce much game, and we find ourselves still in the line one hour later, our end having no luck in putting any birds up. As we reach the end of a plowed field a pheasant is put up and shot. As he comes down he has a leg down, he is possibly a strong runner. Our judge has seen this too, he quickly gives the sign to send the dog. Out he goes in the direction he marked the bird down, through the hedge into a

162

ditch, and there we lose sight of the dog—and once again the helpless feeling of waiting! He is in the area of the fall, we can do nothing but trust him. Quickly the thoughts crowd into our mind of the temptations which can lie in such cover: suppose he is going to put some tempting rabbit out, will he chase? Whistle in hand we wait. Ah, there he is! And as we catch glimpse of our dog the bird he has found rises up in the air and falls ahead on the plowed field. The dog races towards it, gathers it up and delivers it. We have our runner!

We are now walking in an open field, it all looks flat and void, but you feel a tension at your side; across, in front of the line, from a mound of uncut grass springs a hare. The gun at our side is ready, and the hare lies fifteen feet in front, and still. You look down. He asks shall he get it now? You do not move. Any unexpected hand movement to a keen dog, who knows he is well in your favor, can be misunderstood by him. We try to relax, keeping a keen eye by our side. So quickly it all happens; straight down in front of the line the rival, within a short distance of us the dog turns and scents his game; at that split second a dog leaves our side, and you know he is out of the trial; he comes to a frantic call-up on the whistle, and the hare is collected by its rightful retriever. As we walk away from the line we remember number five. He was out of the trial at 9:30 a.m.; we at least had a wonderful run and lasted until 4:30 p.m.; and where is the trial next week?

The trial is over. We meet to see the awards presented and cheer the winner. Our field trials may be run on different lines, but one precious thing we share: the team work of man and dog, and long may it be!

This scene is typical of the activity at a British field trial.

Goldwood Michael, UD, owned by Morgan Brainard and trained and handled by Captain Schendel, was one of the top-scoring early Goldens in the obedience ring.

O.T. Ch. Moreland's Golden Tonka (Ch. Misty Morn's Sunset, CD, ex Moreland's Golden Bonnie), owned, trained and handled by Russell Klipple and bred by William Prentiss. Tonka's career was one of the most spectacular in the history of obedience. Her achievements, described in this chapter, made her one of the most effective ambassadors of the sport.

# 8

# A Short History of Great Obedience Dogs 1945-1983

*"Teresa Winn, 11 year-old daughter of. . ., boarded a Muni bus with her dog and the driver growled, 'You gotta pay for the dog.' Teresa, coolly: 'Just take two punches out of my school pass—he goes to Obedience School.'"*

Herb Caen, San Francisco Chronicle
September 16, 1969

GOLDEN RETRIEVERS have been successful in obedience trials for many years. The first Golden Retriever to earn a UD (Utility Dog) was Goldwood Toby, owned and trained by Rachel Page Elliott, of Carlisle, Massachusetts. Toby's son, Featherquest Trigger, was the first Golden to earn the UDT (Utility Dog Tracking) degree. Trigger was owned and trained by Marjorie Perry of Concord, Massachusetts. Mrs. Perry enjoyed the training, as did Mrs. Elliott, and each dog set a challenge for later performers. Featherquest Trigger competed with another excellent Golden, Goldwood Michael, one or the other earning a slightly higher score on various occasions.

Goldwood Michael was more widely campaigned. He was owned by Morgan Brainard of Rochester, New York, and trained by Captain

O.T. Ch. Top Brass Cisco Kid, owned and trained by Pauline Czarnecki, is the second Golden to earn the O.T. Ch. title. Pauline has since trained two others to the same plateau, and as of this writing owns three O.T. Ch. Goldens.

Am. Can. Ch., O.T. Ch. Sunstreak of Culynwood, TD, WCX, Can. CD (Ch. Sabahkas Alexander of Cal-Vo, CD, ex Ch. Tangelo's End-of-the-Rainbow, CD, WC), owned and trained by Suzi Bluford. Streaker was another with a distinguished obedience record and even had a following of ringside fans.

*Jayne Langdon*

166

Schendel. Goldwood Michael had many high scores and was entered in trials in New England, New York, and other Eastern states, and Washington, D.C., in the years 1945-49.

Another high-scoring Golden in the late 1940's and early 1950's was Ch. Duckerbird Atomic, UD, owned by Duckerbird Kennels. This dog was campaigned in the Great Lakes area, usually Michigan, Illinois and Ohio. Other high-scoring Goldens of the same line were Duckerbird Atomic II, UD, owned by Mary L. Frank. It is my understanding that Mr. Charles A. Frank trained the first Duckerbird Atomic. Max and Mary McCammon owned Sidram Sharmaine, UD, and campaigned him in Indiana, Illinois, and Ohio. In Pennsylvania, New Jersey, New York, and other Eastern states, Betty W. Strawbridge was campaigning Ruanne Gayling's Gaiety, UD. This was one of the high-scoring Goldens in 1956-57. Mrs. F. H. Strawbridge, Jr. campaigned Ch. Ruanne Bali-Hi, UD, in 1957-58. Elizabeth Strawbridge continued the family interest in obedience with Ruanne Yankee Traveler II, UD, in 1956-60. During this time, Charles A. Frank had high scores again with his Duckerbird Atomic III, UD. Mrs. Perry trained another Golden, Golden Economist, CDX (Companion Dog Excellent). Alice and William C. Worley had high scores with Ch. Indian Knoll's Roc-Cloud, UD. This was another Midwestern campaigner.

Thousands of Goldens have earned CDs over the years, and many have continued through the higher classes, such as Companion Dog Excellent, Tracking or Utility. Some of the field dogs have campaigned in the various classes. On the West Coast, many Goldens have been entered and won high scores in obedience trials. Two happy working Goldens on the West Coast, Ch. Sunshine Prince of Los Altos, CDX (Sunny) and Ch. Princess Royale, CDX (Tootsie), were owned by Mr. and Mrs. Arthur Mathews of Portola Valley, California. These Goldens were brother and sister of the outstanding bench winner, Ch. Prince Royal, owned by Mr. Oliver Wilhelm. They were bred by John and Maryanna Railton and all were the get of Ch. Jason of Golden Anno Nuevo, UD. Their grandsire was the English import, Ch. Oakwin Junior. Jason was bred and owned by Mr. and Mrs. James Humphrey of Cascade Ranch, living at that time at Pescadero.

Jason, Sunny and Tootsie would go from obedience ring to conformation ring with equal and successful grace. As Sunny and Tootsie were always shown in the same shows, they had quite a following. Ringside buffs were ever trying to guess which one, dog or bitch, would end up with the higher score. Sometimes each had the top score and tied for first place. Their fine temperaments and good looks made many friends for the breed. Douglas Bundock trained and handled the brother and sister pair.

From 1958 to 1963, Ben Lake's Ch. Ben's Major of Sun Dance was among the top scorers. He was entered in 29 trials and his lowest single score was 198.5. Other scores were 199 and 199.5, and there were 13 scores of 200, the perfect score, as 200 is the highest number of points possible to earn in an obedience trial. Ch. Ben's trials were in Florida, Ohio, and Indiana. As noted by the prefix Ch., many of these top obedience scorers were also bench champions, representing good conformation to the breed Standard. Besides looking good, they obviously responded well to training.

Goldens in all areas continue to excel in all aspects of obedience. It is not possible even to attempt to list the Goldens or any special lines that have been outstanding, as many lines have done well.

The highest and most consistent obedience record of all dogs belongs to a Golden Retriever. He is pictured in this book with his trainers and owners, Mr. and Mrs. Albert Munneke of Hamilton, Ohio. This dog is the famous American and Canadian Ch. Sun Dance's Rusticana, WC, UDT, Can. UD. The breeder was James Mardis, sired by Ch. Indian Knolls Roc-Cloud, UD ex Ch. Sidram Shining Star, UD. The dog was whelped on May 26, 1957, and retired on October 29, 1967, at the age of 10½ years. The WC stands for Working Certificate, which indicates that this Golden could, and did, retrieve shot game on land and from water.

Mr. and Mrs. Munneke had trained another breed, and then had an opportunity to acquire Sun Dance's Rusticana when he was a puppy. They never regretted their interest in training and campaigning this Golden. Rusti was shown under the same judge very few times. His average score over a nine-year period was 197.381. He won first place in 284 of the 534 trials in which he competed. In addition, he frequently tied for first place. He also won the special award of the Golden Retriever Club of America, the Toby-Trigger trophy, which was started in 1963 as a perpetual trophy. This award was set up by Mrs. Arthur Perry and Mrs. Mark Elliott, and named for the first two Goldens to earn the U.D. degree. Because of the interest which Mr. and Mrs. Munneke developed and the many friends they have made, as well as their success as judges and in holding obedience clinics in so many of the 50 states, Mrs. Munneke has been asked to contribute, for this book, some training information on the beginning work in obedience trials and in tracking. Mrs. Munneke's contributions form the succeeding two chapters of this book.

Many people find that they can commence tracking with their dogs soon after the CD (Companion Dog) degree has been earned. Or tracking training may begin as soon as the Companion Dog exercises (basic obedience) have been learned. Mrs. Walters, in the chapter on field training, also indicates that beginning obedience is needed for field work, such as the basic commands heel, sit, stay, etc. Those who wish to go beyond novice work may read Margaret E. Pearsall's *The Pearsall Guide to Successful Dog Training* (Howell Book House, New York). Consult the bibliography at the end of this book for a list of excellent obedience books. You may also wish to join a local obedience club. These may be either informal or organized groups. Many local S.P.C.A. organizations give basic obedience classes from time to time. You will enjoy the improved

The Toby-Trigger Trophy is a perpetual award of the Golden Retriever Club of America. It is given to the Golden owned by a member of the GRCA making the most high scores in any one year.

Mr. and Mrs. Albert Munneke, well-known obedience authorities, with their Am. and Can. Ch. Sun Dance's Rusticana, UDT, Can. UD. Rusti may be considered an obedience authority in his own right. He held a working certificate and has made more high scores over a longer period of time than any other dog of any breed.

citizenship of your Golden and the enhanced dog/owner communication developed.

Jeannie Fox was asked to sum up what has been happening in obedience from 1970 to 1983. Jeannie trained to a *Super Dog* title and continued her interest in obedience over the past approximately 15 years. Her comments follow:

> Training the family pet in obedience makes the pet a more enjoyable, well-mannered part of the household. It also allows the dog and handler to participate in an exciting sport, obedience trials. The typical Golden Retriever is extremely outgoing and trainable. Conscientious breeders are concerned with the temperament of their lines as well as their soundness and conformation. Obedience trials provide a showplace for the trainability desired in the breed. A typical pedigree of a Golden is sprinkled with many obedience titles as well as breed championships and working certificates. Showing in obedience trials allows every dog owner to compete on the level he or she enjoys.

The late Virginia Beauchamp of Vallejo, California, was one of the first on the West Coast to follow the training through Utility and Tracking with her Ch. Sure Shot's Heart of Gold, UD (Sunny) and Heart of Gold's Replica, CDX, TD (Lady). He was one of the first tracking Goldens in the San Francisco Bay area. Virginia felt that once dogs and people have learned to communicate, the communication should go much further than just obtaining the CD title. She expressed her opinion as follows:

> Golden Retriever obedience training misses a real opportunity when the objectives of such training are limited to trialing the Golden. Most of us eventually learn that successful training of a show-winning dog is repetition of simplified sections of a particular exercise, the gradual combining of them with subsequent modeling of a desired habit pattern. Then we smugly think we've trained our Golden. But few of us realize that our dog smugly knows he has finally trained us to behave pleasantly when he jumps or walks or runs in certain ways. The two-legged or the four-legged animal's respective viewpoints notwithstanding, both have acquired a tremendous amount of "savvy" about each other, and nowadays it is considered knowledgeable to call it communication.
>
> How sad it is to see so many fine dogs, and supposedly intelligent people, gain those wonderful legs and degrees and call it finished. This people-dog relationship has just established the foundation for real living and companionship. Listen to our dogs when they talk with eyes, tail, ears—how we can understand with no movement or word spoken. Learn his barks and see how many can be interpreted. What fun it is to talk to him, interjecting all the words he knows, and have someone count the times he indicates by a tipped head or lifted ears that he recognizes them. Learn to read his voice. It may be very important sometime. For instance, once Queenie was outdoors when suddenly I became conscious of her bark—demanding, insistent; danger—it said. And yes, a grass fire was leaping at our fence at wind-fed velocity. She wasn't just a barking dog to me, as she can be at times, but

Am. Can. Ch., Can. O.T. Ch. Bonnie Island Gold Rush Carla, Am. Can. UDTX, WC (Am. Can. Bda. Ch. Cummings' Gold Rush Charlie, OS, ex Bevin's Brandywine), owned and trained by Roberta Anderson. Carla was the first female and second Golden to become a Canadian O.T. Ch. and UDTX. *Roberts*

Bonnie Island Antique Bronze, CDX, TD, WC, Can. CDX, TDX, WC, and Ch. Bonnie Island Gold Rush Carla, UDTX, WC, Can. Ch., O.T. Ch., UDTX and WC, eleven and nine years old respectively, enjoying "the tube" together. They are owned by Roberta and John Anderson and photographed here by Mrs. Anderson.

communicating loud and clear. How glad we were that I could understand her.

A UD, or tracking dog, usually enjoys a run in the field and it's not a bit unusual for them to find and bring back an article with human scent on it. This is communication. "See what I found? Do you want it?"

And how about a seek-back becoming a game that can be frequently played and may sometime be for real. Queenie and I still play "Lost the Keys" when on a long walk, and it delights her to run back and find a lost article— leash, handkerchief, keys, etc. Let's hope it continues just a game—I may lose them yet.

Our gentle Goldens seem far from protective watch dogs, but I have experienced many times my dogs' protective reaction when I was uneasy. One memorable night, I was alone and recent events in the neighborhood left me more concerned than I probably should have been. Communicating this uneasiness to our three Goldens started their nearly all-night tour of protection—pacing through the rooms, checking doors with loud snuffs and low growls. None of us slept much that night.

No child or woman with a Golden that they have trained and lived with need have any doubt about what amount of protection their dog will exhibit should the need arise. And never fear about the dog knowing a need. He'll know all right. But the rest of the time, he'll be the glorious, gentle, fun companion of field and home.

Virginia's commitments to Golden Retrievers and Guide Dogs for the Blind were great. She helped Clarence Pfaffenberger with much of the research and puppy testing. Her guide dog Queenie (Golden Queen of Hesperian) was one of the most trainable dogs she ever had and this dog produced four or five litters of high test puppies for Guide Dogs—more than any other brood bitch for Guide Dogs.

Jeannie Fox's material updating obedience in the late 1970's and early 1980's continues:

The number of Golden Retrievers earning the Utility Dog title has increased dramatically in recent years. Completing this title remains a very significant achievement for a dog and handler. It reflects the trainability and willingness of the dog and the patience and perseverance of the handler. In July, 1977, the AKC instituted the obedience trial championship. Before a dog can earn points toward this title, it must have completed the Utility Dog title. Points are earned for placements of first or second place based on the number of dogs competing in the Open B and Utility classes. A dog must earn at least one first place in Open B and one in Utility plus an additional first placement in either class. A total of 100 points is needed to earn the O.T. Ch. This new title has provided a new area of competition which allows the obedience exhibitor to continue beyond earning the UD.

The first obedience trial champion of any breed was O.T. Ch. Moreland's Golden Tonka owned and handled by Russ Klipple. Mr. Klipple has shown many dogs to obedience titles over the years, but Tonka was by far his most impressive, completing the O.T. Ch. title in just 23 days. During her show career, Tonka was shown in 309 AKC trials in 14 states under 120

Ch., O.T. Ch. Meadowpond Dust Commander (Am. Can. Ch. Bradfield Boomer, UDT, WC, ex Missy of Nottingham), owned and trained by Bernie Brown and bred by Meadowpond Kennels. An obedience superstar, "Duster" led all dogs for the number of O.T. Ch. points for 1981 with 1,159. He was also top obedience dog in 1979 and 1980.

O.T. Ch. Meadowpond Fem de Fortune, WC, Can. CDX (Am. Can. Ch. Bradfield Boomer, UDT, WC, ex Am. Can. Ch. Meadowpond Dazzle's Sparkle, CD), owned and trained by Diane L. Bauman. "Charo" boasts a trial career filled with spectacular achievements including 1st Open in the 1980 Gaines Eastern Regional, Super Dog 1981, three *Dog World* awards, four perfect scores and several HIT wins.

judges. Her record includes eight perfect scores of 200 and 176 High Scoring Dog in Trial awards. Tonka was very successful in the obedience tournaments, winning three Super Dog awards. Most importantly, Tonka was described as a loved companion by Mr. Klipple and his wife.

The first dog of any breed to earn the O.T. Ch. and breed championship was Ch. O.T. Ch. Russo's Gold Rush Sensation. Sadie was co-owned by E. Hamm and L. C. Johnson. She was campaigned mostly in the East. Mr. Hamm did the obedience training and handling.

A very popular Ch. O.T. Ch. on the West Coast was Sunstreak of Culynwood, TD, WCX, Can. CD. "Streaker" was owned and trained by Suzi Bluford. His obedience record was outstanding, but his personality was his winning edge. He was so popular that people followed him from show to show to watch him and Suzi work together.

In the Midwest one of the most successful obedience teams was Pauline Czarnecki with O.T. Ch. Topbrass Cisco Kid. Pauline has also trained and competed with two other O.T. Ch. Goldens.

The AKC honors the obedience trial champion with the highest number of points earned each year. Goldens have dominated all other breeds every year since the Ken-L Ration award has been offered. An outstanding competitor was Ch. O.T. Ch. Meadowpond Dust Commander owned and trained by Bernie Brown of the Chicago area. "Duster" won the award in 1979, 1980, and 1981. Another Midwest Golden competitor won the award in 1982. O.T. Ch. Topbrass Ric O Shay Barty and his owner Sharon Long were honored for the dog's impressive total of O.T. Ch. points.

Goldens continue to compete successfully all over the United States. A few of the top handler-dog teams include Diane L. Bauman with her O.T. Ch. Meadowpond Fem de Fortune, WC, Can. CDX. "Charo" has earned several perfect scores in AKC trials and won some of the major tournaments. On the West Coast O.T. Ch. Miki O Puapualenalena with her handler Janis Teichman was very successful.

A history of obedience for Goldens must include some of the dogs that have earned multiple titles in all the areas of competition offered by the AKC and the GRCA.

One of the most talented trainers is Roberta Anderson (Mrs. John B.). In the past 30 years Roberta has finished titles on many dogs including the multi-titled Am., Can. Ch., Can. O.T. Ch. Bonnie Island Gold Rush Carla, Am., Can. UDTX, WC. Roberta has campaigned her dog in three countries: in Canada, the United States, and Mexico, winning titles in all three. She has also written the obedience news for the GRCA newsletter for several years. She promotes obedience training in her area and stresses enjoying her dogs as companions.

Another very titled Golden is Am., Can. Ch. Ambertrail's Bargello Stitch, UDTX, WC, Can. UDTX, WC, Bda CDX, TD. Stitch is owned and trained by Barbara Tinker and was the most titled Golden in June, 1983. Mrs. Betty Drobrac has completed multi-titles on her Goldens, including conformation championships, obedience trial titles, and field titles such as the WC and WCX.

The number of Goldens earning obedience titles increases every year. As a breed it is outstanding in obedience competition and for companionship.

YET ANOTHER TRIO OF OUTSTANDING OBEDI-ENCE GOLDENS. O.T. Ch. Sancy's Miki O Pupua-lenalena (AFC-Ch. Honor's Dorado of Spindrift ex Rusti-cana's Sancy, UDT), owned by Janis Teichman and bred by Jeannie Fox, is shown above performing in the directed retrieve exercise. A well-known worker, she has competed successfully in trials held in Hawaii as well as in Northern California and is handled by her owner. The dog in the circle is heavily titled Am. Can. Ch. Ambertail's Bargello Stitch, UDTX, WCX, Can. UDTX, WC, Bda. CDX, TD (Am. Can. Ch. High Farms Jantze of Curacao, CDX, TD, WC, Can. CD, TDX, ex Can. Ch., O.T. Ch. Val's Dolly, WC***), owned and trained by Barbara Tinker and bred by Michael Ducross. "Stitch," like so many other Goldens has a truly outstanding obedi-ence record. He was the most titled Golden in 1983 and is handled by his owner. *Korker.* Finally, to the left is Royalridge Nifty Lass, CDX, TDX, WCX (Dual Ch.-AFC Tigathoe's Funky Farquar ex Royalridge Tule Lass, CDX**), owned and bred by Janet S. Trigg and Robert L. Trigg. Another owner-handled, obedi-ence winner, this one was first in Utility A at the 1983 GRCA Specialty with a score of 197. In her list of achievements is the winning of the Mudcreek Flare UD Trophy for the highest scoring GRCA member-owned and bred dog that is owner handled.

*Rich Bergman*

The Golden Nuggets, a California-based obedience team shown following their win at the team class at the 1980 national Specialty. They are (from left): Team Captain Judith Myers with Topbrass Teal of Buckthorn, CDX, TD, Can. CDX; Janet Trigg with Royalridge Nifty Lass, CDX, TDX, WCX; Christine Perri with Barr Harbours Kelly-Girl, CDX, TD, and Judith Asher with Royalridge Tule Lass, CDX**.

More Golden Nuggets—This time from the East: This is the Golden Nuggets Drill Team of the Lenape Golden Retriever Club of Pennsylvania. A truly unique group, its main purpose is to dispense information on responsible dog ownership to the crowds it attracts at local functions and area shows.                    *Robert Grow*

176

There are so many top trainers and performers that a complete listing would be impossible. Records of titles and trial scores are maintained by the GRCA and available as yearbooks updated every two years.

Team competition in obedience attracts many individuals. In team competition four people, each with their own dog, work together with specific exercises. These include some of the novice exercises with additions that suit group performance. At many Specialty shows as well as other shows, people enjoy exhibiting and other people enjoy watching. One such group, the *Golden Nuggets* of California, is depicted herein.

Other groups are made up of individuals who met in obedience classes and decided to work their dogs together. One such group calls itself the *Marching Band*. This group is made up of a talented engineer, a schoolteacher, a photographer, and a disk jockey. These men put together their own costumes, western style— hats, boots, shirts, etc. They enjoyed meeting after work, enjoying friendship and getting their own exercise as well as training and exercising their dogs.

A few years ago in the Potomac Valley, a group of six women and seven dogs formed team groups. These were young women from their mid-20's to mid-30's. While some of the dogs and some of the women took time out for maternity, there were always four that could perform well as a team. They won several first places.

The brace class is less popular. This consists of one handler with two dogs working together. The outside dog, of necessity, works wide for individual competition. For this reason, it is less popular for anyone who wishes to go on to more advanced work such as a CDX, UD, or higher competition.

The Tracking Dog Excellent title (TDX) has further promoted the interest in tracking exercises. These exercises are more difficult and require more training and more talent in the dog than the less demanding exercises required for the TD. Such exercises are useful in themselves and can be used in finding lost children or adults or lost articles. This could certainly be a beginning exercise for dogs that are used in narcotics detection or rescue work.

The AKC limits the TDX competition to five competitors in any given trial or for any given track for the purpose of acquiring the TDX. Refer to Mrs. Munneke's chapter and the bibliography for further information on tracking.

### New Obedience Title: Obedience Trial Champion (O.T. Ch.)

After a dog has earned the Utility title, he can compete for the title of Obedience Trial Champion (O.T. Ch.) by defeating dogs in Open B, Utility, or Utility B classes. The candidate must earn at least three first place ribbons—one from Open B, one from Utility, and the third from either class—until he has earned a total of 100 points. There is no limit to the number of trials in which a handler may compete with his dog, even after the O.T. Ch. title is earned.

Review each year any new rules on obedience competition. Write to the American Kennel Club, 51 Madison Avenue, New York, N.Y. 10010 for a copy of *Regulations for American Kennel Club Licensed Obedience Trials,* including $.25 for postage.

O.T. Ch. Topbrass Ric O Shay Barty (AFC Holway Barty ex Ch. Sunstream Gypsy of Topbrass), owned and trained by Sharon Long and bred by Joe and Jackie Mertens. Ric is a winner of the Ken-L Ration Award in 1982 and Super Dog at the 1980 Midwest regional. His numerous other honors and achievements include a WC and a WCX.

Here is a truly remarkable pair— Toni Gardiner with her guide dog, Flicka. Toni and Flicka received a score of 188 in one of the legs toward the CD. They travel all over New York City and across the United States. Toni is blind. Paul Gabias, a blind friend, and Toni trained Flicka to be her guiding eyes. Flicka has her CD and is now working on Open class exercises.

## Golden Retriever Obedience Champions
### July 1977—August 1983

| *Dog's Name* | *Date Finished* |
|---|---|
| Morelands Golden Tonka (Klipple) | 7/23/77 |
| (Ch. Misty Morn's Sunset, CD, TD, WC | |
| ex Ch. Moreland's Golden Bonnie) | |
| | |
| Topbrass Cisco Kid (Czarnecki) | 7/31/77 |
| (Poika of Handjem | |
| ex Valentine Torch of Topbrass) | |
| | |
| Ch. Sunstreak of Culynwood, TD, WCX (Bluford) | 9/5/77 |
| (Ch. Sabahka's Alexander of Cal-Vo, CD | |
| ex Ch. Tangelo's End of the Rainbow, CD, WC) | |
| | |
| Ch. Russo's Gold Rush Sensation (Hamm/Johnson) | 9/16/77 |
| (Ch. Cummings' Gold Rush Charlie | |
| ex Russo's Wildwood Flower) | |
| | |
| Bonnie Brooks Harvey, WC (Guetzloff) | 10/1/77 |
| (Bobby of Sleepy Hollow | |
| ex Bonnie Brooks Elmira) | |
| | |
| Enchanted Chaparells Tug (Bickford) | 12/4/77 |
| (Honor's Easy Eyeful, UD | |
| ex Enchanted Equadora) | |
| | |
| Amber of Fairlawn Acres, UD (Hart) | 11/6/77 |
| (Ch. Cummings' King Midas | |
| ex Golden Tonia of Wochica) | |
| | |
| Wessala Naughty Nannette (Prouty) | 11/6/77 |
| (Ch. Finderne Square Shadows Fury, CD, WC | |
| ex Wessala Laurel Leaf) | |
| | |
| Andrew (Johnson) | 12/4/77 |
| (Milo of Ben's Major, UD, WC | |
| ex Double J Kim) | |
| | |
| Proud Phrogg of Jocar, UD (Loewen) | 1/21/78 |
| (Brackenhollow's Sir Herbert, CDX, WC | |
| ex Cameo of Brackenhollow) | |
| | |
| Windy's the Forecast (Rowe) | 3/12/78 |
| (Am., Can. Ch. Bradfield Boomer, Am., Can. UDT, WC | |
| ex Sunstream's Little Echo) | |
| | |
| Meadowpond's Happy Valentine (Roberts) | 4/8/78 |
| (Am., Can. Ch. Bradfield Boomer, Am., Can. UDT, WC | |
| ex Kaymoody's Chevron Redsails) | |

179

Beckwith's Indian Summer, TD, WC (Taylor)      5/14/78
(Am., Can. Ch. Bradfield Boomer, Am., Can. UDT, WC
  ex Beckwith's Amiga Mia)

Beckwith's Eta of Spindrift, TD, WCX (Klausman)      7/29/78
(Ch. Beckwith's Tally-Ho, CDX
  ex. Ch. Beckwith's Malagold Omega, WC)

Chance by Milo (Burge)      7/30/78
(Milo of Ben's Major, UD, WC
  ex Double J Kim)

Jason's Golden Shadow (Kerr)      8/26/78
(Glyn Taff's Trojan Lance
  ex Yorkshire's Golden Duchess)

Meadowpond's Tuf Tiger (Parris)      10/8/78
(Ch. Laurell's Especial Jason, UDT
  ex Windy's Little Honey)

Goldenloe's Just Ducky, WC (Couttet)      11/4/78
(Ch. Golden Pine's Courvoisier, CDX, WCX
  ex Goldenloe's Tawny Tiger, UD, WC)

Topbrass Rocky Mountain High (Schillenkamp)      12/15/78
(Poika of Handjem
  ex Ch. Topbrass San Francisco Flame)

Mr. Bo Jangles XXIII (Chaillot)      3/31/79
(Jack of Hearts
  ex Jessica XII)

Sir Duke of Benton (Lystra)      4/27/79
(Glorigold's Jackson Andrew
  ex Susie Redinger)

Vikays Ace of Diamonds (Parris)      6/3/79
(Milo of Ben's Major, UD, WC
  ex Double J Jim)

Double J's Bufflo Bill Cody (Wood)      6/9/79
(Double J's Boozer
  ex Brandy Deseri)

Golden Tobiah of Tara (Illias)      7/8/79
(Gwinn-Dell's King Midas, UD
  ex Gwinn-Dell's Lor' li O'Glorigold)

Ch. Meadowpond Dust Commander (Brown)      7/15/79
(Am., Can. Ch. Bradfield Boomer, Am., Can. UDT
  ex Missy of Nottingham)

Tyler of Rapscallion Ways (Reynolds)                    8/10/79
(Ezekiel II
 ex Heidi of Fenn's Folly Farm)

Quintocks Rick Rack, TD (Keller)                        8/12/79
(Ch. Footprint of Yeo, CD
 ex Hunts Early Bird, CDX)

Lady Windham (Leedale)                                  9/8/79
(Sir Gabriel Shannon
 ex Miss Tally of Brairwood)

Sungold Duke of Brookshire, WCX (Ochylski)             10/5/79
(FC-AFC-CFC Bonnie Brooks Elmer
 ex Sungold Cinnamon Cinder)

Jan's Golden Mandy (Adams)                             10/27/79
(Honor's Easy Eyeful, UD
 ex Dionysus's Golden Odessa)

Am., Can. Ch. Meadowponds Angelic Abbey, TD, WCX (Schulte) 2/24/80
(Am., Can. Ch. Bradfield's Boomer, Am., Can. UDT
 ex Laurell's Jaunty Jinn-Jinn, CDX)

Barr Harbour Wild Muncie (Armentrout)                   3/21/80
(Am., Can. Ch. Golden Pines Courvoisier, Am., Can. CDX, WCX
 ex Casadeloro's Windward Breeze, CD)

High Times Solicitor, WC (Brinker)                      4/6/80
(Holway Solo
 ex Woodridges Daisy)

Meadowpond's Christopher (Klipple)                      4/13/80
(Am., Can. Ch. Bradfield's Boomer, Am., Can. UDT
 ex Laurell's Jaunty Jinn-Jinn, CDX)

Sir Gold Dust of DWC (Carlson)                          4/27/80
(Goldwood Little Raymond
 ex Lady of Bveltak)

Topbrass Ric O Shay Barty, WCX (Long)                   5/3/80
(AFC Holway Barty
 ex Ch. Sunstreams Gypsy of Topbrass)

Pekays Charm Temptress, TD (Brown)                      5/4/80
(Ch. Misty Morn's Sunset, CD, TD, WC
 ex Honor's Pekay Kiss Me Kate, CDX)

Vikays Jiggs (Parris)                                   5/16/80
(O.T. Ch. Chance by Milo
 ex Rimrac's Brinsmade New Tempo)

181

Topbrass Stubblesfield Pippa (Guetzloff)                    7/11/80
(AFC Holway Barty
 ex Valentine Torch of Topbrass, WC)

Lucky Days Gretchen, WC (Baranowski)                       8/16/80
(FC-AFC Bonnie Brooks Red
 ex Lucky Days Spice of Life)

Burlington of Breenway (Freije)                            9/7/80
(Parkewood's Sir Percival, CD
 ex Jubilees Honolulu)

Robert de Brus of Cocopai (Babbitt)                       11/2/80
(Holway Gillie***
 ex Polaris Kristen of Cocopai, CDX)

Honeys Thrupence Goldkist (Hinton)                        12/6/80
(Honor's Pekay About That Time
 ex Trupence Goldkist Kristy)

Pekay's Magic Moment (Miller)                            12/14/80
(O.T. Ch. Topbrass Cisco Kid
 ex Honor's Pekay Kiss Me Kate, CDX)

Brandywine's Rocky Road, WC (Bluford)                    11/30/80
(Ch. Lorelei's Reza Odu, CD
 ex Ch. Brandywine Tansu D'Oro)

Jim-Jim of Fairlawn Acres (Hart)                          2/22/81
(Ch. Cummings' Gold Rush Charlie
 ex O.T. Ch. Ch. Amber of Fairlawn Acres)

Tass of the West (Schmitt)                                3/8/81
(Cajon Brooks
 ex Gold of Misty Mer)

Galway's Sundown Tango, WC (Igleheart)                    4/25/81
(Viking's Golden Lucky Warlock
 ex Thboy's Miss Gobble Creek)

Rustivus Rustler Pool (Pool)                              4/26/81
(Daniel Webster Finley
 ex Lisa of Dassion)

Sancy's Miki O'Paupaulenalena, WC (Teichman)              4/17/81
(Ch.-AFC Honor's Darado of Spindrift
 ex Rusticana's Sancy, UDT)

Zed (Vermette)                                            4/5/81
(Unknown
 ex Unknown)

182

Jamac's Sunnyday Betyar, TD (McConnell)      6/20/81
(Bim Bam Beaux***
  ex High Hopes Pearl Betyar, UD)

Stardust Thunderbolt (Einhorn)      6/20/81
(Ch. Beaumaris Tangleloft Heath, CD
  ex Sunstrem Amber Mist of Slade, UD)

Graelyn Red Rooster (Ford-Wilson)      9/6/81
(FC-AFC Kinike Chancellor
  ex Maid Megan of Memphis)

Jack's Golden Joy (McManus)      9/27/81
(J.P. Casey
  ex Williams Sweet Juliet)

Meadowpond Fcm De Fortune (Bauman)      9/5/81
(Am., Can. Ch. Bradfield Boomer, Am., Can. UDT
  ex Ch. Meadowpond Dazzle's Sparkle, CD)

Amberac's Sunrise Duke (Schneider)      10/4/81
(Topbrass Ad-bib's Rip Off, UD
  ex Amberac's Sunburst Sun-Brave)

Eastgate's Golden Trisha (Bedingfield/Snell)      10/4/81
(Sunrapt Silver Drift
  ex Eastgate's Golden Legend)

Karagold's Magic Marker (Aranda)      2/28/82
(Am., Can. Ch. Bradfield Boomer, Am., Can. UDT
  ex Missy of Nottingham, CD)

Hoadleygold Duster (Hoadley)      2/13/82
(Trailblazer's Jack of Farquar
  ex Trailblazers Lady of Sands)

Gold Country's Lucky Strike, TD (Anderson)      3/21/82
(Ch. Sham-O-Jets Luvamike
  ex Indian Knoll's Cricket's Love)

Wildwood's Autumn Aspenglow, TD (Olshock)      3/27/82
(Ch. Footprint of Yeo, CD
  ex Ch. Wildwood Windemere)

Decoy's Tomboy of Birdan, TD (Hudson)      4/24/82
(O.T. Ch. Windy's The Forecast
  ex Laurells Honors Gibson Girl, CDX)

Meadowpond Tackle (Berger)      5/1/82
(Am., Can. Ch. Bradfield Boomer, Am., Can. UDT
  ex Ch. Meadowpond Dazzle's Sparkle, CD)

Westmont's Natty Bumppo, TD (English)        5/9/82
(Ch. Sundance's Rainmaker
ex Ch. Westmont's Goldrush Dynamite, CD)

Ch. Morgen's Deerfield Panama Red (Lowy)      6/20/82
(Ch. Rush Creek's Guten Morgen, UD
ex Deerfield's Just a Jonquil)

Shannon Shamrock Pfeifer, WCX (Pfeifer)     7/11/82
(Major Red
ex TJ's Golden Cinnamon)

Meadowpond Son of a Gun, UDTX (Phillips)    8/1/82
(Am., Can. Ch. Bradfield Boomer, Am., Can. UDT
ex Heather's Wish Come True, CDX)

Kyrie Gallant Scot (Hartman)          8/21/82
(Kyrie Gesundheidt, TD
ex Ch. Kyrie Larkin, CDX)

Pekay's Effervescence (Brown)        10/24/82
(Ch. Honor's Rebel Yell, CD
ex Ch. Spindrif's Pekay Penny, CDX)

Countryside Striker (Stith)           10/16/82
(Ch. O.T. Ch. Meadowpond Dust Commander
ex Karagold's Autumn Firefly, CDX)

Richess Merri Mindi of Shy-Yo, TD, WCX (Chaillot)  10/30/82
(Ch. Topbrass Durango Brave, CDX
ex Ch. Spannens Lollypop of Richess)

Ch. Gold Rush Wild Trout (Armentrout)     10/31/82
(Ch. Cummings' Gold Rush Charlie
ex Ch. Jungolds Gold Rush Hope)

Vikay's Silverdale Zack (Silvers)        11/6/82
(O.T. Ch. Vikay's Ace of Diamonds, UD
ex Rapid Aigo Smith, CD)

Meadowpond Shana Maidel (Friedman)     11/26/82
(Am., Can. Ch. Bradfield Boomer, Am., Can. UDT
ex Windy's Meadowpond Sabrina)

Topbrass Windjammer (Czarnecki)       11/14/82
(Topbrass Knuckles, CD**
ex Ch. Topbrass Dazzlin' Daisy Slade)

Meadowpond Strut (Czarnecki)        12/18/82
(Am., Can. Ch. Bradfield Boomer, Am., Can. UDT
ex Heather's Wish Come True, CDX)

Shenandoah Golden Jake (Connors/Lam)                    12/19/82
(Ch. Feara's Sun Dance Risen Shine, CD
  ex Hillsdale Hoosier Honey)

Meadowpond California Poppy (Howard)                      4/3/83
(Ch. Topbrass Durango Brave, CDX
  ex O.T. Ch. Meadowpond Angelic Abbey, UDT)

Chaparral Sonic Boom (Buck)                              4/9/83
(Am., Can. Ch./O.T. Ch. Sunstreak of Culynwood, UDT, WCX
  ex Ch. Odu's Bianca of Manorloch, CDX)

Sancy's Georgi Girl, UDT, WC (Ball)
(Ch.-AFC Honor's Darado of Spindrift
  ex Rusticana's Sancy, UDT)

Ch. Pekays Deliverance, UDT, WCX (Patton/Cathey)         5/15/83
(Ch. Misty Morn's Sunset, CD, TD, WC
  ex Honor's High Stakes)

Wynwood Two Double Zera, UDT (Treanor)                    6/5/83
(O.T. Ch. Sungold Duke of Brookshire, UD, WCX
  ex O.T. Ch. Meadowpond Angelic Abbey, UDT, WCX)

Shadow of Sands, Am., Can. UD, WCX (Gregor)              6/12/83
(FC-AFC Chief Sands
  ex Shadowbrook Bittersweet***)

Wynwood Countessa of Windham (Leedale)                    7/3/83
(O.T. Ch. Sungold Duke of Brookshire, UD, WCX
  ex O.T. Ch. Meadowpond Angelic Abbey, UDT, WCX)

Amberac's Boisterous Brett, UD (Garvin)
(Am., Can. Ch. Topbrass Durango Brave, CDX, WC
  ex Amberac's Sangria de Ora, CD)

Morning Sage Cinnamon Toast (Gensmer)                    7/16/83
(Am., Can. Ch. Topbrass Durango Brave, CDX, WC
  ex Morning Sage Malagold Honey)

Gold Country's Timber Flash (Kopecko)                    5/29/83
(Ch. Sham-O-Jets Luvamike
  ex Rainbow's Tupelo Honey)

Ch. Fieldale's Nike of Honeyhill, CDX***, owned and trained by Pat Bixby, has enjoyed success in obedience, the field and on the show bench.

A trio of multi-talented Wyndspelle Goldens have a photo session in the snow. They are (from left) Am. Can. Ch. Jabula Thembalisha, Am. Can. CD; Am. Can. Ch. Sun Dance's Tiger Lily, Am. Can. CDX, OD; Am. Can. Ch. Jolly Jack Frost o'Wyndspelle, Am. Can. CD. Jack Frost eventually became enrolled in the GRCA Stud Dog Hall of Fame. These dogs are all owned by James and Deborah Totten.

# 9

# Novice Obedience Training

*by Edith E. Munneke*

THERE IS NO ONE WAY to train a dog, nor is there a set age when formal training should be started. The sooner a puppy is taught to "mind his manners," the easier he is to live with and the fewer bad habits he can develop. Every puppy must be trained early for his visits to the veterinarian, and he certainly should learn to come when called. Most training schools will not accept a puppy until he is at least six months old.

## The Collar and Leash

Standard training equipment consists of a slip chain collar just large enough to fit over the head. Never allow any part of it to hang down where a puppy can get it in his mouth or catch a paw. As the puppy grows, get a larger collar; it can be inexpensive, but proper fit is important. After the puppy gets used to the collar, he should wear it only while working. The six-foot leash should have a swivel snap, but be careful that the snap is not so large that it clouts the puppy in the head as he moves.

The collar is placed around the dog's neck so that when he is at your left side and facing forward, the end attached to the leash passes *over* his neck. When you put the collar on the puppy for the first time, distract his attention by running with him or getting him to chase a ball. Short sessions accompanied by play will soon get him used to the collar. Now the leash can be attached. Again it must be a game with plenty of fun and coaxing. Patience at this stage is most important. MAKE IT FUN.

When your puppy accepts both collar and leash without objection, you are ready to start training. How successful you will be depends on *you*. If you do a good job, you and your dog will enjoy each other more than ever; if you do a poor job, you will have only yourself to blame.

The fundamentals of dog obedience training are found in the Novice exercises formulated by the American Kennel Club and are used in obedience trials all over America. Each of these exercises has a utilitarian value in everyday life. They are not just tricks. HEEL: Your dog walks close to your left side and sits when you halt. FIGURE "8": Your dog stays close on crowded sidewalks without sniffing people, fire hydrants, or other dogs. STAND FOR EXAMINATION: Your dog allows strangers to touch him. He stands quietly while you talk to a friend. RECALL: Your dog comes when called, sits directly in front of you, and moves to your left side on command. LONG SIT and LONG DOWN: Your dog stays in either position while you attend to other business.

## Home Practice

Once formal training has started, it is most important that some practice is done every day. At first, one person only should do all the training. It should always be fun for both you and your dog, but do not play with him during a practice session. Be firm but keep him happy with praise. Sometimes it seems as if a dog can read a person's mind. He knows when he can get away without obeying the commands of an easy master. Your dog should understand right from the start that you are the boss, and that he must respond to your commands. This understanding should be based on respect and the desire to please rather than on fear and punishment. A correctly trained dog is neither cowed nor broken in spirit. Spanking or other punishment has absolutely no place in obedience training. Never lose your patience no matter how stubborn or stupid your dog seems. Do not practice just after your dog has eaten, nor during the heat of the day in summer. Make the practice sessions more interesting by changing the order of the exercises. Always give commands and signals in exactly the same way. Don't expect perfection at first. You could seriously confuse your dog by attempting too much in too short a time. Teaching your dog is a step-by-step process. Teach each step as thoroughly as you can.

## Commands and Signals

The first step is always the command. If the dog does not respond immediately (and of course he won't at first), force is applied with the leash. Force should generally be followed by praise. The leash is usually held in the right hand in such a way that a little slack hangs below the collar. Corrections are made by snapping or jerking on the leash (often with the left hand), momentarily tightening the collar.

Knowing just *when* and how forceful to make the jerk is an art which must be studied and practiced. Every dog and every situation is different. The jerk should be short, quick, and usually quite vigorous, releasing the tightness immediately. Never pull or drag on the leash. It is always either hanging loosely or being snapped and instantly loosened again.

Jerking is a temporary but necessary correction which must be eliminated as soon as the dog obeys the command satisfactorily without it. Be prepared to use the leash any time your dog fails to respond immediately to your command or signal. Don't forget the praise which should accompany every correction. The commands commonly used are, HEEL, SIT, STAY, DOWN, STAND, and COME. Use exactly the same command and signal every time. Commands may be repeated several times when first teaching a dog an exercise, but eventually he must respond to one command only. Never repeat a command without good reason.

Give commands with a firm but not harsh tone of voice. At first, the tone of voice is more important than the actual words. Make your voice fit the command. COME (pleasantly), NO (sternly), STAY (firmly), etc. Use the dog's name *before* the command when he is to move (Heel, Come, etc.). Do *not* use his name when he is to stay (Stay, Stand). The sit command is discontinued in heeling as soon as he learns he is to sit every time you halt (unless you give the command and signal to stand).

At the proper times you may praise, scold, coax, or pet your dog. He should learn to recognize words like Good Boy, Shame, No, Close, Straight, etc. At first, always use hand signals with Stay and Stand. For Stay swing the left open palm close to your dog's nose. For Stand swing the right palm close to his nose. Body motions become important signals. Always step forward on the *left* foot when you want the dog to move with you. Step forward on the *right* foot when he is to stay.

## Heel and Sit

Say, "Rover, Heel," and at the same time give a jerk on the leash with a forward motion of the left hand so that your dog moves with you. Several increasingly forceful commands and jerks may be necessary. The force of the jerk depends on the dog. DON'T OVERDO IT! Coax your dog to heel close (but not touching) with his shoulders even with your left side. Use sharp, quick jerks of the leash if he lags behind, forges ahead, or is more than six inches from your side. Loosen the leash immediately after each jerk. Praise him every time you jerk him close.

189

Come to a gradual stop and say, "Rover, Sit." At the same time, jerk (gently at first) straight up on the leash with the right hand while you guide and push downward on the dog's rear with the left hand so that he sits straight and on both haunches with his shoulder even with your left knee. The halt command, and both corrections (jerk and push) should all be done simultaneously. You may bend but do not turn sideways nor move your left foot. If your dog is not sitting correctly (crooked, wide, forward, or behind), heel forward another step or two and try it again. Do not adjust your position to that of your dog. Praise him when he sits correctly. Your dog must not move until you say, "Rover, Heel." In practice, vary the length of the Sit from two or three seconds to ten or more.

The ultimate goal is to have the dog sit immediately and straight every time you halt and without command, upward jerk, or downward push (automatic sit). The halt itself becomes the signal to sit. When your dog is ready for this automatic sit, occasionally omit one of the three (command, jerk, or push). Do not omit the same one every time. If your dog sits quickly, omit another, and finally try it without any command or correction at all. Praise him generously when he sits automatically. Be prepared to use the corrections again any time he forgets. If he does not begin to sit immediately when you halt, push or tap down on his rear (not over the kidneys). Don't allow him too much time. A good automatic sit may take several weeks of diligent practice, but its importance cannot be over-emphasized.

### Turns and Changes of Pace

New problems are the LEFT TURN, RIGHT TURN, ABOUT TURN, SLOW, and FAST. Avoid making the turns too fast at first. A short step just before a turn can alert your dog that you are going to do something different. You may use your right knee or foot to help nudge your dog into the LEFT TURN while you keep him close with short, quick jerks of the leash and lots of coaxing and praise. Use the leash to avoid lagging on the RIGHT TURN and ABOUT TURN. Remember that the leash is always either hanging loosely or being snapped and instantly loosened again. The command, Heel, should accompany every snap of the leash.

The ABOUT TURN is always made to the right and at first may be simply a continuation of the RIGHT TURN. Later on, increase the sharpness of the turns. The ultimate goal is military precision. When you halt, see that your dog sits quickly and straight.

Changes of pace should likewise be very gradual at first. Do not let your dog forge ahead or lag behind. NORMAL should be a fairly brisk pace. FAST means at least an easy trot. Use the leash *only* when necessary on either the turns or changes of pace. Praise your dog for every well-done turn, sit, etc.

**Sit-Stay**

Never use the dog's name when he is to stay. Say "Stay," and at the same time, swing the left palm in front of his nose. Always use the left hand for this signal. Step forward on the *right* foot, but at first, slowly and only far enough to stand directly in front of and facing your dog. He must not move. If he seems about to break, repeat, "Sit" and "Stay" more forcefully. If he does break, get him back in the same position *immediately* and say, "Sit" and "Stay" very forcefully. Tap his nose with your left palm as you again give the Stay command and signal. Let him know by the tone of your voice that you are displeased.

Transfer the leash to your left hand as you start to return to your dog's left side. Continue on around in back of him and pass the leash back to the right hand as you come up to heel position on his right side. He must not move. Say, "Rover, Heel," and take a few steps forward before praising your dog.

When your dog seems to understand the command "Stay," gradually move farther away. Keep the leash very loose. Gradually increase the time of the sit until the dog will stay in position several minutes without moving. This will prepare him for the LONG SIT. The SIT-STAY also forms the first part of the RECALL exercise.

**The Stand-Stay**

Your dog should sit automatically every time you halt except when you give the command and signal to STAND. Heel forward and turn sideways (left) toward your dog as you halt, as you would in the breed ring. At the same time, bring your right palm in front of his nose (hand signal for STAND), and say, "Stand." A touch of the left hand in front of the dog's right rear leg is usually enough to keep him standing. Lift him back into a stand position immediately if he sits. Repeat, "Stand" and "Stay" to steady him as you straighten back to the heel position.

When your dog seems steady, say, "Stay," give the hand signal (left palm), and step forward on the right foot. At first, stand directly in front of and facing your dog. Later on, go out the length of the very loose leash. Your dog must not move his *feet*. Repeat, "Stand" and "Stay" *only* if necessary to steady him.

Again transfer the leash to the left hand, move to the dog's left, and circle around behind him. Pass the leash back to the right hand as you come up to position on your dog's right side. Your dog must not move until *you* command him to do so. Heel forward before praising him.

In practice, alternate the STAND-STAY with the SIT-STAY exercise. Never call your dog from the STAND position. Gradually prepare him for the STAND FOR EXAMINATION. The Stand is essential for showing a dog in the conformation ring. Repetition is the key to successful dog training. Each exercise must be repeated over and over until the response becomes almost a reflex to the command and signal. It is possible to over-train a dog, but such a thing is rare indeed. The results of a wrong type of training may sometimes be confused with over-training. Your dog is not a machine. He constantly seeks your approval. If you give him enough encouragement, reassurance and praise, you will probably continue to have a happy and willing worker. Your own attitude is also important. If you are bored with the whole business, your dog is very likely to be bored too. If you are enthusiastic, your dog is almost sure to reflect your enthusiasm.

## Down

Here are a few of the many ways to teach a dog to go down from the sit position. Repeat the command, "Rover, Down," as you put your dog down. Reassure him with praise.

(1) Place your left arm over your dog's back and grasp his left front leg. Hold his right front leg with your right hand. Lift both front feet and move them forward. Block other movements of the dog with your left elbow and knee.
(2) Lift your dog's front feet forward with your right hand; push downward with the left hand.
(3) Force the dog's head toward the floor by stepping down on the leash.

Keep your dog down several seconds; then say, "Rover, Sit." If necessary, jerk up on the leash.

## The Down-Stay

Say, "Rover, Down." Force him down if necessary. Say, "Stay" (do not use his name), give the hand signal, and step forward on the *right* foot. At first, stand directly in front of and facing your dog. Later on, move out the length of the loose leash. If your dog moves, put him back in the same position *immediately*. Speak very firmly. Tap his nose as you again give the hand signal. Transfer the leash to the left hand as you circle your dog. Pass it back to the right hand as you come up to position on your dog's right side. He must not move.

Say, "Rover, Sit." Heel your dog forward before praising him. Gradually increase the length of the Down-Stay. As you and your dog become more proficient, you will gradually eliminate corrections, extra commands, and other temporary aids which you may have been using. You may invent other aids to overcome problems as you find them. Improvement of any exercise may seem like a series of learning plateaus. Days may go by without any apparent change, and then perhaps quite suddenly you may see definite progress.

Am. Can. Ch. October's Foxy Lady, Am. Can. CD (Ch. Sir Duncan of Woodbury ex Ch. Cal-Vo's Nickel Nehi), owned by Kay Gosling and bred by Sharon Smith and Carol Vogel.

Ch. Valhalla's Trowsnest Folly, UDT, WCX, owned by Marjorie Trowbridge.

## The Finish

The FINISH is the final part of the RECALL exercise. It will bring your dog from his sitting position directly in front of you to heel position at your left side. There are two methods of doing the FINISH. Choose one or the other and then *always* use the same method. If you choose the first method, your dog will move to your right, go on around behind you, and come up to sit at heel position. If you choose the second method, your dog will move to your left, turn about, and sit at heel position. The second method may seem flashier, but a large dog may do better with the first method.

METHOD 1 (AROUND THE BACK): Stand directly in front of and facing your dog. Hold the leash rather short in the right hand. Say, "Rover, Heel." (Some handlers prefer the command "By-Me" instead of "Heel.") At the same time, jerk the leash backward and a little to the right as you take a backward step with your right foot. As the dog passes on your right side, change the leash behind you from your right hand to your left. When your dog is behind you, again say, "Heel," bring your right foot back into position, and jerk forward on the leash with the left hand to bring him up to heel position. Say, "Rover, Sit," and, if necessary, use your left hand to guide his rear so that he sits straight.

METHOD 2 (TO THE LEFT): Stand directly in front of and facing your dog. Hold the leash rather short in the left hand. Say, "Rover, Heel," step backward on the left foot, and at the same time jerk the leash to the left rear. When your dog has passed the original position of your left foot, again say, "Heel," bring your left foot back into line, and jerk forward on the leash so that the dog turns and comes up to heel position. If necessary, say, "Rover, Sit," and use your left hand to help guide him into a straight sit. Eventually, he must learn to FINISH with one command only. Eliminate the corrections as soon as possible.

## The Recall

Take your dog to the starting place and have him sit at heel position. Say, "Stay," give the hand signal, and step forward on the *right* foot. Replace your dog immediately if he follows you. Walk to the end of the loose leash and turn to face your dog.

Say, "Rover, Come." The tone of voice is most important. Make your command as enticing and exciting as you can. If your dog does not come immediately, give a sharp jerk on the leash. Do not pull the dog to you. A series of increasingly sharper jerks and more forceful commands may be necessary. Coax your dog to come toward you at a lively pace. As he comes toward you, gather up the leash so there is very little slack. If necessary, use the leash to guide him so that he sits straight in front of you. If he is out of position, move back a step and again have him sit. Praise him when he sits correctly. Eliminate the Sit command and any accompanying corrections as soon as possible. Say, "Rover, Heel," and use the corrections for the

FINISH. Eliminate these corrections as soon as your dog will go to heel position without them.

**Stand for Examination**

To stand your dog for examination, transfer your leash to the left hand as you heel forward. Turn toward your dog as you halt. Say, "Stand," give the hand signal (right palm), and pass the leash back to the right hand. You may also pose your dog as in conformation. When your dog seems steady, say, "Stay," give the hand signal, and step forward on the *right* foot. Go out the length of the loose leash and turn to face your dog. After the Stay, you should not speak or signal to your dog until the exercise is completed. Practice this until your dog is steady, then stand dog without leash, for obedience rules now in force require the stand for examination without leash.

Have someone run a hand over the dog's head, shoulders, and down his back. The dog must show no sign of shyness or resentment and must not move his *feet*. When the examination is completed, return by circling your dog as you did on the STAND-STAY exercise. He must not move. Heel a step or two forward before praising your dog.

Like all exercises, teaching your dog to accept the examination is a gradual process of development. (1) You, yourself, should first examine your dog. Pause several seconds before and after the examination. Pause again when you return to position. (2) Arrange with someone your dog already knows and likes to do the examining. (3) Get many people, both men and women, to examine your dog.

**Figure-8**

The Figure-8 consists of heeling around two people or objects in a figure-8 pattern. The two people (usually stewards) stand about eight feet apart and facing each other. Take your position about half way between them. Your dog should be sitting at heel position. Say, "Rover, Heel," and step forward on the *left* foot. Most handlers go around the left post first (dog on the inside). Allow sufficient room between yourself and the post so that the dog is not crowded. Bump him with your right knee or foot if he does not make the left turns with you. Use sharp, quick jerks of the leash to keep him from lagging. You may take shorter steps as you go around the right-hand post (dog on the outside), and again use sharp, quick jerks with lots of coaxing and praise to avoid lagging.

When you halt, see that your dog sits quickly and straight. He must completely ignore the posts. If he sniffs, tap him on the nose and say, "No." You will heel forward and halt several times during this exercise. In practice, use any two objects as posts (buckets, chairs, etc.). Halt at various angles and see that your dog sits quickly and straight. Walk with your dog on a moderately crowded sidewalk. See that he stays close to your left side without sniffing anyone or anything. At every opportunity, put into practice the exercises your dog has learned.

Ch. Poppygold Ginger Ripple, UDT, and her owner, Mrs. William Carter demonstrate the demanding tracking exercises.

Ch. Mon's Tawny Priscilla Suvarna, UDT, owned and trained by Nick and Suse Hammond, was an obedience star in Southern California during the 1970s.

# 10

# Tracking

*by Edith E. Munneke*

**E**ARNING a tracking title is not as difficult as one might suppose. It all depends on how carefully the dog has been prepared. As in all other obedience work, it is a step-by-step process.

You can have a Tracking Dog (TD) without having earned a CD, CDX, or UD, but previous obedience training certainly makes it easier to teach your dog to track. To pass a test, your dog must follow the track of a stranger for a minimum distance of 440 yards. There is no time limit provided the dog is working. The track must include at least two approximate right angle turns. At the end of the trail your dog must retrieve a glove or billfold dropped by the track-layer.

Again, there is no *one* way to teach your dog to track; nor is there any certain age when a dog is too young or too old. A dog with a Utility title has already been taught many of the fundamentals needed for tracking, so he should be much easier to teach.

Before one can start to teach actual tracking, a dog must be able to respond to all the basic commands like Heel, Sit, Stay, Down, and Come.

In addition, he must be willing to pick up or retrieve an object and return it to his handler and must be able to search out and find an object by scent alone. The earlier your dog has been taught to obey, the easier your task will be. REMEMBER TO MAKE IT FUN! If you keep it a game, you and your dog can spend many happy hours in the fields together.

At first, put your dog on a Sit-Stay while you go out in a straight line and drop the leather object in plain sight. Return and send your dog to retrieve and bring the article back to you. When your dog retrieves every time, you are ready to start the next step.

Now, go out of sight around the house before you drop the article. Be sure your dog does not see you drop it. Make it easy at first, but as he gets better, make it more difficult. He will soon learn to use his nose to find the object.

Now you are ready for the tracking harness and line. Some handlers use a flat leather collar; some even use the choke collar with the line fastened in both loops. We have followed the policy of having special equipment to be used only in the breed ring; other equipment to be used only in obedience; and a special harness to be used only for tracking. A dog soon learns what response is expected when each set of equipment is brought out. IT IS ADDED INSURANCE AGAINST FAILURE.

A tracking harness can be made from webbing or from leather strapping which is fitted to each individual dog. Most any pet store will gladly measure your dog and order a harness. The advantage of the harness is that the pull comes on the shoulders and chest rather than on the neck. The line must be at least 20 feet long but may be no more than 40 feet. It may be plastic clothes-line or flat webbing which is snapped to the collar or harness.

By now your dog has been conditioned to move forward to seek and retrieve an article. He has added to his vocabulary such words as TRACK, SEEK, GO FIND IT, etc. From now on, the tracking equipment should be worn at all times while the dog is working but should be removed as soon as the work session is over.

Don't give up if you have to work alone, but it is a great advantage at this point to have a partner. One person can be the track-layer. It is best to wear leather shoes at first and to take short steps. As the dog becomes more experienced, he should be able to follow a track made by any footgear.

Do not let the dog see the track being made. Inconspicuous green garden stakes make good markers for starting flags and turns. Tramp down a wide enough area at the starting flag so that the dog can easily pick up the scent. You can soon tell how much time and encouragement your dog needs at the post before he is ready to hit the trail. No two dogs are alike. As the handler, your satisfaction comes from learning the work habits of your individual dog so you will know when to encourage and when to correct.

Some dogs track with noses constantly low to the ground; some check for scent with heads high in the air. *KNOW YOUR OWN DOG.* At first, lay a straight track. If you are working alone, after dropping the article, you may have to walk back on your own track to pick up your dog; then you will follow him as he tracks. It may be possible for you to circle back to your dog and then follow the track you have made.

As soon as your dog is steady on the straight track, it is time to add a turn. Let him cast around at the turn to find the scent. Stand still and let him work. If he seems confused, guide him gently until he gets back on the track. You know where the track is, so encourage him to find it. Do not make it so difficult that he loses interest or becomes discouraged. PRAISE is most essential. Once your dog has accepted the fact that you will try to "trick" him with turns, he will look for them and not be confused by them. Be sure that he retrieves an object every time.

It is important that you track in many different areas, in all kinds of weather, and over all types of terrain. Remember that your Tracking test will be made in an unfamiliar area with no dependable cooperation from the weather bureau. It is important that your dog have an opportunity to track strangers because he will not know the track-layer at his test.

It is safer to train carefully and surely step-by-step rather than have to go back later to correct mistakes. You and your dog are working as a team and must have faith and confidence in each other. Remember that in a Tracking test it is the *dog* that has the nose! You will just be along for the walk. If you have trained your dog properly, he, with encouragement from you, will retrieve the object and share with you the honor and glory of having earned a TD.

### New Tracking Title: TRACKING DOG EXCELLENT (TDX)

After a dog earns a Tracking title (TD), he can be entered in a Tracking Dog Excellent (TDX) test without a qualifying letter. Since there is only a starting flag, he must be taught to seek out the direction of the track without the help of a second flag. A total of four different types of articles (billfold, key case, glove, scarf, sock, handkerchief, etc.) must be picked up and returned at the finish of the test. One article will be at the starting flag and one at the end of the track. The other two will be dropped on the track, but no closer than 30 yards from any turn.

The track must cover different types of terrain (low growth, high growth, brambles, sparse growth, heavy cover, bare cover, ridges, valleys, etc.), and may cross roads and creeks as well as fence rows. At two separate places, the track must be crossed at right angles by two cross-track layers, walking together but four feet apart.

The track will be about 800 yards long and aged about two hours. All TDX tests are limited to an entry of five dogs with two judges officiating. This test requires the use of more land and offers a greater challenge to both the club giving the test and the dog and handler working the course.

Ch. Asterling's Tahiti Sweetie (Ch. Gold Rush Judgement Day ex Am. Can. Ch. Amberac's Asterling Aruba), owned by Sylvia Donahey and Mary Wuestenberg (breeder). At the time this book was being prepared, "Brooke" was setting a sizzling pace in the Group and BIS ring. Handled by Ms. Donahey, she has been shown fearlessly from coast to coast and went BB at the 1983 GRCA national Specialty and Group 2nd at the 1984 Westminster Show. In the photo at the top of the page, taken when she was just six weeks old, "Brooke" was already hinting at what was to come.

# 11

# Show Ring
# Competition and
# Other Activities

---

**T**HERE ARE THREE major forms of competition in which the Golden owner may wish to participate. Each of these forms has its merits. The choices will have to do with the convenience to the owner and his major interests. One form of competition should not be thought of as being more important than the other and, as time goes on, one or all three may be the choice of the owner.

BENCH COMPETITION, or bench activities, refers to competition in the show ring in which the dog or bitch is shown against others of the same breed to evaluate its beauty and closeness to the Standard. Usually this competition is in shows *licensed* by the American Kennel Club, in which points may be won toward a championship. Then there are *sanctioned* shows in which no championship points are awarded. This type of show should not be underestimated. It gives the new owner or handler experience in presenting or handling his dog, in acquiring ring manners, and giving the dog some experience in posing and exhibiting. It is also a valuable opportunity for the veteran exhibitor to start his new puppies.

Information regarding registration of purebred dogs and shows is available free of charge from the American Kennel Club, 51 Madison Avenue, New York, New York 10010. Some of the dog food companies have diagrammed charts, showing the succession of classes for dogs and for bitches, the competition for Best of Winners and Best of Breed. It takes only a short time to learn the classes from puppies all the way to Best of Breed. This competition is for purebred dogs only. In filling out the entry blanks, which may be obtained from the various show superintendents or show-giving clubs, the entry form should be carefully followed, indicating the AKC registration number, the registered name, date of birth, class in which shown, owner's name, etc. The form is more or less self-explanatory, including a little note to "please enclose your check for the entry fee" and giving a deadline in which the entry must be in the office of the superintendent. The closing date is usually two to four weeks prior to the show date.

FIELD COMPETITION, as a rule, is more expensive as to entry fees. More travel time is required, as well as considerably more training. This training and form of activity is carefully explained in Chapters 5 and 6. It is an interesting form of competition. C. Mackay Sanderson of England in the 1949 *The Labrador Retriever Club, Stud Book & Record of Field Trials* terms this "the higher form of competition." The term "higher form," refers to the amount of training and experience that goes into preparation for this form of competition. Information regarding the various stakes, derby, qualifying, open all-age, amateur all-age, and limited all-age stakes is found in *Rules and Regulations for Field Trials* and its supplement, published by the American Kennel Club. Prospective participants should request a new rule book each year. The changes may be minor, but they could be important.

OBEDIENCE COMPETITION is the third form of competition. The routines learned in obedience training, whether or not the training is done by the owner or a professional, is to develop better citizenship in the dog that makes for better dog relationships. The advanced classes further this training. Classes in obedience have spread and the competition and interest are high. Most owners find obedience training through local training classes most enjoyable. The dogs like it also, for they learn what is expected of them under distractions. Basic obedience is, of course, necessary for field competition and some owners and dogs participate equally well in both. The time required for training is such that once the basic obedience is learned, the training will be concentrated on one or the other, at least for a time. Novice obedience training and tracking are explained in Chapters 9 and 10.

The classes in obedience competition are Novice A, Novice B, Open A, Open B, and Utility. It is very important to acquire a new rule book each year and note any recent changes. Rules and regulations for obedience trials, like those for field and for show, may also be obtained from the American Kennel Club. An interested dog owner can obtain individual copies of all three—bench, obedience, and field trial rules and regulations—free on request from AKC.

Ch. Kachina's Kamiakin O'Darnley (Ch. Gold Rush Great Teddy Bear ex Ch. Krishna's E.Z. Livin'), owned by Robert Fell and Barbara Fell Weirick. A strong winner, he is shown taking his eighth BIS. This was at the Golden Gate KC under judge Robin Hernandez, handler Jerry Weirick.

Am. Can. Ch. Russo's Pepperhill Poppy (Am. Can. Bda. Ch. Cummings' Gold Rush Charlie ex Russo's Wildwood Flower), owned by Jeffrey and Barbara Pepper, was BB at the GRCA 1979 Specialty under Mrs. James E. Clark. In doing so, she became the first bitch in many years to achieve this honor. She was handled to the win by Elliott More.                                                              *Martin Booth*

In bench competition—or conformation classes, as this phase of competition is sometimes called—one may choose to handle one's own dog or use a professional handler. If you are active and at ease before people, or if you want to gain poise, showing your own dog can be a great pleasure. If you try to present your dog in the best possible way, your dog has a very good chance of being assessed for its true value. There may be reasons why you would prefer to have a competent professional handler present your dog in the ring. At one time professional handlers were AKC-licensed. This is no longer true and one sees the term *agent* with the agent's name included with the dog's entry information. This agent may be paid, or he may be showing the dog free as a favor to the owner. Excellent professionals (or agents) are paid a fair sum varying from agent to agent to handle a dog. Once an agent has done well with a dog and the dog receives a major show win (3, 4, or 5 points), the agent generally continues handling the dog until completion of championship, or until the owner decides to discontinue showing the dog. It is more expensive, but you, at the ringside, may assess your dog more objectively (though this is sometimes hard to do when you love your dog) in relation to the other dogs exhibited. You should remember that dogs do not show equally well each day or for each handler.

Preparation for your Golden before the show is important. A dog should be immaculately clean. This usually means a bath from a week to a few days before the show. The coat should be groomed through combing and brushing so that it will appear most becoming to the dog and show off the dog's body structure at its best. Some dogs may need some slight trimming around the ears, through the neck, or in other spots to give the best possible presentation. The feet and hocks should be neat. Over-grooming or a barbered look is not well-liked among Golden fanciers. But certainly an unkempt look does not make for a good appearance either.

Those who use their dogs in tracking or field work do not like to trim their dogs' whiskers. They feel that this is a mutilation. Dr. Thomas E. McGill, Ph.D., has published an article in *Dog World* which has been widely copied in which he explains why he feels the whiskers should not be trimmed. Under the new Standard adopted by the GRCA in 1982, the cutting of whiskers is discouraged but removal is optional.

The whiskers are often trimmed for the show ring. There is a practical reason for this. The dog not only looks neater, but as the judge opens the dog's mouth to check the teeth and jaws, or passes his hand over the dog to feel the skeletal structure and to check on the dog's temperament and willingness to be touched, the whiskers, which are sensitive, may cause the dog to move uneasily under the judge's hand. Even though you may feel the whiskers are part of the dog's personality, you must decide to leave the whiskers, which are useful in field and in tracking, or whether you will trim them. The whiskers will grow out surprisingly fast. Whiskers are not trimmed on puppies.

Another reason for having your dog very clean (and you would

Am. Mex. Ch. Fireside Splinters & Chips, owned by Mr. and Mrs. Raymond Hendricks, had a long, successful show career. One of his best wins was BB at the GRCA national Specialty under breeder-judge Joseph Dainty. He made this win from Veterans at age 9. Presenting trophy is GRCA President Dixie Akers.

Ch. Thistledue's Shining Star (Ch. Wochica's Okeechobee Jake ex Ch. Goldenquest's Thistledue, OD), owned and bred by Carter Foss. This dog is a multiple BIS winner and is shown taking the top spot at the St. Joseph KC (Missouri) under judge Maxine Beam. *Don Petrulis*

Ch. Brandywine's Sparkling Wind, CD, owned and bred by Ben and Bonnie Gikis, shown winning under Mrs. James E. Clark. *Rich Bergman*

Ch. Foxy Lady Loch of Wil-Lin (Beckwith's Echo of Loch Tay ex Am. Can. Ch. Kyrie Loch Ness of Terra-Hoh), owned by Linda and Willard Hall, was BOS at the GRCA 1976 Specialty under judge Robert Waters.
*Martin Booth*

Ch. Golden Pine's Brown Bear, owned by Mary Luise Semans. One of the most memorable dogs of the late 1950s, he is shown here winning a Group under judge Kenneth Given. The handler was Lloyd Case, closely associated with Goldens for many years.
*Evelyn Shafer*

certainly want the other dogs to be equally clean) is that as the judge passes from one dog to the other, there is little chance of infection, and surely you would not wish the judge to come from a soiled dog to yours. Remember, the judge must judge many dogs during the day. The exhibitor should think in terms of the judge and his busy schedule and make it possible for the judge to see the dog in the best possible light and as quickly as possible. Watching at ringside during a few shows will give the exhibitor a great deal of information. In many communities, there are classes in learning how to handle a dog in the show ring, and it is an advantage for the owner and his dog to attend these classes.

Success in the show ring depends upon both the dog and the handler. A team relationship is most desirable. A dog's show success is a combination of his basic conformation, condition, personality, and the way he projects in the show ring. A great deal of this is natural, but it may be enhanced or limited by the early care and training of the puppy. Some people begin posing the dog almost as a form of play when the puppy is eight or nine weeks old, stroking his chin upward, encouraging him to hold his head high, feeding him at shoulder height to encourage good canine posture, and teaching him happiness on the leash and in walking or gaiting on the left side. An outgoing personality helps, but it does not make up for overweight, poor physical condition, or an unbalanced proportion far from the Standard. For the purpose of conformation competition, judging is based on how closely each dog adheres to the breed Standard, a Standard set for the purpose for which the breed is used. See Chapter 4, the detailed drawings by Mrs. Perry and the discussion by Mrs. Elliott.

Obedience and field competition do not require perfection of form and coat condition. However, even in these forms of competition, a dog in good condition looks better and, if in good condition, usually is more successful in training and trials over a period of time. Naturally, some forms of cover in which field dogs are worked do some harm to the coat. The damage usually is not serious if the dog is combed and checked immediately after training or competition. Certainly burrs and debris should be removed from the coat as soon as the training session or trial series is over. A handler checking the feet of his dog to see that there are no burrs between the toes, rocks or other debris that could cause lameness or pain to the dog, or seeds that could work their way through the coat and damage the skin, is always a satisfying sight.

There are customs in each form of competition which should be learned early. One of these is—do not allow your dog to sniff another as it walks through the grounds or into the conformation ring, obedience ring or in field activities. Sniffing is not only bad manners and takes the dog's mind off his or her work, but can get him into trouble with a hostile dog.

Rules, sportsmanship and the etiquette of these various activities should be learned and observed early.

Dual Ch. Tigathoe's Funky Farquar (AFC Bonnie Brooks Elmer ex Tigathoe's Chicka-saw***), owned by Dr. and Mrs. R. Eugene Ramsay. As the top derby retriever for all breeds in 1973, he won the *Charles Morgan Memorial Award,* formerly known as the *Country Life Trophy.*

208

# 12

# Care of the
# Adult Golden

THE CARE OF THE ADULT GOLDEN may be thought of in four parts: personal attention and training, feeding and housing.

Personal attention, companionship and training are important to any dog and particularly to Golden Retrievers. They enjoy attention from the owner and are enhanced by training, care and companionship, for basically they are personal dogs. This means that the dog should be with its owner on some occasions of travel, in the house and about the yard. And if there are two or more Goldens they often will share the affection of their owners, though each may have his or her favorite.

I recall my first two Goldens whose call names were Candy and Flare. Candy loved me, but she loved my husband a little more; the reverse was true of Flare. These two beautiful ladies would come into the house through the Dutch door. Candy would go to my husband—Flare to me. After a proper greeting, they would switch and go to the other in much the same way as polite visitors would do. Then they would either settle down like well-behaved dogs in the house, or return to the yard.

They enjoyed each other much as happy sisters do, and they were close companions throughout their lives. Both made trips to the mountains, to San Francisco, and many other areas, as did their sons and daughters at a later time. They made friends for all dogs, and especially for Golden Retrievers, sometimes introductions for us, and in many ways added to our vacations, weekend trips or shopping excursions. Both dogs were trained well enough to stay in their place quietly when we were entertaining guests or when strangers appeared, and they were equally willing to stay in their enclosed yards when it was inconvenient for us to have them in the house, or when there were guests who were not interested in dogs. Flare taught many young children to love animals as she was quiet and would creep up to a child, kissing a baby's toes, but never the baby's face. Some of the older children preferred Candy because of her gay and entertaining ways. Other Goldens which came later had their own special place. The showman of them all was Ch. Jewelite's Mr. Swagger, CD, Candy's first son. His personality and outgoing qualities were ever attractive. He passed them on. Flare's dignity, beauty, and great quality have also been passed on. Her great-great granddaughter is still with me, and gives me much pleasure.

Others who have had Goldens have made them personal friends in the same way, and the Goldens pictured in this book whether bench champions, field champions, obedience dogs, or legend figures have been the better for this personal attention. Their owners have been rewarded by the giving and receiving of affection from their devoted Golden friends.

**Feeding**

Food for the Golden should be well-balanced and sufficient in quantity to maintain the dog in good condition. There should be a small amount of fat over the rib cage, but not excessive. The diet should consist of some commercial dog food such as kibble or meal, meat and cottage cheese or milk products, a hard cooked or scrambled egg two or three times a week, and an all-purpose vitamin-mineral maintenance supplement, since it contains all vitamins and minerals necessary for a warm-blooded animal. Excessive vitamins are undesirable and an unnecessary expense. Vitamins A and D are retained in the body and if taken in excess can become toxic. However, a lack of any supplement may impair the health and well-being of a dog, since the pattern of a dog's diet is much less than that of a human who usually has three varied meals a day. Heart, kidney and liver may be desirable, and important additions in the dog's diet, but should not replace all-muscle meats, as they do not contain enough fat. Special tidbits such as an occasional baked potato, a bit of leftover gravy, or even a few vegetables may be added to the diet. A few people prefer to use cooked ground rice mixed with the meat and milk products, rather than the commercial kibble which usually adds bulk to the dog's diet. A Golden Retriever is rarely allergic, but sometimes may be to a few products, and rice may be substituted for dry dog food if necessary.

Bones are not necessary, but if used they should be clean marrow bones that cannot be splintered and any spoiled bones should be picked up each day and discarded. Fish bones (other than canned salmon bones), fowl or chop bones should not be used as they may splinter and puncture the alimentary tract.

Should there be one or two feedings a day? There are differences of opinion on this and, while one complete feeding is enough, some dogs appear to benefit from two feedings a day. This means dividing the total amount of food into two parts, possibly the larger feeding in the morning and the snack-like feeding at night. The feeding schedule of any dog can be adapted to suit the schedule of the family.

Protein balance should be maintained in any case. There are many forms of proteins. There are proteins even in wood fibers which are undesirable, though some dogs will enjoy chewing their dog house or a board. For food, however, it is not the thing. A dog is a warm-blooded animal and needs the same food elements as humans, except that sugars and white breads should not be part of his diet. Complete proteins, such as meat combined with the protein and calcium of milk products, give a balanced diet when mixed with a commercial dog food. Calcium in milk products is better absorbed by the dog than dry calcium powder such as some bone meals. These, when given in excess, are excreted and carry off other essential food products with them. There are several good commercial dog foods on the market, both canned and in dry form. They may be combined with some of the nutrients mentioned in providing a varied and balanced diet. Canned dog food is preferable while traveling as it is easy to carry and easy to use. Because of its high water content, it is not as inexpensive in a total diet as one might believe.

Hard exercise should never immediately follow a meal. This will make a difference in the feeding schedule for dogs which are to be used in hard hunting or in special training. A dog should have had a chance to let his food settle and to eliminate before starting hard exercise. After hard exercise the dog should not be given excessive amounts of water, and should be allowed to rest before eating a large meal, though a small amount of food or water may be desirable. Dr. Donald Collins, in his *Collins Guide to Dog Nutrition* (Howell Book House, New York), advises that a dog which has been hard hunting for three or four hours should be given four ounces of protein (either meat or a meat mix) and allowed to rest for at least twenty minutes before resuming the hunt. If a protein is not available, a candy bar will do.

It is now believed that dogs benefit from vitamin C—included in the all-purpose vitamins formulated for human use. Chewing a few lemons or oranges may give a dog vitamin C. However, buying them for a dog does not add anything essential to his diet. Such fruit from my own trees makes great, and harmless, toys for my Goldens. Possible excess of vitamin C is easily excreted. One of my champions enjoyed picking tomatoes, but others left those red love-apples alone.

For generally good manners at your own mealtimes, a dog should not be given tidbits from the table, or encouraged to snatch things from the hands of children. As early as six or seven weeks a dog should be trained to allow anything to be taken from his mouth. There are two reasons: one, it

Many owners prefer to feed their Goldens on a platform to prevent their dogs bending too far to get at their food. Bob and Janet Trigg have found that a few cement blocks do the job for their Hollybriar Royalridge Cheer.

"Friends". *Bill Huffman*

could save the dog's life if it picked up an undesirable object; and two, a dog growling over the food pan is not pleasant or safe for humans or other animals.

A dog should eat more or less at shoulder height. It is preferable that a dog the size of a Golden Retriever not eat off the ground. This is important for posture and particularly for a show dog, which should always carry itself well. Generally speaking, both the food dish and the water dish should be somewhat elevated. This table may be the back steps, a few bricks, or a wood platform. It should go without saying that food dishes and water pans should be kept scrupulously clean. A few dogs learn to drink from a patent faucet. Such a faucet may be an advantage in mild climates, but should not be used when winters are extremely cold because it might freeze. A dog needs to be taught to use it.

## Housing

The problems of housing a dog depend to some extent on whether there are one or more dogs, and if the dogs are of different sexes. While many dogs live very happily together, there may be a time when it is very wise to separate them—bitches, for example, during their heat period.

The quarters for the dog should include a fenced yard which may be a run of any shape, a yard within a yard of his master's property. There should be a suitable dog house within that enclosed space. This yard should provide both sun and shade. The reason for a special yard for the dog is to give him protection and security when the family may be away or when there may be visitors who may not enjoy dogs or who may be allergic to them. In any family there are times of emergency, such as illness, when it is better, and safer to have the dog in its own special quarters. Conditioning the young dog to such a yard makes for easier handling at a later date. According to Clarence J. Pfaffenberger, in his book *The New Knowledge of Dog Behavior* (Howell Book House, New York), a puppy adjusts to a yard at an early age. A dog can even be taught not to bark in his own yard.

The floor of the yard may be cement, gravel, or even grass. Cement, of course, is easier to clean and maintain. The dog should not have to live in the yard all the time; he should have some part in the family life and routines, as mentioned in the first section of this chapter. In general, the fencing should be on the inside of the posts so that the fence will be pressed toward the posts if the dog leans against it, unless this fencing is very strong. Such an arrangement allows space for landscaping the yard which makes for a more attractive appearance. Some sort of plant which has few enemies, requires no spraying and does not have blossoms that attract bees is suitable for landscaping the dog yard. On the West Coast, laurel is ideal. Check with your nursery for other types of plants which are hardy and may be pruned easily.

Many people prefer a duck-board or slotted platform near the opening of the dog yard, as dogs tend to like to lie by the opening. Often such a duck-board may be by the entrance to the dog house, as it forms a deck for sunning or airing.

The dog house may be simple or elaborate, and the thickness of its walls will depend upon the climatic conditions. In mild climates the dog house may be made of light plywood with an opening on the long side to permit the dog to enter and go further in out of the wind. In cold climates the dog house should be insulated. The dog house should be up from the ground, three to four inches, so that rain or storms will not flood the interior. The roof may slope slightly, but should be reasonably flat, as many dogs enjoy the top of their house for sunning.

The opening should be four to six inches from the floor in order to contain cedar or pine shavings which make a very satisfactory and inexpensive bed. Some form of bedding is needed to prevent the elbows from rubbing. Another type of flooring may be a bath mat or washable carpeting—either of which may be taken out and washed from time to time. Some indoor-outdoor carpeting, however, may be undesirable because of some chemical reactions to urine, detergents or other materials. The dog may express some choice in this matter as some insist upon taking out any rug and using it as a toy. Pine shavings, which are popular as bedding material, should be changed frequently, or they may become a flea haven.

For the one-dog family, space may be arranged in the family room, patio or wherever his sleeping quarters may be. A yard, however, should be essential. Clarence J. Pfaffenberger has pointed out that a puppy will adapt to an area enclosed by a small lightweight fence, but if allowed to roam free as a puppy he will find it difficult to adapt to a fenced yard as an older dog. The long-range requirements of ownership should be considered early.

People who have two or more dogs will develop their own best kennel facilities. An ideal one on the West Coast which handles four to six dogs was developed by James and the late Bonnie Humphrey of Soquel, California. This is a block of runs with a cement floor. There is a foot-high cement wall between each run and this wall serves as the base for the fencing which separates the runs. Adequate drainage facilities are provided in each run. At the end of each run there is a roofed-over, shelflike arrangement, up from the ground, or floor, of the run and enclosed on three sides. This gives the dog protection at all times and gives him his own house. The dog soon learns to jump upon the shelf where he may enjoy the wooden floor in warm weather, or a box of shavings in the winter. There is a drop let-down plywood door which may be used in stormy weather for protection. Such an arrangement is easy to clean and maintain.

In any arrangement, individual drainage facilities are better so that in washing, the water does not go from one run to another. The terrain and conditions will determine the location of the drainage exit to its own septic tank or sewer. In areas in which there are wild animals which might approach the dog yards or even invade the dog runs, different facilities

Am. Can. Ch. Sadie's Sundance Kidd, CDX, WC, Can. CD (Ch. Brandywine's Dusty Dandy, CDX, ex Aurora's Sunshine Sadie), owned by Jack and Jamie Warren and bred by Ray and Robin McCarthy.

Ch. Chaparral's Limited Edition (Ch. Three J's Calif. Okee of Braevue, CD, ex Ch. Odu's Bianca of Manorloch, CDX, OD), owned and bred by Terry, Julie and Jennifer Hubbs. Jennifer, a junior handler, took the dog to its title fom the Bred-by-Exhibitor class. *Jayne Langdon*

Ch. Tempo's Frontier Bronco (Ch. Sun Dance's Rarue ex Ch. Tempo's Nassau Miss), owned by Hank and Michelle Arszman and Vivian and George Wright and bred by Peter and Sheilah Huser. Winner of the 1981 national GRCA Specialty, he is also a multiple BIS winner.

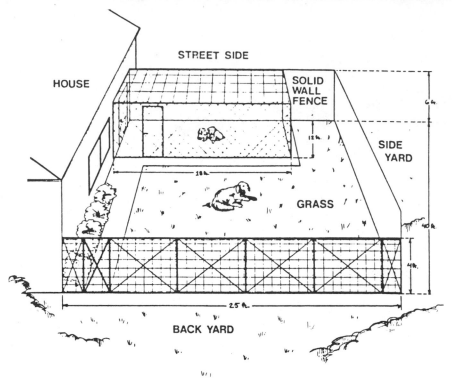

Diagram of the yard and kennel for the Smithaven Goldens. This is where the puppies start! *Courtesy June and Elizabeth Smith.*

The actual facilities at Smithaven illustrating good use of available space for the small breeder. Wise planning has resulted in a comfortable, secure facility for three or four grown dogs and the conduct of some breeding activity.

would be needed. Where winters are severe other arrangements would be needed. Where winters are severe other arrangements would be needed. In some cases people may prefer locking the dog in its own dog house or crate, but this requires that the dog be released early in the morning. For most, indoor-outdoor facilities for the convenience of the dog are preferable.

In any dog yard there should be a place for fresh water. This may be a pail hung a little distance above the floor, but easy for the dog to reach. Some dog yards are covered with either wire, wooden or aluminum roofing. The Smithaven yard and run presented here is an excellent facilitiy for three or four dogs. There are two additional covered runs with dog houses for bitches in season or visiting dogs. These runs are on another side of the property to prevent dogs and bitches from close contact when bitches are in heat.

In severe climates, heavier plywood and warmer conditions are important, for dogs cannot protect themselves against subzero weather. In extreme climates, some form of heating is desirable as protection from cold weather, and perhaps air conditioning, or certainly shade, in the summer. Golden Retrievers are hardier than many dogs and do enjoy the snow, but any dog exposed to wet and cold needs a dry, warm place in winter and a place to avoid the extreme heat and sun in the summertime.

Emphasis has been placed on the importance of a dog yard or dog run. It is not desirable to tie a Golden to a post or any other stationary object for too long, or from day to day. A clothesline or running wire is not a dog run. The frustration developed in the dog from lunging at the end of the rope or wire may affect his ability to receive training, as he learns to toughen up his neck and shoulder muscles at the end of a rope. Such an arrangement, if continued, may interfere with the physical and emotional development of the dog and make housebreaking more difficult. Confinement at the end of a rope is especially serious if the yard is so located that the dog may be teased by anyone passing by.

The dog is a happier playmate when released from its own yard and brought into the house. He soon learns to know his own location, and readily takes his place with the family.

## Indoor Manners

Even in the best Chamber of Commerce weather anywhere cold and rainy days occur and the hardiest outdoor dogs enjoy the warmth and dryness of the house in place of their covered kennels at such times. Once inside, Goldens will often develop a particular fondness for a special piece of furniture or area of carpet. My Ceilidh adopted a leather chair which, over a period of time, she shaped to fit her own preferences. Chas, on the other hand, preferred his slip-covered pad in the bedroom and would even accept a top innerspring mattress and bedspread if given the least encouragement. Goldens become possessive of their own "special spot,"

Remember how big a Golden puppy will become when you allow it on the furniture. However, if you'd like to share your comfy recliner with your Golden pal, "Reka" and Bill demonstrate how easy it can be.

It's easier to groom a dog on a special table made for the purpose or on the top of its crate. In either case the grooming surface should be fitted with non-skid material for the comfort of the dog. This takes the strain out of the groomer's back and makes thoroughly inspecting the dog more convenient.

and may or may not be inclined to move when human company visits.

Ceilidh's leather chair also raises another point—the problem of young puppies choosing a good piece of furniture for their chewing. Ceilidh's daughter, Tangerine, preferred the sides of the leather chair to a chew stick (fortunately, the upholsterer had two matching skins—for the sides and a new cushion.) Although its actions can be irritating, a young dog should only be punished when caught in an unacceptable action. A stern "No" is an effective and non-physical way to express your displeasure, for dogs are very sensitive to change in voice tones. Preventive measures should be taken as well. Chew sticks and other toys may avert interior disaster. Furthermore, young pups, like small children, need supervision and a watchful eye. It is wise to "dog-proof" the house by removing valuable or dangerous items from the puppy's reach. If a young dog is left alone in the house, it should not be for a long time. This is precisely the time when a well-constructed dog yard is needed.

## Grooming

Frequent grooming is needed. Daily combing and brushing is desirable—once or twice a week is a must. This may be done with a steel comb and a stiff brush, such as is used for scrubbing. If one feels inclined, an English bristle brush or other elaborate equipment may be used, but this will depend upon the taste and pocketbook of the owner. However, a Golden will enjoy a simple combing-out. The attachment of a hand vacuum cleaner or other type of vacuum cleaner used for brushing upholstered furniture or cleaning out the car is especially suited for grooming the Golden Retriever. It may take a little training to adapt him to the sound of a vacuum, but he soon discovers how nice the air feels and enjoys this ideal tool. It is especially good for the Golden who spends a good deal of time in the house, as it saves many dog hairs from getting on hardwood floors or rugs. Once a week or every other week with the vacuum attachment is not a serious chore, but does help both dog and owner.

Trimming about the feet and toes is desirable as it keeps dirt and debris from accumulating. Any burrs, grass, foxtails and other items should be removed from the coat immediately after the dog has returned from the field. If the dog has been in water or mud, he should be hosed down at once. This will not only make the dog more comfortable but may save the owner a visit to the veterinarian. If it has been extremely cold and wet, the dog should have a warm place upon returning home. One excellent handler who has had great success in field trials takes his dog into his hotel room after rough and cold weather competition and gives him a warm bath to loosen up the muscles. He then dries him with a warm towel. After this, the handler takes his own shower and dinner.

Grooming for the show ring requires very little more. A bit of thinning of the hair around the ears may be needed, and a bath and jacket to keep the coat flatter. (see chapter on Competition.)

The toenails should be kept reasonably short. Working dogs or dogs kept on cement usually keep their toenails worn down, but if not, they should be filed or clipped with the usual dog toenail clipper. The shorter nail is less likely to split, but care should be taken not to clip too closely.

Any dog should be inspected by a veterinarian from time to time. Teeth should be kept free from tartar. Immunizations for distemper, hepatitis, rabies, parvovirus and other communicable diseases should be maintained. A check for worms should be made from time to time through the analysis of a stool specimen by the veterinarian (flotation). In areas which require special attention, such as areas in which heartworm is a problem, more frequent checks are needed. Your veterinarian may be both your own and your dog's best friend.

Ears should be kept clean and free from dirt, insects and foreign objects. Learn to clean your dog's ears and to check them at least once a week. Consult your veterinarian on how to properly clean the ears.

One of the reasons why many people like a Golden is that the breed is generally a hardy one and requires no special stripping or grooming other than a bath from time to time when he becomes soiled. Naturally a dog that enjoys digging will have to be washed more frequently than one who doesn't. And a dog working in lakes or creeks with soft bottom will need more washing than one which is in a well-kept yard or in and out of the house frequently.

If the dog's quarters are kept clean and the dog is groomed, there should be no problem with pests such as fleas or ticks. If these do occur, rid the premises and the dog of these pests through more frequent grooming, washing and care of both dog and premises. In some areas insects are more prevalent and more care is needed, particularly if a dog is exposed in tick areas. Check with your veterinarian on how to control this. A dog in clean condition is more fun to have around, and he is less likely to have unhappy skin conditions which may be hard to prevent and harder to cure.

## Exercise

Exercise is important for any dog and particularly for a Golden Retriever, though Goldens which were bred to sit quietly and wait for commands do not require the exercise of the pointing breeds, the setters, the racing dogs, or sight hunters. Exercise does keep up muscle tone and keeps the dog in better condition; this is important to the dog's health. Young and adolescent puppies as well as adults, benefit from a walk on leash in city or country with their owners. Golden Retrievers enjoy swimming, retrieving and other exercises used in hunting or obedience. Candy, our first, enjoyed a little free swimming just for fun, and Chas, some twenty years later, loved a short swim after the serious business of retrieving or bringing in his bird.

Few areas in the United States today have places where a dog should be allowed to run completely free, as they may come in contact with wild animals, wild dogs, or urban conditions which are dangerous to people and more dangerous to the individual dog. Besides, such free activity may violate the laws or ordinances of the community. The individual owner gains respect for himself and for his dog by observing the rules that communities feel necessary to make, whether these rules have to do with dogs in sheep country, dogs molesting deer and other wild animals in a national park, or dogs invading a neighbor's lawn.

A device called a "Retriev-R-Trainer" is a good item for both exercising and training a Golden Retriever. It allows one to propel a training dummy at selected distances on land or water; and it saves the throwing arm. A companion may enjoy throwing or discharging the dummies for you. The noise is about the intensity of a 22-caliber rifle, so it is not possible to use this device everywhere. On weekend trips or drives one frequently finds small roadside lanes in which the training may be done. A courteous request to a farmer will get you into many fields. We have never been refused, but the dogs were on leash when we asked and the farmer knew we would make good if an accident occurred.

Think in terms of how to work the exercise in with pleasant or recreational activities of the family. Our beautiful puppy, Swag (later Ch. Jewelite's Mr. Swagger, CD) learned his retrieving in a small fishing creek. As early as four to five months of age he learned to cross water and land—then water and land again. Some of these distances were small, but the area included swimming water and a small island in the middle of the creek, making two water entries and retrieves from a second piece of land. Later on he was able to do retrieves at longer distances, but he had learned as a puppy that retrieving was important, and to continue on to his fall, and not to turn around at the first change of terrain. Crossing water twice, and two types of terrain in the same retrieve, can be important in hunting or for field competition. It can be easily taught, however, with exercise. Such exercise was good for me and good for the dog.

Ch. Flarewin Ceilidh's Tangerine, owned by Gertrude Fischer, was Winners Bitch and Best of Opposite Sex at the Western Regional Specialty show of the Golden Retriever Club of America under judge Joe Tacker enroute to her championship. She was handled by Tony Gwinner. She represents over twenty years of breeding and traces back to Chs. DesLac's Lassie and DesLac's Lassie II. *Bennett Associates.*

Breeding dogs and raising puppies are demanding both physically and emotionally, but when a breeder's efforts result in delightful puppies, the satisfaction is great indeed. Such a puppy is six-weeks-old Flarewin's Happy Boy (Dual Ch. Ronaker's Novato Cain ex Ch. Flarewin Ceilidh's Tangerine), bred by Gertrude Fischer. *Dorothy Carter*

# 13

# So You Are Thinking of Puppies

---

$G$OOD PUPPIES, those that are a pleasure to have, that are easy to place and will give satisfaction as adults are the result of much planning by the owners of the bitch. Careful thought and analysis of the bitch or dam, her mate, the inherited genes, her care from puppyhood on and her care during the gestation period—all these are factors that fundamentally influence the future litter.

Several books including *The New Art of Breeding Better Dogs* and *The Joy of Breeding Your Own Show Dog* (Howell Book House, New York) go into detail on out-crossing, inbreeding and line breeding. For each of these methods of breeding there is much to be said, though ideally an out-cross which works is much to be desired, as it may give strength to a litter and form the basis for returning to close or line breeding at a future time. In any event, the dogs in question should be analyzed from the standpoint of skeletal structure. Breeding very large to very small may present mechanical problems in the mating act. Besides, it may result in disproportionate animals, as the progeny may inherit the head of the one and the body of the other. While one might breed a bitch to a slightly larger dog, one would not use extremes as the type would be too different to give a predictable uniformity at maturity. But skeletal structure and soundness and general proportion are of first consideration. Breeding should always be toward the Standard.

Breeding light colors to a deeper color usually results in a spectacular gold color in the offspring. Very light bred to light colors may emphasize the light undercoat and give a washed out or a too pale tone.

The coat colors in Goldens may be less predictable in puppies than in some other breeds. The colors across the face and the ears are clues to the mature coat color. Many puppies that will be darker later on, or a rich gold color, may be a light or a medium beige at birth. Some knowledge of the color typical of the breed in the past and those specified in the American Standard should be kept in mind regardless of the beauty of a single individual. In some animals and in some breeds of dogs, extremes or unusual variations in color may be associated or occur with undesirable traits in other areas, traits that may be passed on or may even be lethal. This may be true with other forms of mutations. The average breeder who thinks only of Mendel's Law of recessives and dominants may be unaware of, or unable to check in his dog, some of the technical genetic factors. All characteristics are not inherited according to Mendel's Law. Some are more complex in the inheritance pattern. Recessives are not always completely recessive. He may not know whether his dog or bitch is allelic or heterozygous and what is of concern when the individual is called homozygous.

These are technical concepts which are explained in detail in such books as *An Introduction to Medical Genetics* by J. A. Fraser Roberts (Oxford University Press) and in Frederic Bruce Hutt's *Genetic Resistance to Disease in Domestic Animals*. In Mr. Hutt's book, examples are given as to how these inherited situations affect various domestic animals and some effects in some breeds of dogs. Mr. Hutt explains on page 27 how certain grey colors in sheep may be associated with lethal or other serious disadvantages. He cites the findings of French Zoologist, Cuenot, as reported in studies of the yellow mouse. Such mutations are lethal in the early stages of gestation. Yellow is not the usual color of mice, but does occur. Mr. Hutt also explains conditions of hemophilia in dogs and shows examples of a hemophilic puppy. Ojvind Winge has traced and shows the pattern of inheritance of coat colors and special marking in several breeds of dogs, but does not have studies on Goldens.

Von Willebrand's disease is a bleeding disease affecting both male and female dogs. While it is not common in Goldens, it does occur. Unlike many genetic diseases, this can be bred out in one or two generations. Dr. W. Jean Dodds of the Public Health Department, Albany, N.Y., has completed many studies on von Willebrand's disease and other forms of blood problems, including hemophilia.

It is not the purpose of this book to go into a long, complicated explanation, but it is important to call attention to the average reader that it is advantageous to consider seriously a breeding program even if he plans to breed but one litter. For those interested in further reading, refer to the bibliography at the end of the book.

Again, it is important to breed toward the Standard in color, form, intelligence and temperament, knowing the history of the breed.

Ch. Pele of Flarewin, owned by Jack Martin and handled by James McManus. *January*

Ch. Pepperhill's Golden Pine Irish, owned by Nancy Kelly Belsaas (with whom she is shown), G. Cortesia, M. Flynn and Pepperhill Farms. "Irish" was bred by Jeff and Barbara Pepper.

There are sometimes throwbacks of small amounts of white, such as a dot on the head or toes. Usually such pigment has just been slow to develop and these marks disappear by the time the puppies are three months old. Small amounts of white on the chest seldom change and are not considered a serious defect, though where this does occur the animal should be mated to one of a solid color. (See Chapter IV.)

Temperament and response to training, both of which are closely related characteristics, are thought to be inherited, though environment plays its own part. One of the several tests for Guide Dogs for the Blind, San Rafael, California, includes a test for shyness. If these tests are failed, the puppy is no longer considered for later training. Yet, the most important tests are vision and retrieving. These two characteristics are known to the individual dog owner by the time the bitch would be old enough to breed; in fact, these traits would show up by the first six to eight weeks in the life of the puppy.

A puppy's parents are more important in terms of genetic influence than its grandparents and the grandparents are more important than the great-grandparents. It is important to consider the pedigree and the lines and what these lines stand for. The novice might need to seek out someone familiar with the characteristics of those dogs in the background to determine this. These traits are more important than impressive titles. Many excellent dogs are not shown on the bench or run in the field or obedience trials. The participation in these activities does indicate how well a particular animal performs in the various types of competition. Still, titles alone, without consideration of other items, should not be the sole consideration in breeding. Titles are not as helpful in selling the puppies as is sometimes believed. In California, for example, some of the finest lines and most beautiful dogs are used as personal dogs and never compete. Their owners, like those who introduced Goldens in the Northwest in the 1930's, prefer the beautiful and competent dogs for themselves and are not thinking of competition any more than they think of competition in well fitting clothes or a comfortable home.

First of all, consider the bitch and what she lacks, as no dog is perfect. Does she need tighter feet, shorter ears, a better topline or a more outgoing personality (we assume that no shy dog will ever be bred)? Now consider the male. Do his strong points counterbalance her weaknesses? Is he also strong in her good points? The owner of the male should likewise consider these points if he allows his dog to be used, for it is no credit to any stud to have mediocre puppies.

The veterinarian and veterinary radiologist will be most helpful in assessing the skeletal structure. For many people this is now routine. X-rays are taken of the hip structure of the dog and often of the shoulders, spine and leg joints to check on the various possibilities of inherited structural faults (dysplasia among others). The importance of dysplasia should not be overlooked, for while it may not seriously affect the mobility of a single dog, future generations may inherit the disease in more serious form, and may become crippled. If carriers are mated repeatedly, soon many dogs may be affected causing disappointment to owners and lessening of breed quality.

Because of their importance, all x-rays should be re-evaluated by experienced veterinary radiologists. Most veterinarians are aware of these problems. While skeletal faults are not common in Golden Retrievers, they occur in any breed and especially in medium- to large-sized animals of all breeds. Dogs which will be expected to live an active life in the family, hunting, or working, need sound physical structure.

Both sire and dam should be free from skeletal faults. In addition, they should be checked for eye defects, such as hereditary cataracts and progressive or central retinal atrophy. This can only be properly done by a certified canine ophthalmologist who specializes in hereditary eye diseases.

Many conscientious breeders also require a brucellosis test within six weeks of breeding time. Brucellosis is a venereally-acquired disease affecting dogs, cattle, and swine. It may cause sterility in either the male or female, spontaneous abortion, and death in the litter. Veterinarians can check for brucellosis in their offices.

Once a decision is made and the time is set for the mating, a small informal contract should be written concerning the stud fee, repeat mating if no puppies result, or any other situations. A formal standard stud contract may be used. If the dog is listed in more than one name, or in community-property states, the dog is considered part of the total estate and the contract would help clear up any obligations and refresh a memory if there were any questions at a later time.

The female is customarily taken to the home of the male unless arrangements have been made to have the breeding take place at a veterinary hospital or a kennel experienced in these matters. Before the mating the bitch should be inspected during her heat period to determine that there is no infection. A vaginal smear should be taken to indicate the optimum time of mating as this will vary a little with each bitch, although in general it could be said that the best time of ovulation and most receptive period for the bitch is between the ninth and twelfth days of her period. There may be one mating, or it may be desirable in young bitches to repeat the mating after 24 hours. More matings are undesirable in view of the short gestation period of 63 days.

The care of the bitch during pregnancy as well as her care and feeding throughout her life before the pregnancy have a bearing on the ease of giving birth, the quality of the puppies, her ability to nurse them well and her general health and appearance at the time the puppies are available for placement. Her food intake for the first four weeks of pregnancy will be about the same as usual, moving the quantity and protein content up 50 to 60% from the fourth week on. Many good breeders add one multiple vitamin capsule, that is, a maintenance vitamin, to the daily food. Standard vitamins, for human consumption, are best. Feeding excessive vitamins and minerals is unwise. A good diet for a pregnant bitch consists of a commercial kibbled dog food or a good-quality dog meal, fresh meat or cooked meat, and cottage cheese in about equal proportion to the meat. To this may be added some liver and two or three hard-cooked eggs each week. The amount of food will be determined by the size of the bitch, whether she is working during the early part of the pregnancy, and the climate. Dogs apparently absorb more calcium from cottage cheese or buttermilk than they do from dry calcium. They also benefit from the correct balance of phosphorus (from the meat) and the calcium (from the cottage cheese) which combines to become calcium phosphate so essential in the development of bones and teeth. There are other benefits from milk proteins and meat proteins. From the fifth week of pregnancy to the time of whelping, the food should be divided in two rations, one in the morning, and one in the evening. This way the bitch will be more comfortable and the nutrition will be spread over a longer period of time. Any special problems should be discussed with the veterinarian. She should be checked by your veterinarian at least once or twice during the gestation period. Throughout pregnancy the bitch should have a reasonable amount of exercise. Walking is good and her normal activities, whether hunting or other types of exercise, may be continued. Only during the last three weeks of the pregnancy should heavy hunting, hard water entry, swimming and jumping be avoided. Remember that she will not know that she does not balance well and that she can suffer internal injuries in her willingness to please. (For additional information, see "Pregnant Bitches and Neonate Puppies" in Appendix C.)

Rectal temperature should be taken during the mid pregnancy period to determine the bitch's normal temperature which would ordinarily be about 101° F. During the last week of pregnancy take rectal temperature readings morning and evening. In most bitches the temperatures will drop two or three degrees about 48 hours before the puppies arrive. Then the temperature starts rising again and the puppies will be due in a few hours. The question arises whether you checked the temperature when it first went down or later and whether you picked up the rise in temperature when the rise began. There are some bitches which may whelp as early as the 56th to 60th day. In this case, temperatures may or may not fluctuate. Others may not give birth until the 65th day. After this period, it is advisable to consult a veterinarian.

X-raying a pregnant bitch a day or two before her litter is due may also be advantageous. The resulting picture will more closely tell the time when a bitch can be expected to whelp and may indicate the number of puppies in the womb. This last point is important due to the varying sizes of the puppies and length of delivery time.

Many people feel that the bitch tends to look for a nest or to tear papers or become restless just before the puppies are due. This may be true, but if she has enjoyed her own special chair in the living room or her own spot at the foot of the bed, she may consider this perfectly satisfactory. However, if she is seeking a place of privacy under the rose bush or the neighbor's hedge, this just wouldn't do for convenience and supervision. So the whelping box should be in order several days ahead of time and the bitch should be introduced to her new bed. Some remarks about the whelping box and plans for making one are included later in this chapter.

It might be necessary to tether her in the whelping box a few minutes or a few hours during the day so that she will become accustomed to it. This is easily done with her usual collar and leash and a staple on the edge of the whelping box. Obviously she should not be left unattended for long in this position or at this time.

If things appear to be normal, the whelping may be done at home. As the puppy emerges from the vagina, lift up the puppy, remove the sac or placenta, free the mouth from any liquid, cut the cord (using sterile scissors) not too close to the puppy, dry off the puppy. If the cord is cut first, the puppy will drown or die as he breathes through the cord while in the sac. Place the puppy on a warm towel. It is not necessary for the bitch to eat the placenta.

If the whelping lasts over a long period of time, it may be wise to allow the first puppies to nurse before all are delivered. *Colostrum*, the first milk-like substance consumed by the puppy during nursing, is vital to its health and welfare. See that first the puppies are not crushed during the birth of later ones. After nursing, they should be placed in a box separated from the mother.

Consult with a veterinarian as to the advisability of an injection to cause the uterus to shrink and expel any placenta or pieces of placenta immediately following the whelping.

### Danger Signals—When to Call a Veterinarian

If the bitch appears to be in labor or is having labor contractions, and yet no puppies are appearing, possibly the birth canal is not expanding and she may need some help. Long continued contractions may tire the puppies and the bitch and it would be possible to lose both dam and litter. A veterinary service should be called at once. If several of the puppies have been delivered but there is a general slow-up between puppies of an hour and a half to two hours, get help at once. A Caesarian section may or may not be needed, but the need for medical advice is definitely indicated.

Temperature of the bitch should be taken in the morning and evening for several days after the whelping to be sure of the bitch's health and ability to nurse the puppies without adverse effects to her and to the litter. This should be routine for the first three or four days.

Crying puppies mean cold or hungry puppies. Check each puppy to see that it is not too far away from the dam. If it continues to cry give it some supplementary feeding. Temperatures can be taken of a very young puppy if there is reason to doubt its well-being. Again, professional help may be needed.

It is not the purpose of this chapter to go into all of the specialized medical situations which can arise, but, rather, to give the reader comprehensive information, and to alert him to any possible complications so that medical help may be had before it is too late. Most Golden births are normal, but there is always the possibility of an exceptional pregnancy or unique situations in any litter. The size of the average Golden litter is such that some supplementary feeding may be desirable to protect the litter and the bitch. Such supplementary feedings insure optimum nutrition and quality of the puppies so that when they are ready for placement, each will go into its new home with the bloom of health.

*Summary:*

1. Check health and soundness of skeletal structure of dam and sire before the heat period when breeding is planned.
2. Arrange breeding contract.
3. Check bitch during pregnancy.
4. Prepare whelping box.
5. Watch food intake in amounts and quality.
6. Check temperatures.
7. Consult veterinarian regarding normal conditions.
8. Alert veterinarian to be ready in the event of complications.
9. Have scales for weighing puppies (see weight chart).

**The Whelping Box**

Specifications and a drawing for a very good whelping box are given. This particular box is large enough for comfort for both bitch and puppies and yet is narrow enough so that anyone taking care of the puppies may bend over the side to pick up the puppies and change canvas or papers. Still, the box may be disassembled and the whole thing hung on a flat surface until needed at another time. Do not use indoor-outdoor carpeting in the box as the carpeting contains a chemical that can injure the delicate skin of an infant puppy.

The whelping box should be assembled several days ahead so that the bitch might become accustomed to it and might use it as a sleeping bed.

Several layers of newspaper should be put in the bottom of the box, and over this a canvas (20 ounce or "G.I." canvas) should be placed. The canvas gives the puppies traction so they do not slide when they are nursing or start moving about. Soft sheets or blankets that wrinkle easily are not as desirable. The canvas feels warmer than paper or boards for the puppies and it may be changed daily and washed in an ordinary washing machine.

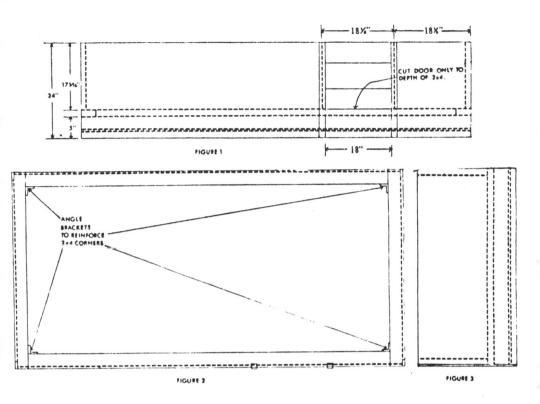

FIGURE 1

ANGLE
BRACKETS
TO REINFORCE
2nd CORNERS

CUT DOOR ONLY TO
DEPTH OF 2nd.

FIGURE 2

FIGURE 3

Very young puppies "piling" as they sleep. In the first few weeks of life, puppies will huddle for warmth as well as security. Eventually they become less dependent on each other but still need the closeness of litter mates for proper emotional development.                              *Dorothy Carter*

When the puppies are approximately three weeks old, they begin moving to the second section of the whelping box (which need be covered with newspapers only) and use it for urinating and defacating. It is often amazing to note how quickly puppies appreciate the advantage of being clean and it is interesting to watch which ones seem to learn first.

One may think that the assembly of a whelping box is a project which can be done in two hours, but it takes quite a bit longer. Anyone handy with a saw, such as an electric saw, and a drill may assemble it from scratch. However, the components can be ordered from a lumber company with the holes drilled in such a way that it need only be assembled. This extra service, of course, makes it more expensive; therefore, a choice must be made between convenience and time in preparation. No paint or stain is recommended for use on either the in- or outside. Paint, if it contains mercury or lead, could be harmful as the puppies start chewing.

### Building a Whelping Box

Specifications, list of materials and construction directions for an excellent and easily assembled whelping box:

Purchase the materials indicated.

Assemble with reference to the figures as follows:

In all assembly, it is advisable to drill pilot holes for the screws. Panel 1 is the most complex, so let's take it first.

The door cut-out should be made first using a jig saw or saber saw. Use measurements from Figure 1. The object is to end up with a slight narrowing of the opening toward the bottom, so that the slides will go in and out easily.

After making the cut-out, saw the piece removed into three sections as shown, so that as the pups grow, you can drop in another section to keep them in the box.

Place the 1″ x 2″ x 24″ pieces in place on either side of the opening on the outside of the box allowing ⅓ of the material to overlap the opening. Place a 17⁵⁄₁₆″ x 1″ x 2″ on each side of the opening inside the box with the same ⅓ overlap. Clamp the inside and outside 1″ x 2″s together with ¼″ ply in between and drill holes through in the top and bottom of each for the 2″ long bolts—insert bolts and attach wing nuts on the outside. Place one 77″ x 2″ x 4″ flush against the bottom edge of the 17⁵⁄₁₆″ x 1″ x 2″ leaving 3¾″ clearance at each end and 5″ clearance from the bottom edge. Note the 2″ x 4″ is mounted on its narrow side.

Panels 2 and 4 are identical: Mount 1″ x 2″ x 17⁵⁄₁₆″ on each edge flush with the top. Attach the 2″ x 4″ x 48″ flush up to the bottom of the 1″ x 2″s and you should have 5″ clearance from the bottom. Refer to Fig. 3.

Panel 3—mount a 2″ x 4″ x 77″, 5″ from the bottom and 3¾″ in from each end. Screw together.

From the new litter of today will come tomorrow's stars of the field trial, the conformation ring and obedience competition. Time and development will determine which worlds these puppies will grow to conquer.

Ch. Roxanne Summer Rose, Am. Can. CDX, WCX, owned by Stephen and Cathine Seagrave, observing her litter of 15 on the deck of a hot tub. Two years later two of this litter were WB and RB at the 1983 Western Regional Specialty. *Stephen Seagrave*

Panel 5—The bottom of the box is most easily assembled by forming a 4' x 8' rectangle on the floor using the 46⅜" 1" x 2"s with the 8' x 1" x 2" placed flush against them. Stand the 1" x 2"s on edge and lay the ⅜" 4" x 8" sheet of plywood on top of the 4" x 8" rectangle formed by the 1" x 2"s. Screw floor to its supports.

*Final Assembly:*

Place panels 1, 2, 3, and 4 around the floor panel 5. Tilt up into place and screw the edges of panels 1 and 3 into the edges of panels 2 and 4. Six-inch spacing on screws gives adequate strength. Nails can be used if the box is never to be dismounted for storage, but screws make storage much simpler, as the box can be knocked down to 4 easily handled pieces for storage on your garage rafters.

Use the four angle brackets to strengthen the corners where the 2 x 4's meet. (Fig. 2)

The 1" x 4" x 48" board will just fit between the 2" x 4"s and the floor and is jammed in to provide a divider between the pups' living/sleeping area and their newspaper bathroom.

| Purchase | Makes |
|---|---|
| 1  4' x 8" sheet ⅜" const. grade plywood | 1 4 x 8 sheet ⅜" ply |
| 2  4' x 8" sheet ¼" const. grade plywood | 2 2 x 8 sheets ¼" ply |
| | 2 2 x 4 sheets ¼" ply |
| 4  ½" x 2" angle brackets and screws | 4 ½ x 2" angle brackets |
| 3  8' 2" x 4" | 2 2 x 4 48" long |
| | 2 2 x 4 77" long |
| 1  10' 1 x 2 | 6 1 x 2 17 ⁵⁄₁₆ long |
| 3  8' 1 x 2 | 2 1 x 2 24" long |
| | 2 1 x 2 8' long |
| | 2 1 x 2 46⅜" long |
| 1  4' 1" x 4" | 1 1 x 4 48" long |
| 4  2" long ⁸⁄₃₂ bolts, with wing nuts | 4 2" bolts with wing nuts |
| 6  dozen ¾" #5 round head screws | |
| 16  screws for brackets flathead | |

## Puppies—The First Eight Weeks

For the purpose of this book it is assumed that the puppies are normal, that the condition of the bitch is normal and that the litter is from six to nine, possibly 10 puppies. Seven or eight is the average litter in Golden Retrievers.

The first few days of their lives the puppies nurse almost constantly. The bitch will hesitate to leave them except for a few minutes to relieve

For a healthy Golden litter the only quiet moment is mealtime.

More often this is the typical scene.

Eating is too serious a business to bother about the photographer—even approaching from the back.

Golden Retrievers usually make excellent mothers. Mrs. J. T. Blackburn's bitch, shown here, was the dam of this robust litter of twelve.

"On the March!" These puppies, half English-half American, are owned by Jane Davison.

*Dorothy Carter*

Ch. Pele of Flarewin challenges one of her puppies to a game of "tag."

herself or to get needed food. She will need at least three good meals a day during this nursing period with plenty of liquids, such as milk or meat broth, in order to maintain her milk supply. She may not have enough nipples to supply all of her puppies and she, herself, may rotate them. Each nipple does not yield the same amount of milk from hour to hour so it is difficult to know how much each puppy receives. Is the puppy at her breast for food or for warmth, or both? Either is important. If the litter is large (nine or more) or the bitch's milk supply not abundant, it may be necessary to supplement the feeding of the puppies from the second or third day on. This may be done with a special formula made up of powdered simulated bitch's milk and warm water. This product, under brand name, may be bought at pet stores or drug stores. Or the formula may be a regular baby formula of one cup of evaporated milk, one cup of water and one teaspoon of white Karo syrup. A premature baby's nursing bottle may be used, holding individual puppies in your hands or on a towel.

If by any chance she misses one in rotation, the owner will have to give such a puppy additional food and arrange for half the litter to nurse, then the next half. This will necessitate removing part of the litter and placing one half in a box while the others nurse. In litters of 10 or 12 it may be necessary to more or less rotate hand-feeding and nursing. While they will nurse a little when returned to the dam, they will not attempt to drain so much. At the next feeding time select the other half for the hand-feeding. In this way each puppy receives some of the bitch's milk and all have some supplementary feeding.

If a puppy is an ineffective nurser or if a large litter demands supplementary feeding, a technique called tube-feeding is beneficial. This is an effective way to get the proper amount of milk into the puppy's stomach, and it takes less time than bottle-feeding. Be sure to consult a veterinarian for the proper technique and formula. It is also worth remembering that the ineffective nurser may become the star of the litter once on solid food.

The puppy should be returned to the mother who will lick off the excess milk. She must lick the puppy, for the puppy cannot eliminate at first without the massage by her tongue. This is how nature has provided for caring for the early elimination needs and cleanliness of the puppy. If for any reason the dam is unable to do this for the puppy, the owner would have to massage the groin and anus of each puppy with a gauze bandage dipped in warm water.

Many puppies benefit by the addition of vitamins. The best are human baby vitamins such as Poly-Vi-Sol, one drop per puppy per day at the time of feeding or nursing.

The greedy, roughneck puppy may have to be restrained or limited in his feeding time as the days advance. Small puppies need additional food or more feeding time. At this early stage, who is to know which is the best puppy and the one that would suit you or another owner best?

At nine days, add strained baby meat (beef) to the milk formula until it becomes a cocoa color. Meat is very important to puppies at this stage. Puppies will actually eat meat off the finger of the owner or off a spoon; however, the finger will allow for a sucking motion. Meat placed in the milk is also satisfactory. A puppy of nine days may be held on the hand on a towel and can actually lap warm liquids such as milk-meat liquid mix from a sauce dish tipped and held in the other hand. The puppy must be supported with one hand to prevent its sliding. It is rather fun to see which one is a lady or gentleman and eats in a neat fashion, or which wants to plunge in, both feet and nose. It may take two or three feedings for some. Return it to the mother and she will lick the puppy and enjoy the puppy meat-mix as dessert. The puppies get a little wet during this process, so chilling should be avoided.

Puppies should be weighed daily and the weight recorded on a weight chart. In this way, the owner will know which puppies may be gaining too much or too little. The puppy which gains too little either requires supplementary feeding (tube feeding) or the attention of a veterinarian. A five-pound postage scale may be used the first few days—follow with a 25-pound kitchen scale, using a shoe box to hold the puppies, or use baby scales. Your veterinarian will appreciate the weight record, and you will know your puppies better.

At the end of the second week, a small amount of baby cereal may be sprinkled into the milk-meat mix. The puppies will still enjoy ending with the liquid. During the third week more cereal may be added and at the end of the third week ground, semi-cooked extra-lean beef may replace the strained meat or baby food mix. About this time puppy meal or small kibble should replace the baby cereal.

Why this extra-lean meat? Puppies eat a great deal in relation to their size, as they are growing very fast. They are shifting and adjusting to new foods while still getting a large supply of their dam's milk. Any excess fat that there might be in the average hamburger meat can produce a loose stool which is hard to handle. If diarrhea or loose stools occur, important nutrition may be eliminated and lost to the puppy. Besides, it's just plain hard to stop as well as messy to clean. By this time the owner will need to give some assistance to the bitch and not leave to her the entire problem of her special form of housekeeping.

Shall we discuss how to mark the puppies? There are lots of ideas, but only one works. And it may be as hard for the new owner to face as cutting off Johnny's first curl. Get out the sewing shears or hair clippers and hold the puppy. Start with all the males. One is put in the box without any mark at all and he is Mr. No-Mark. The next male should have a little hair about a quarter of an inch wide and an inch or two long clipped from his right hip, but just the hair—not the skin. He becomes Mr. Right-Hip-Mark. The next male the right shoulder. The next, the left shoulder, and then the left hip. You may have to go to the tail or make a double clipping if most of the litter should be boys or girls. Repeat the same thing with the bitch puppies. The

## WEIGHT — MARKING CHART

Clip hair to identify the puppies. Clipping must be repeated every ten days to two weeks. Check birth weight and daily thereafter. (Continue weight chart for 7 weeks.)

| DATES | | | | | | | | | | | |
|---|---|---|---|---|---|---|---|---|---|---|---|
| **Male—** | No Mark | | | | | | | | | | |
| | Left Hip | | | | | | | | | | |
| | Right Hip | | | | | | | | | | |
| | Left Shoulder | | | | | | | | | | |
| | Right Shoulder | | | | | | | | | | |
| | Tail | | | | | | | | | | |
| | Right Hip (double clip) | | | | | | | | | | |
| | Etc. | | | | | | | | | | |
| **Female—** | No Mark | | | | | | | | | | |
| | Left Hip | | | | | | | | | | |
| | Right Hip | | | | | | | | | | |
| | Left Shoulder | | | | | | | | | | |
| | Right Shoulder | | | | | | | | | | |
| | Tail | | | | | | | | | | |
| | Right Hip (double clip) | | | | | | | | | | |
| | Etc. | | | | | | | | | | |

Weight increase indicates growth and development of the puppy. Weight gain should be from 1 to 3½ ounces per day. Check weight approximately the same time each day. If puppies fail to gain each day, add additional food—tube or bottle feeding—between nursing. If puppy loses weight, contact your veterinarian.

At six weeks, a puppy's most important activity is a thorough exploration of the world around it. Note the identifying shoulder clip on this youngster.

Nancy Belsaas with her home-bred puppy, Jameson. Nancy has been active in Goldens since childhood and was best junior handler at Westminster in 1958. With husband, Dean, she continues enthusiastically on behalf of the breed.
*Fox & Cook PhoDOGraphy*

"Happiness", owned and bred by Peggy Strange.
*Dorothy Carter*

hair soon grows, and in two or three weeks the clippings must be repeated. It is a very good way to identify individual puppies in checking weight, alertness to reactions and later on when they are playing in the yard. This clipping method is used at Guide Dogs for the Blind at San Rafael, California, to identify the puppies as they react to the testing programs.

Any owner will find this method of marking to his or her advantage in watching the development of the puppies, as they change very rapidly from day to day. It becomes a great advantage at the time the puppies are viewed by prospective new owners. Anyone seeing the puppies for the first time may be confused and not recognize them individually save for size and color. If the puppy has been selected and is not to be delivered immediately, the purchaser may sign a card indicating his or her choice, such as Mr. Right-Hip or Miss Left-Shoulder-Mark. Then this one may be considered as promised, or perhaps to be reserved for future choice, leaving the rest of the litter available for selection. When the new owner returns to pick up the puppy, it will be easy to identify his choice. Puppies grow at an amazing rate and in a week's time a puppy will have changed, save for his mark.

One of the chores during the entire eight-week period is the clipping of the toe nails. In a ten-puppy litter this makes a lot of toenails to clip, even though only the sharp tips are taken off to prevent scratching the mother. The usual clippers for grown dogs are too large for small puppies. Small nail clippers that can be bought in a drug store are ideal for taking off the sharp tips of puppy toenails. If dewclaws are to be removed, this should be done in the first few days in the life of the puppy. Removal of dewclaws, although optional in Goldens, is preferred by some hunters.

During the fourth and fifth weeks, the dam will find it uncomfortable to nurse the puppies as they are big, their claws are sharp, and she begins to tire of her chores. But the puppies should remain to some extent on their mother's milk until six weeks as they gain some immunity through her milk, and the relationship of dam and puppies is important to their emotional development, ability to receive training, and their relationship to other dogs as revealed in puppy tests. (See Pfaffenberger, *The New Knowledge of Dog Behavior,* Howell Book House, New York.) By six weeks the puppies may be completely weaned as they will have gradually shifted off the mother's milk to their new food.

Six-to-eight-week old puppies require three to four feedings per day, preferably two of milk-meat-kibble (meal) mix morning and evening, and the mid-day feeding of milk, cottage cheese and cereal. Hard cooked egg and small amounts of cooked ground beef liver should be added to one of the meals or used three or four times a week. Raw eggs should not be given to dogs, particularly young puppies, as raw eggs are colloidal in dogs and so tend to remove minerals and vitamins during excretion. Tuna (either oil or water packed) may be used for variety.

Continue some form of vitamin-mineral (all purpose maintenance) throughout life. Vitamins used for humans are desirable because they include all the vitamins such as Vitamin D and minerals in a good proportion for warm-blooded animals. Excessive amounts of powdered calcium or excessive Vitamin D and A may be undesirable. Conversely, the lack of any supplement is undesirable.

Specific amounts are difficult to give as the amount of milk of the dam and the size of the litter varies. The puppy will usually turn its head away even at eight or nine days when it has had enough. Occasionally, as mentioned before, there is a greedy puppy who will never stop—or the little explorer who could care less about food. For these extremes, adjustments must be made. *No puppy should be allowed to become overweight* as its bones are soft and too much weight is harmful to its feet, joints and general development. A too-thin puppy may lack for food just when he needs it most. Puppies at the age of eight weeks will eat almost as much as a full grown dog because of the great rapidity with which they are developing. Each day in the life of the puppy in this period of its life equals about twenty days in the life of a child as far as its nutritional development is concerned, so the loss of a day or two can be serious.

At 12 weeks one meal, preferably the noon meal, can be eliminated and the total feedings should then be divided into one morning and one evening meal until the dog is six months old. Many breeders continue two feedings through the first year. The activity of the dog and the rate of growth determine the amount of food. A layer of fat over the ribs is desirable, but not a very thick layer.

There are several books which go into more detail in the feeding of dogs which will be of considerable interest. For those who wish to study the subject of dog feeding in greater detail, *The Collins Guide to Dog Nutrition,* by Donald R. Collins, DVM (Howell Book House, New York) is highly recommended.

Chop bones, chicken bones, and fish bones should not be given to the puppies. A fresh marrow bone may be given during the teething period, but it should be a fresh bone each time, and never allowed to become dirty or lie around for more than a few hours.

The whelping box is not the whole solution to caring for young puppies, though an ideal whelping box is suggested. Commercial dog supply houses have portable, wire puppy pens in which the puppies may be placed for additional exercise and airing. A similar arrangement may be made at home out of wire fencing and arranged so that it will bend as a panel screen. Papers may be placed on the floor of the wire pen to keep the puppies off cold cement and also to expedite cleaning. Shavings may be sprinkled over the papers to absorb moisture. The feeding may be done in these pens when the puppies are four weeks old.

Such a pen may be moved about so that puppies accustom themselves to different surfaces under their feet. This also contains the puppies for short periods of time. Naturally as the puppies grow older they could push such a fencing pen over unless it is secured in some way.

Ch. Holman's Mister Charley, owned by Gertrude Fischer, had six Best of Winners placements enroute to his championship. He is shown with his handler Tony Gwinner.

*Johnnie McMillan*

Am. Can. Ch. Sutter Creek Cloverdale Erin (Am. Can. Ch. Cloverdale Bunker Hill Seth, OS, ex Can. Ch. Goldenquest Sutter Creek Lyric, Am. Can. CD), owned by Jane Zimmerman and bred by Susan Breakell, shown winning the Sporting Group at Tidewater under Virginia Hampton.

*Stephen Klein*

243

The trained eye can find many indications of what a young puppy will be when it is a grown dog. This extremely typical baby is Golden Comet of Flarewin. Note the correct expression, the muzzle, eyes, ample bone and overall balance. This same puppy, when grown, won well in dog shows and field trials.

Eileen Oshiro with her young hopeful, Golden Pine's Bronte Suntory, contemplating the prospects of a bright show career ahead. *Richard Oshiro*

In summer heat such a pen should not be left too long in the sun and may be moved from sun to shade. In very cold or sub-zero weather, of course, the puppies cannot be left out for any time at all. Golden Retrievers have very good coats as puppies and from six weeks on can tolerate 50 to 60 degree temperatures provided they are dry and under a roof. They cuddle for the cold and spread apart for the heat. Even at six weeks they will enjoy a romp on the grass and may be tested with recently killed pigeons as early as six or seven weeks.

## Feeding Puppies from Birth to Eight Weeks

The following has been a successful formula, used by many for the feeding of Golden Retriever puppies. While it is somewhat expensive it more than pays for itself in the condition of the puppies at the time of sale.
*Normal delivery and normal conditions:*

| | |
|---|---|
| 1st day: | Allow puppies to nurse from their dam each day. |
| 3rd or 4th day: | Start one drop of Poly-Vi-Sol (same as for human infants). Give one drop and place back to mother's breast. Vitamins with one meal. |
| 10th day:* | Add strained beef (any good baby meat) to milk formula. |
| 14th to 16th day: | Add small amount of cereal such as Pablum or puppy food put through a blender to milk-meat mix. Puppies enjoy thickened milk but prefer to end a meal on straight liquid. |
| 21st to 23rd day: | Add a little more puppy food and some semi-cooked, ground extra lean beef in place of the strained beef, or you may shift to junior meats before starting the ground, extra lean beef. Add liquid to a bowl of milk-meat-cereal mix as the puppies like to end on liquid. |
| 28th to 30th day: | Gradually increase the food as needed. Do not overfeed. Add cooked egg yolk to milk-meat mix. Puppies will now probably be on two meals per day, plus their dam's milk. Some may be on three meals. |
| 5th week: | The puppy should be on meat-milk-cereal feeding and continue on its mother's milk though she will be starting to wean them. |
| 6th week: | The puppy should be on three to four meals per day. Morning and evening feeding of milk-meat-cereal. Noon feeding of milk, or milk-cottage cheese and some hard cooked egg, and meal. Possibly a fourth snack such as a little meat or kibble with barely enough milk to moisten it before bedtime. |

*Puppies may eat out of a dish by the ninth day if the puppy is held on a towel and a dish held in the opposite hand is tipped so that the puppy may lap. They can do this even before their eyes are open though they are too young to support themselves easily. By the end of the third week, two or three of them may eat from the same pan. Layer cake pans, taped bottom-to-bottom, make excellent feeding and water dishes for puppies. They do not tip over, are a suitable height and are inexpensive.

Puppies should be returned to the mother as soon as they have been given any supplementary feeding and she will clean them off. They may be wet and must be kept out of any drafts.

The amount of food will be determined by the size of the litter, the amount of milk of the dam. Adding some milk and some meat, particularly the meat, produces a puppy with a harder, better muscular development than just milk and cereal, which alone tends to develop a soft, mushy puppy.

In the third week step up the vitamins to two drops. In the sixth week you may substitute a human vitamin such as Stewart's Formula. Use maintenance vitamins, not extra-strong ones. The mineral-vitamin mix contains Vitamin D and calcium. The puppy also receives calcium from the milk. An all-purpose mineral-vitamin mix is best for dogs.

Cottage cheese and/or tuna (occasionally) may be added to the noon meal.

Ground cooked beef liver may be added from the third week, a little each day or three or four days a week. Some use traces of liver from the eighth day.

Raw egg whites should never be given, as these are colloidal in dogs and tend to sweep out all minerals and vitamins for the day from the young puppies' intestines.

Puppies may be fed from individual dishes or three or four puppies around a pan. Of course, pans must be washed thoroughly after each feeding.

After the fourth week puppies should have water available at all times.

Greedy puppies may have to be taken away from the feedings to prevent them from becoming too fat. Smaller puppies or more social puppies may have to be encouraged to eat more often.

Small puppies may require two or three feedings from their second day in addition to their mother's milk, using a premature infant's bottle or tube feeding.

The bitch should be fed three times a day from the time the puppies are whelped until she completes the nursing. Her food should include substantial amounts of milk, liquids, meat, cottage cheese as well as meal or kibble, and she should have her single vitamin tablet per day, such as a human maintenance vitamin. Extra calcium and other materials should not be added without the advice of a veterinarian in specific instances, as the milk-cottage cheese-meat takes care of her needs and that of her puppies during nursing.

The bitch should not be given any booster shots for distemper or other shots during the nursing period. Check anything of this sort or any unusual rise in temperature with the veterinarian, who has some experience in animal nutrition.

The suggestions for a whelping box and for the feeding of the puppies from birth to eight weeks are ideal which make it easier to handle a litter of puppies and easier to be specific in regard to estimating a desirable diet.

For example, the whelping box could be smaller or a frame might be used. The main purpose of a whelping box is to have some form of confinement for the bitch and puppies, particularly for the puppies, so that they will not stray too far from the dam. The supervision is easier. People have used a child's playpen and other equipment. Some people have used a six-foot square rather than the four-by-eight whelping box. The square is harder to handle, as the owner would have to walk around the box and could not easily bend over to pick up a puppy. If the box is too small, there is a risk of the bitch's crushing the puppies. Besides, the puppies would find it difficult to set aside an area for their toilet.

When the puppies are four weeks old, the feeding may be done in a portable wire pen. This is a great help in caring for puppies or adjusting them to various locations, or just confining them while they are small enough to get lost. However, puppies from four weeks on will profit if the weather permits, from different conditions under their feet. This makes a suitable confinement area when taking the puppies out one at a time for testing. Some people may have adequate space or a kennel area making these extra pieces of equipment unnecessary.

The basic feeding is bitch's milk, other milk such as cow's milk, and meat proteins plus cottage cheese and cereal. If available, there is no reason why venison, lamb, if not too fat, and other meat proteins could not be used. In farming communities, owners may make up their own cottage cheese mix. The puppies may be fed curds of milk, as lactic acid in the milk and curds actually have, in effect, partially "predigested" the milk which makes it easier for the puppies to tolerate such a diet this is another reason why buttermilk might be used for puppies over six weeks old, as well as for adult dogs. In European countries some version of sour milk is used in more or less the ways mentioned above. Meat such as pork and bear meat should be completely cooked if used for either puppies or grown dogs.

Mixtures may be cooked up including meat scraps, kidneys, heart and muscle meat to make a broth. This is a great deal more work and harder to proportion than shopping at the supermarket, as could be so easily done in the optimum suggestions for feeding. While one man has compared these methods to treating the puppies in the same way as driving up in a Rolls Royce to The Savoy in London, or Trader Vic's in San Francisco—there isn't all that difference in price, though there is in convenience. People who have freezers will have been able to buy meat and obtain cottage cheese at quantity prices. Even chicken meat, completely removed from the bones, is sometimes less expensive than beef or lamb products—but some red meat is needed. Field trial people might object to feeding any kind of fowl, as some think that even cooked fowl might encourage wrong habits in the field. Uninspected horse meat should always be cooked.

If rabbit meat is used the meat should be cooked and removed from the bones, as rabbit bones are easy to splinter and could harm the intestines of dogs, especially puppies. Care should be used in preparing wild rabbits, as the vermin on some rabbit fur may be hosts for tuleremia, which is a serious disease in both humans and dogs. Use gloves in skinning and care in disposal of hides. It is possible to vary the feeding as long as the general pattern and balanced proportion of meat protein, milk, cereal and fats are used in the puppy diet or the diet of a grown dog. Many commercial puppy and dog foods are excellent, but even these are improved in flavor by adding some of these other items, but not in such proportions as would seriously unbalance the food. Meat broth, meat and milk products do not keep as well as dried food. This is one of the reasons for adding them to the dry mixture which is reasonably well-balanced with carbohydrates, roughage and minerals.

Yes, puppies are expensive to raise—but, for most, the personal satisfaction of raising a well-bred litter more than offsets the cost. (For additional information, see "Feeding Suggestions for Goldens" in Appendix B.)

## The Obligations of Puppy Seller and Buyer

The obligations of anyone offering Golden Retriever puppies for sale should be to present healthy, active puppies from sound parents. The puppies should be from a bitch which has been maintained in good condition, and they should be checked for health at the time of delivery. Each customer should receive a health record of the puppy he is buying. On this record should be shown any worming (if such has been needed, as all puppies do not require worming), any immunizations such as for distemper, hepatitis, leptospirosis, and parvovirus—or any medication the puppy might have had. Due to local situations, other types of immunizations may be preferred, but at any rate, the new owner should have complete information. All this is an advantage to the seller as he is presenting the full facts and circumstances of the puppy's life to the new owner.

The seller will wish to include some notes on what the puppy has been fed and what it will need in the next few weeks, as well as the date or dates when additional immunizations are needed. This may be in the form of a health history or a chart entitled "Keep a Medical Record of Your Golden." Perhaps some information on housebreaking, general care and training should be given the new owner. The seller may make up his own notes or use some of the excellent publications put out by various quality dog food companies. Booklets on training or on the breed Standard are an advantage to the new owner.

It is well-advised for the seller to check on how the puppy is getting along after the puppy has been in its new home for one or two weeks, and again when the puppy is a young adult, as this is the only way the seller can check on his breeding program. After all the work and time that has been put into the development of any puppy, the breeder would like to assess the results.

A few sellers go to considerably more work in testing the puppies' retrieving ability. Birdiness, body sensitivity, hearing, and other important characteristics are clues to the character of the adult dog. In the selection of an older puppy or dog, both birdiness and bird-sense may be checked in actual field conditions and perhaps response to the gun. In this way selections may be made for specific purposes such as field work, obedience or other uses. Such tests may be made by a dedicated breeder whether he is a breeder of a single litter or more. Whether he is a hobby fancier and breeds for the purpose of improving the breed and to produce puppies for his own use and the use of friends, or whether he is a large commercial breeder, such testing will be to his advantage. In the case of the occasional breeder, he does not count the cost of his own time. Time and care are given as a labor of love, and he may do an exceptionally fine job and produce exceptionally fine dogs. This can also be true of the one-time breeder. This is the difference between a dedicated and conscientious person and the so-called "back-yard-breeder." All dogs are in the back yard some of the time, but the unkind connotation of back-yard-breeder applies to the unknowing and careless breeder who is thinking only of a little pin money. He is the one who does not assume responsibility for the breed quality and breed Standard, and the placing of puppies in homes where the puppies will be a delight and satisfaction to their owner. The one-time breeder may not realize the importance of the care needed. The large commercial breeder for whom this is a livelihood or an extra business venture, is forced to consider the costs in relation to production, and may not have the time for all these tests. On the other hand, if a commercial breeder is to stay in business, the quality must be maintained, and as in any other business, there are those who are careless and those who are conscientious.

The seller should provide the proper American Kennel Club registration papers for the new owner. The seller may wish to use a theme name as a prefix to indicate a particular litter or a particular breeding much in the same way as a registered kennel would use a registered name. Attached to this theme name may be the name which is the choice of the owner. For example, the breeder may wish to use a theme name such as "Oak Bay" to which the owner could attach Oak Bay "Jason" or Oak Bay "Huntress" or Oak Bay "Golden Torch." Some breeders name all the puppies and register them, then transfer the registration to the new owner. This is really a matter of preference, but it does have an advantage of

Favor, at 3½ months, lends a hand with the gardening. A daughter of the English import Ch. Shargleam Ferryman ex Ch. Smithaven's Rousing Rhet O'Ric, CD, WC, she collected five majors by the time she was two and a half years old to become Ch. Smithaven's Firm Fav O'Rhet, owned and bred by June and Betty Smith.

Tigathoe's Joshin' Me, a true water lover, owned by Chris Repasky.

helping to check on the relationship of the dogs at a later time, or follow the competition of litter mates or related dogs.

If a puppy is to be sold on time payment plan, the transfer of ownership is customarily withheld until the last payment is made. If, for any reason, no papers are to be given with the puppy, this should be so stated in writing with the reason why, and a copy should be retained by the buyer and one given to the seller. It is best if the seller and the buyer sign both copies. Occasionally, a very nice animal has mismarkings, or there is some unusual situation, possibly undescended testicles (which rarely happens). Then a notation may be made on the registration application sent to the American Kennel Club, naming the fault, and the registration will be of a limited type. In this way, an otherwise useful animal could be shown in obedience but could not be bred, or at least no puppies could be registered from this animal. Such situations are isolated but can be checked between six and eight weeks of age, and could be of concern to both seller and purchaser. These conditions should be reflected in the papers or the bill of sale.

According to common practice, if puppies become ill within a week after delivery, or some unusual circumstance comes about which is clearly or even likely to have had its inception before delivery, the seller is expected to return the money and accept return of the puppy. This involves further medical checks, etc. Of course, it would go without saying that the puppy yard and kennel conditions should be immaculately clean at all times.

Any other responsibilities on the part of the seller have to do with his own interests and agreement with the purchaser. If he promises a show puppy, or a puppy which will accept training, etc., this is an arrangement between him and the purchaser, which possibly might be set down in writing. At any rate such arrangement should be clearly understood at the time of the sale. Usually the price is higher in such cases, but the return of the dog should be accepted if such promises have been made, or some suitable adjustment for both buyer and seller is needed.

*Summary:*

1. Place or sell only healthy puppies with complete health records from sound and healthy parents.
2. Provide history of all medication.
3. List when medications, if any, are due again.
4. Include feeding directions.
5. Provide American Kennel Club registration application, or written statement that such is forthcoming. If the latter is given, explain why this is not available at the time of sale. Follow this up.
6. Provide pedigree.
7. Follow up the puppy in the new home, but do not be a pest.

The buyer also has responsibilities. The most important is to make up his mind on what he really wants—whether an attractive personal dog for himself or his children, whether he wishes a field trial prospect, a show prospect, an obedience dog, or a combination of all four. Nobody who selects a pet is interested in an inferior dog. The buyer looks for an adaptable, personal animal that is reasonably within the breed Standard and with the temperament and adaptability to fit into the varied interests of family life. If it is for children, it means an active dog and one of which the children may be proud. If the buyer is interested in a field trial dog or show dog, he will be interested in the testing program, the scenting or marking ability of the dog and such outgoing qualities as are best suited to his purpose.

It is unfair of the buyer to say that he wishes a pet for his children in the hope of getting a lower price, and then to start a breeding kennel with a dog which has been sold primarily for temperament without regard to other considerations. Such an animal may not have the gift to transmit those qualities which improve the breed. Rather, the dog should be enjoyed for itself and another purchased for a breeding program. This is in no way meant to downgrade the usefulness and help of the dog that has been dear to the family even though it has serious or disqualifying faults and should not be shown—neither should it be bred. Nor, is this meant to downgrade the excellent dog which becomes the winner although it is the last one in the litter to go.

In one case the buyers were looking for another breed and happened onto a top Golden puppy that was the last of his litter. This puppy grew up to be Ch. Beau Jack, UD, and his owners made the most of him in obedience and in the show ring and continued to enjoy him as a personal dog.

Few sellers can promise and none can guarantee a future show winner or guarantee a field trial winner, and the buyer should not ask for a commitment of this kind. However, he can check on the dog's birdiness, interest in retrieving, and reactions to loud and sharp noises if he is interested in a field trial dog. He should also check the pedigree which is some indication though not the whole story. If he wishes a show dog, he will be very much concerned with the proportions of the puppy though all puppies do not grow up to their puppy promise.

The buyer interested in show activities might do well to buy an almost grown dog whose proportions and showmanship have developed to the point of better prediction. Such a dog is hard to find and expensive to buy, but occasionally it may be found. When such an opportunity is presented, the buyer should take it at once. Changes in family situations sometimes make such a dog available. There are several true stories that might be cited, but they are still the exception.

The same might be true in selecting an obedience dog, but generally speaking, the alert puppy which has been developed in the family, and brought along gradually becomes the greatest obedience success, particularly for one who is able to train and enjoys the training. This may also be true of a field trial dog. But in many cases, the combination of success in various fields may also have a bearing on success in the others. A field trial dog must be faster than an obedience dog or a show dog. While speed is not as important as accuracy, it may mean that little edge in the decision between the average and the great in field trials.

The buyer should expect and ask for the items listed in the summary of the seller's responsibility as listed above. The buyer then has the responsibility of checking out the animal with his own veterinarian, following through with the immunizations, training, housing, and care. This means a fenced yard, proper housing, and the observation of ordinances regarding animals in his own neighborhood. It means care when the dog is taken in the car, and medical care and grooming when needed. If any unforeseen problems do come up, they should be taken up with the breeder first, as he should be interested in the outcome.

The buyer will do better buying directly from the breeder. If the breeder is sincere, he will have noticed many things about the puppies which indicate their character, and he can be most helpful in assisting the purchaser to make a selection. Straight-forwardness on the part of both is desirable. But in the end, the purchaser must make the selection on the basis of the puppy or dog that appeals to him most, for this is the one he will enjoy training and having around.

## The Golden In Its New Home

Puppies usually enter a new home at seven to eight weeks of age. At this time its new habits are formed. The first two to three weeks with the new family are important in socialization and establishing good habits. This is an optimum time for learning (see Chapter IX in Pfaffenberger's *New Knowledge of Dog Behavior,* "Some Critical Periods in the Life of a Puppy"). Even older dogs will need to relearn some of the rules in a new situation.

Teach the puppy its name. A poor name learned is better than a perfect name delayed too long. In teaching the name, the come command may also be taught. Two people positioned several feet apart may enforce the name and the come command by calling the dog with a happy sound, a hand-clap and the dog's name. When the dog comes, praise it and offer a small reward. The second person should repeat the name and the word "come." Do this four or five times, relax, then repeat at a somewhat longer distance. Be careful not to exhaust the puppy. In three or four days, the puppy will know its name and the command to come.

Start the housebreaking. Housebreaking can be accomplished in two or three days to two weeks, if you take the time. The puppy must be taken outside upon awakening, after eating and following hard play. In general, a puppy will need to relieve itself every half hour to hour. After it has taken care of its duties, return the puppy to the house with extravagant praise. Do this even if the dog must soon be returned to its outside yard. In this way, the puppy learns the reason it was taken outside. Use the same area and the same door as much as possible. The puppy will quickly learn to indicate when he needs to go out-of-doors. If the dog is not successfully housebroken after two weeks on this routine, a medical check of bowels and kidneys is advisable.

Teach the puppy to let you take anything out of its mouth. This can be accomplished in a game-type format with the command "give." Hold your hand below the dog's mouth and say, "give." Praise the puppy and he should drop the item into your hand. A marrow bone makes a good toy with which to teach this command. A dog may need to give up an item which could be harmful to its health, or a child's toy; if the animal becomes a hunter, it will be required to give the bird on command.

Teach the puppy to lie on a towel or bath mat on the left side of your major chairs so that it knows that the left side is the love side and the left hand the petting hand. You can reach over the side of the chair and pet the dog. It will quickly learn to place itself in this position. The left side is the side on which a puppy should learn to heel; it is the side on which the dog goes down the street for a walk; it is the show ring position and the side which most hunters prefer, though some prefer the right side. This exception may be taught at a later time if needed. With the dog at your left when walking down the street, you can stop to greet a friend and keep yourself between the animal and your friend. If your friend also has a dog, there will be two of you between "Jason" and "Goldie," so no sniffing or unfriendly situations develop.

In the house, a puppy should be trained to have good manners. This means he must not be allowed to chew on furniture or to play with pillows or clothing. He should also be trained not to jump up or to sit on your lap without invitation, for these actions will no longer be cute when the dog is grown and weighs 60 or 70 pounds or if he is wet. The puppy should be taught that all four feet belong on the ground. Most bad habits can be quickly cured or avoided if the puppy is correctly trained at an early age.

Whether the dog is a trained hunter, champion show dog, or the family pet, it should be trained to ride quietly in a car. A dog's proper place is either in the back seat (without a leash) or in a crate. The first trips should be short to accustom the dog to the motion. Good manners must always be encouraged—no jumping from the back to the front seat, no barking at passing dogs or people, and no chewing on the upholstery. While driving, the windows should remain slightly cracked or closed to prevent any kind of unfortunate accidents from occurring, but it is imperative to crack open the windows if you must leave the dog in the car for any length of time. If the dog is to leave the car with you, it should be trained to wait until the leash is attached and it is given the command to come.

When training your Golden puppy, remember that a cold, harsh voice can damage a young animal's self-esteem as much as serious physical punishment, for which there is little excuse. Express your pleasure and affection through stroking, a happy voice, and with food rewards especially favored by your dog. Positive reinforcement is a much more effective means of training than physical punishment. The best sources for additional information on early puppy training are Margaret Pearsall's *The Pearsall Guide to Successful Dog Training* (Howell Book House, 1973) and Joachim Volhard and Gail Tamases Fisher's *Training Your Dog: The Step-by-Step Manual* (Howell Book House, 1983).

## A Check List for the New Puppy

*Medical List*

1. Keep a medical check list. Place on the calendar when the next medication or shots are needed. These may be for distemper, hepatitis, parvovirus, rabies, etc. Check for heartworm if it is a problem in your area. Take stool specimens to your veterinarian.
2. Learn to take the dog's temperature.
3. Keep the dog well groomed. This includes regular brushing, checking the ears and nails, and bathing when needed.
4. Keep fleas and other parasites under control.
5. Maintain a good, healthy diet. Give adequate amounts but do not overfeed.

*Training*

1. Teach the dog its name; train it to come and to give.
2. Immediately housebreak the dog.
3. Do not allow a puppy to play too roughly with his kennel mates or an adult dog. Remember the joint bones of a puppy are soft and rough play over a period of time can cause damage hard or impossible to repair.
4. Train the dog to ride in the car, to sit in the back seat or adjust itself to a crate if you are using a station wagon or truck.

*General Manners*

1. Distraction is the best method to cure an undesirable habit. Substitute toys and chew sticks for expensive or dangerous household items.
2. Actions that are acceptable and cute for a puppy may become annoying when the dog is full grown. Train the dog not to jump up, not to play too roughly, and to distinguish which furniture is his and which is off-limits.
3. Remember, your puppy is a retriever and likes to bring things to you. If he brings you your diamond necklace or mink coat or a dirty sweat sock, show your appreciation and thanks—but substitute a string of large wooden beads or a chew stick instead!!!

Anna Adams and her Guide Dog, "Roxanne," enjoy a walk on the 11-acre campus of Guide Dogs for the Blind in San Rafael, California. Following close behind are Sandy Tupper with "Geiger."

# 14

# The Golden Retriever as a Dog for Leading the Blind

SOME 35-40 YEARS AGO, various institutions for training dogs to lead the blind used several breeds successfully. Some working, herding and sporting breeds, as well as non-sporting dogs, were used, and some continue to be used today. A dog gives so much more mobility and independence to the blind individual that many dedicated dog owners are happy to see representatives of their breed lead such constructive and helpful lives.

Several breeds were experimented with and a breeding program developed to select more carefully, as puppies, dogs that would be successful and responsible in this work.

A leader in these programs, and especially in the breeding program, was Mr. Clarence J. Pfaffenberger, who was active in dog training and in Guide Dogs for the Blind at San Rafael, California. The work is well documented and described in his book, *The New Knowledge of Dog Behavior,* (Howell Book House Inc., 1963). Mr. Pfaffenberger won several Guggenheim fellowships and worked carefully over a considerable period with scientists and geneticists in developing both a breeding and a training program. The book is well worthwhile for anyone interested in developing a dog of any breed, particularly a medium-sized dog, whether it is to be used for a personal dog, hunter, field or obedience trials.

Through these studies and repeated checks under controlled conditions and tests by experts, information was obtained as to the inherited abilities and optimum training times for several breeds. It was especially valuable in discovering inherited traits, abilities, and capacities for training in puppies from six to twelve weeks of age. Predictability of adult success in selection of these puppies was improved approximately 700 per cent.

These studies indicated which dogs and which lines produced the most successful guide dogs. There was an exchange of information and breeding stock with some other organizations in the United States, in England and in Australia. This exchange of breeding stock furthered the quality of the guide dogs used in all three countries.

In my first years of Goldens, when Goldens were somewhat new to this area, it occurred to me that they would be successful for leading the blind. Goldens enjoy a close personal relationship to their owners, yet are successfully trained by both owners and professionals. They are also adaptable to some changes in ownership. One day, when driving through the Stanford University Campus, I gave a ride to a blind student and his guide dog, and, although he loved his own dog, he remarked how he enjoyed the feel of my dog's fur. Though I never again saw the young man after I drove him with his dog to the dentist, when there were puppies, I offered one to Mr. Pfaffenberger, and this was successful Golden Genie. After Genie, there was June, and then later my husband and I gave an entire litter from two champions, and we were pleased when each of the litter made it through the testing program. This litter became a basis for breeding stock. At this time there were other breeders who gave puppies from their very fine litters. Some supplied stud services from field and show stock. Bonnie and Jim Humphrey gave Atlanta of Golden Anno Nuevo and then Sue, two brood bitches, and later supplied a stud in Dual Ch. Cresta Gold Rip for Sue. Many counted their litters as though there had been only five or six, and gave one or two first selections to Guide Dogs. Others supplied stud services from field, obedience, and show stock. Among these was FC-AFC Rocky Mack. Virginia and Nathan Beauchamp had a lovely small bitch, Hesperian Queen, descended from handsome Ch. Prince Copper of Malibu and Ch. Oakwin Junior. Queenie supplied five litters for Guide Dogs. And many breeders are still donating puppies and services, and offering only the best puppies.

The research through the study and use of these dogs as they developed and responded to training is so important that, whatever the gift, the gift seems small compared to what was accomplished here. This research furthered the use of dogs for training in this particular field and much of it applied to training in other dog uses and associations. Without the dedicated volunteers, this work would not have been possible. Such work is without price, for some of these people have given weekly service for ten or twenty years.

Marjorie Grinnell, 86, and her Golden companion, Bruce. Once active with Guide Dogs for the Blind in the testing and research program, she selected a Golden as her personal companion upon retirement. This photo was used in the publication of the San Francisco Humane Society to illustrate the importance of pets for senior citizens and those living alone.

259

Kevin Hurley, 4-H Club Guide Dog puppy trainer, and a young Golden destined to become the eyes of a sightless person. Kevin is typical of the many 4-H boys and girls who train future Guide Dogs in basic obedience and normal good manners. They take the dogs as young puppies and keep them almost a year. At that time they return to Guide Dogs for the final training and preparation for their life's work. *Emil Gumper*

A philanthropist and a leader in field trial work, Eloise Heller Cherry (Mrs. Guy), was very active in early guide dog work and wished to see all programs advanced. A knowledgeable person, she has trained and run her own Chesapeakes and Goldens in trials. She suggested an improved arrangement for the early care and training of selected puppies that tied in with the experimental work, in that 4-H Clubs might be interested in a puppy-raising and training program. Many young people are unable to participate in a large animal project because of lack of space and facilities, but have the space and time for caring for and developing these puppies. These young people train and care for puppies from the end of the testing period when they are twelve weeks old until they are about twelve months old.

The training given by the 4-H boys and girls consists of basic obedience and family training, such as heeling, sitting, staying and going about in cars, adjustments to home, street noises, and other unusual circumstances while under control of the 4-H puppy raiser. When possible, the Golden is given the opportunity for other forms of transportation, and of course in the home training, as the puppy, then later as a guide dog, is supposed to sleep beside the bed of its master. These experiences make adjustment and adaptation easier to situations the dog will experience as a guide dog.

Some service clubs defray the feeding and other costs when these expenses are a problem for an interested youngster. The 4-H projects develop skill, observation, and interest and ways of working together. The sadness of giving up their charge is dispelled by their joy in achievement when they attend a graduation of a class of blind people and are invited to present the dog to the blind person who becomes the new owner.

When the dog reaches approximately one year of age, it is returned to the Guide Dog Kennels. Females are spayed following the first heat period, unless they are to be reserved for breeding. Males are castrated after they are fully mature. Then the professional trainers at Guide Dogs begin the intensive training period. Following this, the dog is trained with its blind master. The sightless person lives in the facilities at Guide Dogs, where rooms, dining rooms, etc., make possible a residential situation while the new dog and master adjust and learn to work and go about together. The living costs while at Guide Dogs, and the dog, are without charge to the accepted sightless candidates.

In some cases outcrosses have been shared in this country and in England. Labrador Retrievers, German Shepherds, and Golden Retrievers make up the majority of dogs used in the San Rafael school. Goldens are used in several other schools as well.

Guide Dog owners vary in occupation. For example, one guide dog belongs to a student, who writes that her Golden Retriever made it possible for her to continue her education at the University of California Extension Division and at San Francisco State College, where she will get her degree.

261

At both colleges Belle and her owner have been complimented on Belle's classroom manners. But at "State" Belle made her presence known twice. The first time was during a discussion of cadavers. The class was groaning and squealing, and then Belle, the little joker, sat up and put her cold, wet nose against the back of the girl sitting just in front. The second time was when the professor as he himself said later, was practically insulting the whole animal kingdom—and Belle got to her feet and shook disdainfully at him. Belle's help made possible the training to bring out this student's natural ability. And now Belle makes it possible for her to travel from one part of San Francisco to another, continuing a useful life and supporting herself and her young daughter.

Another Golden Retriever with some famous field trial grandparents, has the distinction of having what is believed to be the oldest mistress to obtain a guide dog. At the age of 77, she needed a fourth Guide Dog, and with Norva's guidance, she is able to go about the San Francisco Bay area continuing her work as a designer.

Other stories could be told of success with Golden Retriever guide dogs: for a Korean veteran in Portland; another in Denver; a young Hungarian refugee in Portland; and yet another for a young family man, who has been able to continue a successful law practice.

The following article, "Teaming Up—Dog Day," was written by Jennifer Bassing, who is employed at Guide Dogs for the Blind. The article tells about the all-important day on which the student receives the new dog. Permission has been given by Miss Bassing as well as by the Dog Writers' Association of America for the use of this material which appeared in the July, 1983 *DWAA Newsletter*.

> There is a day in every class cycle at Guide Dogs for the Blind, Inc., that goes by a special name. It is called *Dog Day* and, as you may have guessed, that is the day on which the blind student receives his or her Guide Dog. . .
>
> For the first couple of days of class the instructors have assumed the role of "dog" in order to teach the students basic Guide Dog handling and commands. . .
>
> The evaluations that precede the final matchmaking are thorough. Every part of the blind person's life is taken into account by the Guide Dog staff who ultimately decide which students get the dog.
>
> Does the person travel by bus frequently? Are there children in the blind person's family? Other pets? What about work situations? Guide Dogs have been teamed up with people in just about every field from attorneys to musicians. . . For example, a fast-moving Guide Dog might not be suitable for a senior citizen who walks at a leisurely pace; whereas an active college student will need a dog that is ready to go off to class on a moment's notice.
>
> The instructors who have trained the string of Guide Dogs about to enter class know the dogs inside and out. They also make it a point to get to know the human half of the proposed team before the final match is made . . . it is a decision reached with complete confidence that the right dog is being paired with the right person.

On the afternoon of Dog Day, right after lunch, the students wait in their rooms to be escorted to the instructor's quarters. One at a time they walk down the dormitory hallway. On the return walk to their rooms they will each have a new companion . . . . a Guide Dog.

The rest of that afternoon is spent in laying the foundation for a long and happy working relationship. The students are advised to talk to their dogs, play with them, get the feel of them. . .

The next day it's back to work, this time with a real four-footed guide in lead. From early in the morning until late afternoon the students and their dogs work six days a week practicing and refining all the elements of their teamwork . . . these teams are called units.

The units begin with workouts in quiet suburban neighborhoods, advancing to the active downtown section of San Rafael, California. . . Among the workouts scheduled is one to San Francisco's winding Chinatown neighborhood where obstacles and distractions abound—a true test of the unit's skill.

Two instructors and a class supervisor are with the students during the workouts. As the 28 days of the training course tick away so does the need for reminders from the instructors to correct or praise a dog.

The last few days of class include "freelancing" periods when the students have the opportunity to shop and walk at will in areas of San Rafael. By the end of the course that earlier anticipation at meeting their new Guide Dogs has turned into eager enthusiasm to return home to enjoy the additional mobility the dog provides.

On graduation day . . . the puppy raisers have been invited to officially present the Guide Dogs to their new masters and mistresses. Instructors and staff are present to share this special time with the students. Friends and families gather . . . for a ceremony that is informal in nature but rarely leaves anyone with a dry eye.

The next day a new class arrives and the Guide Dog story begins all over again. Dogs doing what they do best: befriending and helping people and making all of our lives a little better for it.

Goldens can do more than retrieve ducks! This remarkable trio of Golden sled dogs is owned by James and Deborah Totten and consists of Am. Can. Ch. Jabula Thembalisha, Am. Can. CD; Am. Can. Ch. Sun Dance's Tiger Lily, Am. Can. CDX, OD and Am. Can. Ch. Jolly Jack Frost O' Wyndspelle, Am. Can. CD.

# 15

# Pleasure and
# Legends

THE PLEASURE OF HAVING A GOLDEN has many facets. Jeanne Parkes, who had the Squawkie Hill Kennels in New York in the late nineteen-forties, liked the feel and stroking of Golden fur, and the wonderful temperament of so many of the Squawkie Hill Goldens she bred She used to send her friends and puppy purchasers a small news sheet, *Squawkie Hill Golden Friend.* This little paper contained the appreciative comments of those who had and were enjoying the "Golden friend(s)" which had come from Squawkie Hill. Few of these sheets are now in existence, yet they would give an interesting bit of history for many, as well as some of the stories of the inventiveness of the Goldens and maybe some of the inventiveness of the owners of that time. When Mrs. Parkes developed a terminal illness, the news sheets were discontinued. The Squawkie Hill Goldens were many things to many people, as are the Goldens of today. But Goldens are liked for their companionship, gay ways on walks, or as hunting companions. At home they are ever-nice to have around. They are gay and "full of beans" outside and ladies and gentlemen inside—whether in the home, hotels, or when travelling.

While many of the Golden legends are interesting to read and re-read, the story of Torch, which has been added to this edition, is a lesson in survival. It should also be a warning to trappers, who should pick up their traps at the end of the trapping season and account for each of them in an accurate inventory. This same accident could have happened to a child, who probably would not have survived. Torch's fur coat helped.

## Torch

On a March day in their Midwestern home, Torch and two kennel mates, unable to resist a romp in the snow, "escaped" from their runs. The two older dogs returned later that same day but Torch did not. After several weeks of searching, Torch's owners gave up hope of ever finding her.

Nearly a month after her disappearance Torch was discovered in the woods by a young girl. Encompassed by a circle of bare earth, Torch was caught by a front foot in an animal trap. She had eaten all the snow and every leaf and twig she could reach during the weeks of her gruesome ordeal. At first her rescuers were fearful that the emaciated bitch would be dangerous to approach. But upon being released, her tail wagging, Torch affectionately expressed her appreciation to the girl and her parents.

Due to the cold weather there was no gangrene, but the bones and tendons were irreparable. Less than a year old when her promising show career was cancelled by a negligent trapper, Torch's front leg was amputated at the shoulder.

Altered in body, not in spirit, Torch went on to be the first three-legged Golden to earn a GRCA working certificate. She became a GRCA Outstanding Dam by producing several bench champions, one obedience trial champion son, and two FC-AFC great-grandchildren. Strong will, resourcefulness and love of life have been reproduced by this survivor. *Story courtesy of Joan Pollack*

## Jumbeau

Mr. W.R.W. had a Golden called Jumbeau, for he was a big fellow and weighed nearly ninety pounds. The Golden was at home hunting in the Ruby Marshes of Nevada or breaking ice at 20° below zero in the icy lakes when duck hunting near his home in Montana; he guarded the briefcase and travel bag of his owner on busy Grant Avenue in San Francisco when his owner left him stationed outside the store, while W.R.W. went in to shop. No one ever knew whether the travel bag contained only a change of clothing or ore samples from the gold mines of his owner. But Jumbeau was ever a companion and friend. He could be depended upon to stay where placed among the many shoppers passing in and out of the busy store. There were many admirers of this handsome Golden with the noble face, and it was his dignity that gained the respect of the passers-by. (See W.R.W.'s own story later in the chapter.)

## Tangerine and Other Favorites

For others, the beauty or the companionship are the important things. Personality and trainability are the things that are important traits for the personal dog, for these mean adaptability as well. These are also traits that

266

are valuable for competition in various activities. The following stories, now legends, are based on facts and actually did happen, more or less, as they are set down. Perhaps the imagination of the owners or those wishing to please have colored their accounts to some degree; perhaps also the friends of the owners, wishing to please, have endowed Goldens with achievements they have known or imagined. Only recently, I was showing young Tangerine to friends. As I bent down to move the block holding the gate, Tangerine was lifting, from the top, the ring of the ring-latch with her nose. This was an imitation of what I had done many times, so she knew this meant petting and freedom for her in the orchard playground. She knew how to open other gates—just raise with her nose a 2″ x 4″ six-foot bar and use her front paw to push. She loved the orchard best just after a heavy watering of the trees, but I preferred clean feet in the house. There are stories, however, of Goldens who have learned to use the door mat before entering the house. Or, did they just walk across a rug strategically placed?

Though Tangerine (Tangie) is a rough-neck tomboy in the orchard and an excellent water and field dog, she is a lady-like traveller, endearing herself to other riders. She retains her place without fuss or comment, no licking of the necks or collar-nibbling of those in the front seats. She is as well-behaved in motels and hotels as a much-indulged child visiting grandparents just before birthday or Christmas gifts are asked for. All of these things make for a great fun dog and happy companion. Tangie numbers among her ancestors Flare, and Am. Can. Ch. Des Lacs Lassie, CD, a Best-in-Show winner, and an outstanding hunting retriever. But it is her personality that made her the choice from a litter of seven and which, in combination with her conformation, accounts for her becoming a champion of record. Days for hunting need no longer be put aside for her show activities.

Shauna names among her direct ancestors Ch. Prince Royal of Los Altos, yet the things her family love best about her are her clever ways, happy days on camping trips, in the yard and at play with the son and daughter of the house, as well as her trips with the family in their sail boat. The boat sleeps six, and Shauna is one of these. She does need some special equipment, so her owner and skipper built a small gangplank which lets down on the shore. When Shauna indicates her need for a run, the boat is sailed in near shore and down goes the special gangplank. After a short run, back up the gangplank Shauna comes, the plank is raised, and off go all the sailors. Sometimes Shauna takes a swim with her four-member family and, although she loves all of them, she seems to love one best—her master and trainer.

Another favorite is the story of our Golden hostess, Candy, who minded the house when we were gone and was our beloved pet, hunter, beautiful swimmer, and puppy teacher. A young man came to the door. Candy, who had come to the door and moved aside a curtain, was asked (so it was told) if Dr. Fischer was home. She left the entrance door, returned, moved the curtain aside and shook her head from side-to-side. Neither my husband nor I were there, but the story was told by a young freshman liking Goldens, or seeking favor.

The legends that follow might be added to by others. These have come to me.

### Kip

My name is Kip and I am a Golden Retriever. I love the children of my owner and master and, most of all, I enjoy the opening of duck season at Tule Lake, California. This is where I had my first opportunity to show what I could do and also to make up, in a way, for the loss of my half-brother, Beau Jack.

Beau Jack was the first Golden Retriever that my owner had ever had. He made a place for all Goldens in the home of my master, a rancher, a gentleman, and a hunter. Beau Jack was ready for the Derby Field Trial Stake when he was eight months old because of his natural ability and the interest and time which my owner had devoted to him. Just before a fun trial was to be held on our place, preceding a licensed trial nearby, Beau was killed in an accident through no fault of my boss.

A few months later, I arrived to take Beau's place and also to make a place for myself. My owner's small son loved me and, at first, called me Beau, but soon he loved me for myself and he and the baby soon called me Kip and Kipper. I went hunting in the fields with my boss and he seemed to like me too, but ever in his mind was my talented half-brother. I kept on trying, knowing that some day I would have a chance to show what I could do; after all, it was because of Beau that I had such a nice home.

At last my chance came when I was 10 months old. The opening of duck season at Tule Lake has always been a special event for my boss. Each year he spends the first week of duck season there. It is his real vacation. We drove through the night to be there at the opening hour. This I enjoyed, as I have always liked riding in the car.

Finally the time for shooting began. At first I thought that I should retrieve for everyone, as I had always done all the retrieving in practice at the ranch. But my boss explained, "No! No!—just for me and my group." The first day was wonderful and I never had had so many ducks to retrieve. Some were small and some were large, and my boss seemed to like best the ones he called greenheads or mallards. These were bigger than the ones he called teal. That day, each of the four men got their limit and I was lucky enough to find each bird and return it to them, even though some birds fell in cattails and rough grass in water which required both wading in the mud and swimming among the reeds.

The next day was the same, and my boss said I was surely learning fast, and again they got their limit.

On the third day, I felt pretty good, for so far no bird had been lost; however, I had had more work, as another man joined my boss, making five hunters for me.

268

Doing what the Golden was bred for—Kip bringing in a duck.

These four dogs owned by Mrs. Patricia G. Corey with whom they are pictured, constituted the first team of Golden Retrievers ever to win Best Team in Show at an American dog show. They are (l. to r.) Ch. Fancy, Ch. Candy, Ch. Tabby of Goldendoor and Ch. Lorelei's Sam.

Late in the afternoon, I went out for a long fall on water and brought in a crippled mallard, as I had been taught to "take it, hold, carry and deliver." When I was just back on land and well on my way in, what should happen but another shot when I was only about 50 yards from my boss, and down in front of me dropped a huge bird that looked about like a pillow on the playroom sofa. It smelled different, and this one began to hobble off. What should I do? I could not let go of my quacking greenhead, but this was surely something my boss wanted or he would not have dropped it.

I circled around the big bird, keeping my hold on the winged mallard, which was quacking all the time, but I knew I was holding him gently, as I had been taught and as I knew from instinct to do. I circled twice and then knew what to do—just sit on him and hold him until my boss arrived. Were he and his friends pleased when they saw me use my head, holding carefully the crippled duck in my mouth and sitting on the honker (my boss called it that) just enough to keep him from travelling away.

The words, "Kipper, you are my dog," told me that both Beau Jack and I each had our own place in my master's heart.

Later on, he called the breeder and said that there had been 157 ducks and one honker retrieved by me during that week.

Since then, I have made two other trips and am now looking forward to my fourth season and will look forward to more. I have been in some shows and have two majors. I hope some day to have the time for shows to finish my championship, as have both my mother and father.

I have had many interesting experiences, but the duck and goose story is my master's favorite. Mine, too!

## Rocket

Rocky had pretty good manners as a puppy, but now and then he could not resist the tumbling waters of the spring creeks as he took long walks with his master. One day, he saw an especially inviting pool, so in he dove. When he came up, he had a rainbow trout in his mouth, which he presented alive and unharmed to his master.

Rocky looked much abused when his master tossed the trout back into the creek and said, "No, Rocky, two more days 'til the season opens."

## Rochanne

Rochanne was the happy companion of an only child who had waited six months for her in order to get just the Golden Retriever she wanted. The girl, now a light-opera starlet, continues to enjoy her 9-year-old Golden and remembers with pleasure one of the ways in which Rochanne helped her.

As girls do, at one time she borrowed a sweater against her mother's wishes. Rochanne also disapproved of the sweater, and showed her displeasure in a way that made the sweater unreturnable.

A short time later, Rochanne took a walk with her mistress. In a vacant lot, Rochanne suddenly stopped, dug into the leaves, and uncovered a ten-dollar bill which she delivered to the girl. The sweater was replaced, thanks to Rochanne.

## Ch. Prince Copper

Prince Copper was a young fellow on the bench at a big two-day city show. Everyone loved to pat him, and he enjoyed all the attention. One of his new friends dropped her watch without realizing it, but Prince knew just what to do. Over the watch went his paw, and there it stayed whenever new people came up to pat him.

In time, his owner came back to him, and Prince willingly allowed the watch to be taken. Via the loud speaker, the owner had a chance to thank Prince for its return. Truly, Prince was a Golden *watch* Retriever.

## Coquette

Coquette, or Coki, to her junior mistresses, went visiting with her family over a bleak New Year holiday. While the senior members were enjoying a pre-dinner get-together, the youngsters went to play on the sandy beach. They did not take Coki along. Soon it began to grow dark and the children were nowhere to be found. Judy and Cindy, only four and five years old, were just a little young for a stroll down the beach in the early darkness with the tide coming in. Mr. G., Judy and Cindy's father, had heard of children lost in the hills above his home and had trained Coki to track or go for his children in the neighborhood when they should come home from play. The tracking training became important now. His first action was to call Coki and, at this time, put on her tracking harness and say, "Find Judy! Find Cindy!" Down the darkening beach they went, first down low on the sand toward the incoming waves, then farther up toward the rocks as children go when attracted by different things. Coki led her master farther and farther down the beach, quartering as she went. She passed the first house, then back again, then past the second and on down the beach. Finally, about two miles down the beach, there was a fourth house lighted. Coki turned up the walk, up the steps, and onto the pier to the front door. Coki's owner rang the bell and was greeted with, "Did you come for two little girls? I was just going to phone others in the cove to see who might have guests."

Yes, Coki was before and then a most loved Golden lady.

## Jumbeau

It gets pretty cold in Marysville, Montana, where Jumbeau has been W.R.W.'s happy hunting companion for a long time. Bill has this to say about his Golden:

"The only reason I keep a top Golden is to have a hunting dog. I would not take a present of the best bench-show Golden in the country if he were not a top hunting dog.

"To me, a Golden has to have the guts to get ducks out of the swift-running Montana rivers in December when they are half frozen over. I have one that I will put against any National Field Trial winner, when it comes to breaking 200 yards of ice to reach a duck. His name is Jumbeau. He is a top pheasant dog. He minds at home and in the hunting field, and takes direction perfectly. I do not run him in field trials, although he was one of the coming Derby dogs when I bought him. I want a big, strong dog to get ducks in hard going. He will not get any more water in the car or on you than a smaller, weaker dog, and you will not have to leave ducks in the marsh because your dog cannot fight the heavy salt grass. The duck season is short enough without being spoiled by a beautiful dog that cannot bring in the game because his makeup and lipstick are not the right shade. Now, Jumbeau is bench-show caliber, as he is a very beautiful and perfectly formed dog, but he weighs 90 pounds—all muscle. If I want a lap dog, there are other breeds I would choose instead of trying to make a good hunter into a lap dog.

"My dog hunts in Ruby Marshes in Nevada, in the Dakotas, in Montana, and across the line in Canada. He gets up against all kinds of black Labs and other dogs. I have yet to be ashamed of him. Just two years ago, several ducks were dropped 200 yards from shore in a frozen pond before I arrived. Two black Labs, both Field Trial Champions, refused to break the ice out that far. The boys asked me to send Jumbeau. It took him 15 minutes per duck, standing on his back legs, swimming and breaking ice, and he got all five ducks, breaking a separate path each time. The temperature was 5° below zero. I say, 'Breed them with guts and power and hunting nose.' Who wants a lap dog the size of a Golden?"

Jumbeau not only had prowess as a hunter, but could be a city gentleman as well. He walked down the streets of San Francisco and Seattle, heeling closely at his owner's side. On one occasion, he waited outside a large store on Grant Avenue in San Francisco while his owner shopped. People walked around Jumbeau, giving him a pat, but he never moved as he cared for his master's travel bag.

## Flare (Ch. Des Lacs Lassie II)

Flare lies more quietly than in the past. She likes to be invited to her meals. We both know that she will miss the hunting season this fall. She no longer is kenneled outside, but she has her own clean white rug beside my bed. Her beautiful face is now silver gray, though her ears are the bright gold of the days when she won in the shows and ran in the field. We both recall an exciting wet weekend with lots of game which she retrieved, and the following week, with a bath between, when she brought down the house at a fashion show at a hotel on Union Square. All eyes turned to see

Madame Flare come down the ramp with her head held high, carrying a rhinestone purse, white gloves, and wearing a double rhinestone necklace—one of which was her championship collar. Flare, with her great dignity and poise, provided the proper spoofing for the paid guests who could afford, and those who could not afford, the luxury clothes which had preceded her.

Her puppies have starred on the bench, in the field, and as personal dogs. Her fourth litter of eight puppies became the basis of breeding stock of Goldens for Guide Dogs for the Blind.

She still places her feet with the grace of the past, but now she climbs into the low-set car, instead of jumping quickly to the high seat of the cars we used to have.

We both know that time is short for her, and no other will quite replace her. Yes, the almost sixteen years have been wonderful years for me, and I believe, for her as well.

Can. Ch. Flarewin Tangerine's Brave, WC, CD (Am. Mex. Ch. Combo Gold Rush ex Ch. Flarewin Ceilidh's Tangerine), owned by Mr. and Mrs. Dennis Reid and bred by Gertrude Fischer.

This beautiful study, Tommy and Sunshine, owned by Bill O'Malley, is an award-winning photo and expresses, better than any words, the bond of understanding between children and young puppies.

# 16

# Children and Goldens

---

SELECTING a puppy or a dog for children is an important event in the life of any family. It is something which should be talked over, discussed, and a decision made as to whether the dog will fit into the family and be enjoyed by the boy and/or girl in the family. Some children need an animal as a special friend, and a few children have little interest in animals and perhaps should not have one; but for the child who really enjoys them, there is no substitute. For this child the Golden may be that special friend and confidante—a confidante who never gives him away or repeats a story to come back in another version. Children may need to be taught puppies are not an inanimate toy and need attention and affection and that safety precautions must be taken to protect their new puppy and the dog throughout its life. That care and attention will be returned in affection and companionship by the animal. Children of eight or 10 years may attend a children's training class. There are many of these in relation to 4H Clubs or various civic and recreational groups which plan various activities for children.

The dog gives companionship for the child who is home alone or adds a special type of camaraderie in sports and hobbies, or on vacation. The Golden for a child should be an alert, active dog, suited to the varying moods of the child, active enough to follow him in play, and a dog willing to be on his own in its family yard or run when the child must be in school. Many interesting things develop in the conversation between parent and child regarding the dog. Information regarding feeding, care and training can be the vehicle for confidences and general contacts between parent and

Spring Oaks Tucker (Ch. Holman's Mister Charlie, WC, ex Hoppe No. 9), owned by Steve Baker, 13, and bred by Jackie Armstrong, delivering a chukar to his owner. The youthful hunter likes to combine riding and hunting, so Tucker has been trained to deliver downed birds to the hunter on horseback.

child and other adults, as well as giving the child something to discuss with other children.

The choice as to whether to get a male or female puppy is always an important question. If it is a young boy who will train the dog for hunting, there are some advantages to the male, as the male would never have to remain at home during the short pheasant season because he cannot be with other dogs; but a female is customarily a little smaller and may fit better into the car. Another point, if a female is the choice, are there young children who might open the door and let her out during her heat period when you would not want mongrel puppies or any puppies at all. Will there be sufficient money to kennel her during this period to keep her safe?

If puppies are something that you would like, why not make the most of it by including some interesting genetics, a research and consideration of the various mates for her, and a plan for enjoying the puppies and having the best possible litter that can be planned. To say "just puppies" and breed to the most convenient male is to eliminate much of the responsibility and educational advantage that can be gained from a complete thinking-through of the situation which includes the care of the bitch before, the actual mating, the care of the bitch during pregnancy, the placing of the puppies, whether for sale or as gifts, and the selection of the puppy which the family will wish to keep. All this will make for more interest and make some of the work of caring for the litter less tedious. There may be, of course, problems in supplementary feedings, the way of presenting the puppies for sale, immunizations, registering the puppies, etc.

There would also be the follow-up for a short time after the puppies are delivered. Many friends may be made, but it is important to see that there are no enemies made from puppy placement. To think only of the mechanics of birth is to short-change the values and, to some extent, downgrade the companionship and responsibility toward the animal which becomes the chum, the childrens' friend, and the beloved pet.

If breeding is a problem in the area where the family lives, then a dog, not a bitch, should be the choice.

As a pet, the dog will enhance the children's games and hobbies and many of the children's trips. For example, two girls found their Golden became a very photogenic model for their new camera. He also learned to sit in a new boat as a water skier followed behind. Ch. Riv-Kits Mr. Mingo was a patient companion of his young mistress, Lisa, and always kept her a safe distance from the water's edge.

Jennifer enjoyed her 4H Club work and learned to handle her own Golden Retriever in the Junior Handling class. She was able to compete for first place ribbons handling her Golden in the show ring with professional handlers. She had several ideas as to what constituted the right costume for the show ring. She wanted her hair out of her eyes so that she would not miss a signal from the judge. She preferred a pleated skirt or culottes so that it would not interfere with her action when gaiting or posing the dog. There

Sally Fletcher, 15-year-old junior handler, with Am. Can. Ch. Culynwood's Spirit of America, CDX, WCX, Can. CD), owned and bred by Lynn Fletcher. Sally took this dog to BOS at Golden Gate over an entry of 116.

MacLean's Dream Come True, UDTX, WCX, Mex. UDT, Can. CD, accompanies her teacher owner, Linda Heizman to school. Linda writes: "True is amazingly gentle with the shy kids or those that are afraid, yet eager to play with the active ones. Even on the playground, she is always fair, being sure that all the kids have a chance to throw the ball for her."

The Golden Retriever can suit the needs of any age hunter. Ch. Jewelite's Mr. Swagger with a young friend. This was Donovan Fischer's favorite dog.

were other things that she thought of herself which gave her a chance to develop, in a way, a little different from her sister. She learned to be at ease with the public and before others, and this gave her poise in speaking to people of different ages. Likewise, Doreen entered successfully both breed and obedience competition.

Inca Gold (Rusty) enjoyed the ocean beaches on San Juan below Lima, Peru. He was the first Golden in the area and he became a beloved dog in the company town and was the beloved pet of the neighborhood children. A non-doggy neighbor became his slave when Rusty prevented the neighbor's year-old baby from crawling off a deck with a 50-foot drop. Rusty just held on to the dress until the owners came out. He had heard "No! No!" near the edge of the deck, and applied this to the baby. So Rusty became to them The Inca of San Juan and Lima, a suitable title for his Peruvian home. He was a long way from his birthplace, Arcata, California, where he had been one of Mr. Jack Martin's puppies whose dam was Ch. Pele of Flarewin and his sire, Dual Ch. Craigmar's Dustrack.

"Playmates—Jenny and Hanalei"
Jennifer Gamble and her puppy, Flarewin Hanalei, bred by the author. Jenny has assumed most of Hana's training as well as the major responsibility for her general care. While she is the pet of the entire family, she is Jenny's closest confidante.

Mean Joe Green of Rocky-Vue (FC-AFC Bonnie Brooks Red ex Holway Joyful), owned by William Wandelear and bred by Carma Futhey. He is shown with his owner-handler after scoring a double—winning both an Amateur and an Open All-Age Stake at the same trial. Winning a double is rare and looked upon as a great achievement. *Snyder*

Topbrass Ace In The Hole (Topbrass Cotton ex Woodridge's Hannah), owned, bred and handled by Jacquelyn Mertens. At the GRCA Specialty in October 1983 this pair won the Ralph Boalt-Stilrovin Memorial Trophy. *Snyder*

## Appendix A—Important Information to
## Golden Retriever Owners

### The Golden Retriever Club of America

The Golden Retriever Club of America Inc., (GRCA) was formed for the purpose of furthering the breed. The Club has an annual national Specialty show each autumn. At this show it conducts conformation judging; a field trial in which derby, qualifying, amateur and open stakes are run; and obedience trials which include Novice, Open and Utility classes and Tracking.

GRCA is the only breed club to hold, year after year, a two- or three-way event licensed by the American Kennel Club. In addition, the Club sponsors an AKC-licensed spring all-breed field trial which is held in various areas in the United States.

To reach the current GRCA secretary, write to the American Kennel Club, Inc., 51 Madison Avenue, New York, NY 10010, or to the Editor of the Golden Retriever column in *Pure-Bred Dogs,* at the same address.

The Golden Retriever Club of America publishes a newsletter for its members, *Golden Retriever News,* which carries articles and news items of interest to the owners of Golden Retrievers, be they breeders, exhibitors, field trial or obedience enthusiasts, or just members of the fancy for the enjoyment of the Golden Retriever as a family companion.

### Orthopedic Foundations for Animals, Inc.

This nonprofit organization, commonly known as OFA, is set up to collect and disseminate information concerning orthopedic diseases of animals, to establish control programs, to finance research, and to receive funds and make grants to carry out these objectives.

OFA's basis of its Dysplasia Control Registry is the original plan conceived and carried out for approximately two years by the Golden Retriever Club of America, Inc.

At the start of work in OFA, there were nine participating breed clubs. Three years later, there were 38, with more becoming interested. Today, almost every breed is represented.

In early 1971, there were over 11,000 X-rays of all breeds in the Dysplasia Control offices. X-rays in the early spring of that year were coming in at the rate of over 500 per month; by the early 1980's, the rate had tripled.

Headquarters of the OFA Dysplasia Control Registry are at the University of Missouri, 817 Virginia Avenue, Columbia, Missouri 65201. OFA welcomes all inquiries and questions. You may write for free information. Also available is a kit on how to position, take X-rays, identify and ship X-rays by local veterinarians. A fee of $10 is charged for this referral service.

## American Kennel Club Titles

*Conformation*

| | |
|---|---|
| Champion | Ch. |
| Dual Champion (conformation and field championships) | Dual Ch. |

*Obedience Titles*

| | |
|---|---|
| Companion Dog | CD |
| Companion Dog Excellent | CDX |
| Utility Dog | UD |
| Tracking Dog | TD |
| Tracking Dog Excellent | TDX |
| Utility Dog Tracker | UDT |
| Utility Dog Tracker Excellent | UDTX |
| Obedience Trial Champion | O.T. Ch. |

*Field Titles*

| | |
|---|---|
| Field Trial Champion | FC or FTC |
| Amateur Field Trial Champion | AFC |

Championship titles such as Ch., O.T. Ch., FC, AFC precede the name of the dog. Obedience titles follow the name of the dog.

## Golden Retriever Club of America Awards

| | |
|---|---|
| Working Certificate | WC |
| Working Certificate Excellent | WCX |

(These refer to tests in the field conducted under GRCA regulations.)

| | |
|---|---|
| Outstanding Sire | OS |

(An OS has sired five or more champion or utility offspring or two FCs or one FC and one conformation champion.)

| | |
|---|---|
| Outstanding Dam | OD |

(An OD has produced three or more champion or utility offspring or two FCs or one FC and one conformation champion.)

Hall of Fame

(Applies to outstanding show, field, or obedience competitors.)

*Has passed WC or WCX test.

**Has placed in a licensed field trial.

***Is a qualified Open All-Age dog. This, of course, means placements in licensed field trials.

Such titles as Best of Breed (BB), Winners Dog (WD) or Winners Bitch (WB) or class wins are honors that belong only to a particular dog at a particular show. Other titles become a part of the dog's name.

Titles achieved in other countries by American dogs are usually indicated by a letter or abbreviation for that country such as Can. for Canadian and Mex. for Mexican. Few mainland United States dogs compete in the Hawaiian Islands or the British Isles because of the long quarantine period.

## Appendix B—Feeding Suggestions for Golden Retrievers

A dog should have a well-balanced diet, consisting of good protein, such as milk, cottage cheese, meat, or cooked eggs, some cereal, such as a good commercial dry food, cooked brown rice or other useful carbohydrate. It is desirable to moisten the cereal with vegetable water, for example, from cooked spinach, tomatoes or peas.

In general, the diet should be simple, but it should include more than just dry dog food. Some dogs will indicate when they have had enough and will not overeat. Others will *not* do so. It is preferable to keep your dog in *good weight* but not *overweight,* which affects its health in many ways. Likewise, a dog that is too thin is likely to be nervous, and will not attain its best potential.

### EIGHT-WEEKS-OLD PUPPY

*Morning Feeding:* semi-cooked ground chuck or ground round in water with dry food plus some cottage cheese or milk

*Mid-day Feeding:* cottage cheese, dry food, milk and a hard-cooked egg

*Evening Feeding:* same as morning feeding

*Snacks:* Snacks are not necessary for a dog. A snack may be used, however, in training when teaching the dog its name, for example, or when it is learning to come on recall, to sit, etc. A snack can be a reward for good behavior. The best snacks are dry or cooked pieces of liver, which should be as small as the tip of your finger. You may use a piece of kibble in lieu of the liver, or a small dog biscuit. If it has been necessary to stretch the feeding over a long period of time, the dog may have a small feeding with less liquid at bedtime. This helps to keep the puppy dry.

*Rewards:* Some form of cooked liver is desirable from time to time. Small bits of liver are good to use as rewards in training, whether early puppy training or new routines in the later life of the dog.

### General Notes on Nutrients

Puppies may be given toasted brown bread in preference to white bread. They should not have raw egg white, as it is colloidal in dogs and its jelly-like consistency absorbs the minerals and vitamins, and sweeps them through the dog's relatively short large intestine. The *hard-cooked* white is acceptable. The whole hard-cooked egg may be given the dog, as it is a good source of protein and Vitamin A.

There are many opinions on vitamins and additives for dogs' diets. An over-supply of either calcium or vitamins is not desirable. Cottage cheese will provide the necessary calcium. This, in combination with meat, produces calcium phosphate, which makes up teeth and bones. An excess amount of dry calcium, when excreted, takes other nutrients with it. Since Vitamins A and D are retained in the body, if given in excess, they can be toxic. In areas of colder weather, more Vitamin D is needed during winter than, for example, in the Southwestern United States.

Such human vitamins as a multiple mineral vitamin with iron are easy to give. They are in proper proportion for warm-blooded animals. Vitamin C is now thought to be necessary for the first year of the dog's life, approximately 100 mg. per day. All-purpose vitamins contain 50-60 mgs. per tablet. To them may be added a tablespoon full of orange concentrate (such as frozen orange juice) or two tablespoons of tomato juice in the feeding each day. Where oranges are plentiful and inexpensive, a quarter of a large orange or one-half of a small orange can be given to the dog as a food supplement and as a toy. Excess Vitamin C is not desirable, even though it does not accumulate, as does Vitamins A and D.

## Treats

When baking potatoes for the family, bake an extra one for the dog. Meat drippings may be added to the potato, but sour cream with chives is not essential. On that day cut down the amount of kibble a little. Such things as a baked potato or scrambled egg with toast may be of great advantage when traveling and regular dog food is unavailable. Even an ice cream cone and potato chips may be given on a long hot trip if the dog refuses other food. Small amounts of vegetables (tomatoes, peas, or other cooked vegetables) may vary the dog's diet.

## Commercial Dog Foods

There are many good commercial dog foods, but they are always made from less desirable meat mixes and some materials not suited for human use. Canned foods are expensive, as they contain a high percentage of water, but they are convenient when refrigeration is not available for fresh foods. Canned solid horsemeat or chunk horsemeat is the best of the canned meats; canned beef and chicken are also good. The horsemeat is usually leaner and may need to be supplemented with meat drippings or with oil in small amounts (1-2 tablespoons, depending on the age of the dog). ALL PORK PRODUCTS OR BEAR MEAT SHOULD BE WELL-COOKED, as these meats may cause trichinosis in dogs as well as in humans.

## Bones

Young animals may be given marrow bones as they like to chew on them. Remove some of the marrow, which contains enough fat to cause a loose stool if an over-supply is given. As soon as the bone is soiled or dirty,

Ch. Gold Rush Great Teddy Bear (Ch. Cummings' Gold Rush Charlie ex Ch. Golden Pine Glorybe's Angel), owned by R. Ann Johnson and Diane J. Smith, was BB at the 1978 GRCA Specialty and is shown here with Larry Johnson. *William P. Gilbert*

Ch. Camelot's Noble Fella, CDX (Ch. Wochica's Okeechobee Jake ex Hammerlock's Amber Topaz, CDX, Can. CD), owned by Margaret Zonghetti and Kay Bickford and bred by Patricia Herschman. Shown with handler Robert Stebbins, this dog is a multiple BIS and Specialty winner. *John Ashbey*

throw it away. Do not allow the dog to keep the bone for several days, because it will spoil. We assume that dogs do not read well at this age, and are unfamiliar with the fact that old bones can attract bacteria and become rancid.

### Three to Six Months

At three months the puppy will tend to refuse the noon meal. When this happens, divide the three meals into two feedings—morning and evening. By age six months, The Golden Retriever should be on two meals a day. Some owners use a two-meal feeding schedule throughout their dog's life. Continue to use meat, cottage cheese, dry dog food, at least three hard-cooked eggs per week and vitamin supplements.

Because the dog's rapid growth rate slows down as the dog matures, use proportions that keep it in good weight, but not overweight. This is particularly important in males, as an overweight male can sometimes become infertile or difficult to breed.

### Six Months to One Year

The dog's growth rate continues to slow down, but this development varies in individual dogs. The growing dog still requires quality protein and vitamins, as well as the nutritionally balanced dry food. There are special dry foods for the first year of the puppy's life. These should be supplemented with some fresh foods as indicated above. At the end of the first year, the special puppy foods can be discontinued, and a regular, balanced dry dog food can take their place. Do not, however, neglect the use of some fresh foods.

### Year-Old Dog

Whatever the number of feedings, the food should be sufficient in quantity and quality to maintain a dog in good physical condition, neither too fat nor too thin. Some people prefer morning feedings: this is a better time for them to feed the dog rather than in the evening, because th owner's morning schedule is more likely to be regular than the unpredictable evening hours. If the dog is fed *only* in the evening, he may develop the habit of barking if the evening meal is delayed too long.

### Active Work or Training

A dog which does hard work, such as training or several hours of field work, requires more meat and quality protein than a less active animal does. In cold weather, the dog wil require more food for providing additional body heat.

Two moderate meals per day, in the morning and in the evening, are usually better than one large meal when the dog is in a training schedule, because the dog should not receive too heavy a meal just before or just after hard work. Nor should he receive a large amount of water immediately before or after working. A few short drinks are preferable to a large amount of water.

Dogs which have been hunting for three or four hours, however, need a snack of four ounces of quality protein, and a 20-30 minute rest before continuing their hunting activity.

Two top professional trainers believe the dogs stay in much better physical condition during their training if they are fed twice rather than once a day.

*Note:* John Schulte, D.V.M., has reviewed these feeding instructions and considers them excellent. Dr. Schulte has made special studies of nutrition in animals, particularly dogs and horses.

## Pregnant Bitches and Neonate Puppies

1) Normal feeding first four weeks but increase portion of protein in relation to starch. This means higher meat, cottage cheese and egg content.
2) Wheat germ daily, 1 tablespoon, either cereal or wheat germ oil (Vitamin E). This may be included in the dog's food.
3) Vitamin-mineral preparation with iron. May use 1 adult tablet of all-purpose vitamin-mineral preparation which combines all elements in proper proportion. Must include phosphorous, calcium and Vitamin D, all the B's, G and iron. You may also check with your veterinarian for special instructions.
4) Feeding should include one or more ounces of liver daily. This may be beef liver, lamb liver or cooked pork liver. Usually cooked liver is more palatable to the dog.

   Dr. Shearon Smith of U.C. Davis feels that liver "can make the difference." She advises 60 percent additional protein from the fourth week of pregnancy to term. This means cooked eggs, meat, and cottage cheese in addition to regular kibble.
5) Do not give excessive calcium unless advised to do so by your vet as the cottage cheese, milk, meat, and all vitamin-mineral preparations should take care of this. A preparation such as is given to pregnant women is often desirable. While a baby is larger than a puppy, it has nine months to develop whereas a litter of puppies has only 63 days.
6) After three or four weeks divide feeding 1/2 A.M. and 1/2 P.M.
7) Daily exercise is desirable, but no swimming after fifth week.
8) Consult your veterinarian regarding any question concerning your bitch and her pregnancy.
9) Do not worm during pregnancy except in emergencies as recommended by your veterinarian. Worming should have been done three or four weeks before the bitch came into season and rechecked

before breeding, as the bitch should be known to be clear of worms at the time of mating. However, if the bitch had round worms in early puppyhood they may encapsulate and will come out in the puppies.

10) Check temperatures during pregnancy. Often temperatures drop from normal (101) to 99 or 98, 12 to 24 hours before puppies are due, but sometimes there is no drop. Puppies are due 63 days from time of breeding but may come as early as the 56th day or as late as the 65th day.

11) Have your veterinarian check your bitch shortly after the whelping to be sure all puppies have been delivered and there is no likelihood of infection. If there is any lameness or dullness, check bitch. Again, temperature should be taken. Occasionally calcium shots are needed at this time as process of nursing sometimes causes calcium depletion. This vet check may also include taking blood samples for a nomograph to determine when puppies will need first distemper shots. Nomographs are common on the East coast, not practical on the West coast.

12) During nursing, maintain feeding three or four times daily of high protein, including meat, cottage cheese, cooked eggs and water, all-purpose vitamins and minerals, unless otherwise advised by vet. Bitch should be maintained in good health for herself and for best presentation of puppies. For large litters, supplementary feeding may be necessary, either bottle feeding or tube feeding, to supplement puppy's food or to care for ineffective nursers.

13) Mark puppies with hair clipping in various locations and weigh puppies daily to check weight gain. Five pound postage scales can be used for the first week or two, then move to kitchen or baby scales.

14) *Do not overdo supplements. Excess can be harmful.*


## Selecting a Golden Retriever Puppy

1) When you buy from a breeder, you should be able to see one or both parents of a litter. You will also be able to see the conditions under which the puppies are raised.

2) The parents of the puppy should be free from hip dysplasia as well as other joint problems. Their hips should have been X-rayed and the X-rays referred to the Orthopedic Foundation for Animals (OFA) and rated "good" or "excellent." Or the X-rays could be reviewed by a certified radiologist, not just a layman or veterinarian in normal practice. This will not guarantee perfect hips in the puppy as an adult but the puppy will be more predictably sound.

The parents of the puppy should have been checked by a canine ophthalmologist to ensure that they are free of hereditary eye diseases. The ophthalmologist will be checking for juvenile cataracts, progressive retinal atrophy and other hereditary eye diseases.

Ch. Shargleam Ferryman (Nortonwood Checkmate ex Shargleam Amethyst), owned by Barbara Dismukes.

Ch. Golden Pine's Gradene's J.D., CDX, WC, Can. CD, OS (Ch. Misty Morn's Sunset, CD, TD, WC, OS, ex Ch. Golden Pine's Punkin Pi, CD, OD), bred by Mary Luise Semans and owned by William J. Dean, shown with handler Janet Bunce.

The parents should be free from genetic bleeding diseases such as hemophilia or von Willebrand's disease. Von Willebrand's affects both males and females, and is best checked by having blood samples prepared and sent by a veterinarian to Dr. W. Jean Dodds in Albany, New York. Such testing is not available in many areas so it is not always possible to get this check done.

3) The puppy should show balanced conformation and an outgoing personality, although you could arrive just after the puppy had sacked out from hard play and not get an accurate first impression.

4) Upon looking over the litter, select one or two puppies that you like best—take the first one aside, then another and see if it will retrieve or pick up an object such as a leaf, a birdwing, a ball, a wadded-up paper towel, or a glove turned partially wrong side out so that it forms a wad. The puppy should pick up the item and carry it happily and with style. Sometimes the puppy will even return it, indicating superior, natural ability as a retriever.

The puppy should be able to follow a string in play much as a kitten would. This will give some clue as to the puppy's eye coordination. The puppy should be able to do these things at the age of six or seven weeks. Some do it younger.

5) When playing with a puppy and rolling it over, it should play back at you, not run away as if it were hurt.

6) Try a sharp whistle or handclap and see if the ears lift, as this indicates good hearing. Check response to sound. The puppy should be alert but should not panic. If it does shy away, it should return to investigate.

7) Ask yourself if you really do like the puppy and if the puppy seems to respond to you.

8) Now you may review the Standard in relation to the puppy or puppies of your choice such as breadth of head, eye and ear set, gait, etc. Puppies are not well coordinated at this age, but you can tell something about their fronts—straight front legs, hocks, gait, etc., and color. Color should be last. The preferred color is golden although dark is acceptable. Most hunters prefer the darker colors as this blends in better with cover, is easier to maintain, and most importantly, has been the characteristic color of the best hunters and field trial dogs both current and past.

For show purposes, the medium gold is best. From time to time, however, a dog of outstanding conformation and personality will win regardless of color. Then for a time, this color will be associated with that of a winner and thus become fashionable. But just as important as color are the many other considerations that make for a winner such as gait, general conformation, style, and showmanship. Proportion and balance are basic to any successful show dog.

9) In males, testicles should be descended at seven to eight weeks. In rare cases, the testicles may descend as late as 10 to 14 weeks. This is

Am. Can. Ch. Golden Glo's Valentine, OD (Ch. Misty Morn's Sunset, CD*, TD, WC, OS ex Ch. Copper Kettle's Glory Gobler, CD*), bred and owned by Don and Marilyn Sturz and shown with her handler Donald Sturz, Jr. She was BOS at the 1977 Specialty and has made a commendable record of wins. *Jim Callea*

Ch. Goldwing Blues Boy, CDX, WC (Ch. Gold Rush Great Teddy Bear ex Ch. Goldwing Rhythym-N-Blue), owned by Dennis and Fran Haney, Joyce Davis and Leslie Dove (breeder). "Josh" is a BIS and Specialty winner and is shown in the ring by Ray McGinnis. *Rich Bergman*

exceptional and there should be some price adjustment on a dog with undescended testicles, as such a dog should not be bred. A dog with one or two undescended testicles cannot be shown in conformation but could participate in obedience or field trials.

10) It is the dog itself and what it means to you that is most important. No one can guarantee a "winner" in a litter of puppies; some are just a little more predictable than others. The show ribbons fade, but the personality and trainability of the dog are what make for a happy companion that is a joy to live with.

11) A reliable and dedicated breeder will help you but, in the end, the choice must be your own.

12) Review "The Official Standard of the Golden Retriever" in Chapter 4—"The Breed Standard—An Analytical Discussion."

13) For responsibilities of the seller and buyer, see Chapter 13.

14) Have a complete veterinary health check performed by a qualified veterinarian. Information on all medication the puppy has received should be available from the seller.

15) It is assumed that both parents of the puppy were free from brucellosis at the time of breeding. However, the puppies are unlikely to be healthy or even alive if either parent had brucellosis.

Ch. Sprucewood's Chore Boy (Am. & Can. Ch. Golden Knoll's King Alphonzo ex Am. & Can. Ch. Chee-Chee of Sprucewood), owned by Mrs. Henry Barbour and bred by Mr. and Mrs. Millard C. Zwang. Chore Boy was one of a litter of nine; all became champions. *Frasie photo.*

# Selected Pedigrees

---

Sire: Giltway Strike

                                                                 Rockhaven Tuck
NFC King Midas of Woodend
Glittering Gold
Ch. Rockhaven Harold
Rockhaven Queen
Chiltington Light

**CH. DES LACS LASSIE**

Dam: Maryann of Roo Roix

                                                 Ch. Rockhaven Rory
Beavertail Bruno
Ch. Rockhaven Glory
Ch. Goldwood Pluto
Ginger of Roo Roix
Belinda of Willow Lake

---

Sire: Goldwood Toby, UD

                       Ch. Rockhaven Rory
Ch. Toby of Willow Lake
Rusty Heger
Ch. Rockhaven Rory
Goldwood Ditt
Ch. Sprite of Aldgrove

**FEATHERQUEST TRIGGER, UDT**

Dam: Banty's Pluto of Bushaway

                       Ch. Rockhaven Rory
Ch. Goldwood Pluto
Ch. Sprite of Aldgrove
Rockhaven Tuck
FC Banty of Woodend
Rockhaven Judy

---

Sire: Ch. Stilrovin Shur Shot

                                              Ch. Rockhaven Rory
Stilrovin Bullet
Patience of Yelme
Eng. & Am. Ch. Bingo of Yelme
Gilnockie Coquette
Can. Ch. Rockhaven Russet

**CH. GOLDEN KNOLL'S SHUR SHOT, CD**

Dam: Kingdale's Toast

                                              Gilnockie Beppo
Tonkahof Admiral
Ch. Tonka Belle of Woodend
Ch. Beavertail Butch
Amber Lass
Whitebridge Judy

Rory of Bentley
Ch. Michael of Moreton
Aurora
*Sire:* Ch. Speedwell Pluto
Ch. Cornelius
Speedwell Emerald
Wherstead Beau Monde
**ROCKHAVEN BEAU BRUMMEL**
Ch. Balcombe Boy
Ch. Haulstone Dan
Balcombe Bunty
*Dam:* Saffron Chipmonk
Speedwell Nimrod
Ch. Dame Daphne
Guiding Star

Ch. Heydown Gunner
Eng. Ch. Cubbington Diver
Onaway
*Sire:* Eng. Ch. Marine of Wooley
Ch. Balcombe Boy
Balcombe Pride
Balcombe Bunty
**ROCKHAVEN JUDY**
Ch. Michael of Moreton
Ch. Speedwell Pluto
Ch. Speedwell Emerald
*Dam:* Can. Ch. Rockhaven Lassie
Speedwell Barley
Am. & Can. Ch. Wilderness Tangerine
Ch. Wilderness Maud

Digger of Golden Valley
Stilrovin Terry Lee
Stilrovin Bride
*Sire:* Stilrovin Bearcat
Pirate's Sundust
Bonnie of Bear Creek
Country Lassie
**FC-AFC, CAN. FC STILROVIN TUPPEE TEE**
Ch. Lorelei's Golden R.
Ch. Lorelei's Golden Rockbottom
Lorelei's Golden Tanya
*Dam:* Pink Lady of Audlon
Masterpiece of Yeo
Masaka of Wynford
Wynholes Gaylass

Normanby Balfour
Rory of Bentley
Columbine
*Sire:* Eng. Ch. Michael of Moreton
Triumph
Aurora
Amber
**AM. & CAN. CH. SPEEDWELL PLUTO**
Binks of Kentford
Eng. Ch. Cornelius
Balvaig
*Dam:* Eng. Ch. Speedwell Emerald
Rufus of Everest
Wherstead Beau Monde
Wherstead Russet

Peter of Woodend
Beautywood's Buckshot
NFC Sheltercove Beauty
Sire: NFC Beautywood's Tamarack
Ch. Rockhaven Rory
Goldwood Sunset Jill
Whitebridge Judy
**DUAL CH. & AFC CRAIGMAR DUSTRACK**
Ottershaw Sunhaze
Yester Beam
Poppy of Merrymount
Dam: Sundust Girlie
Stubbings Golden Dandylyon
Golden Dawn of Dryden
Dorothy Dean


Michael of Woodend
Ch. Speedwell Pluto
Speedwell Emerald
Sire: Rockhaven Tuck
Haulstone Dan
Saffron Chipmonk
Dame Daphne
**NAT. FC KING MIDAS OF WOODEND**
Gilder
Stubbins Golden Goblet
Sewardstone Tess
Dam: Glittering Gold
Speedwell Andrew of Stubbings
Stubbins Golden Anchor
Stubbins Golden Lass


Michael of Woodend
Dual Ch. Stilrovin Rip's Pride
Gilnockie Coquette
Sire: Ch. Lorelei's Golden Rip
Jeff of Chateau d'Or
Greenfield Jollye
Goldenfields Mollye
**CH. & AFC LORELEI'S GOLDEN ROCKBOTTOM, UD**
Ch. Alexander
Missy's Great Michael
Twin Hill Sparkler
Dam: Lorelei's Golden Tanya
Ch. Headisland Peter
Dale
Glenisland Caroline


Ch. Speedwell Pluto
Rockhaven Tuck
Eng. Ch. Saffron Chipmonk
Sire: FC Goldwood Tuck
Eng. Ch. Kelso of Aldgrove
Ch. Sprite of Aldgrove
Rorina of Aldgrove
**FC PIRATE OF GOLDEN VALLEY**
Gilnockie Dan
Rockhaven Pluto Boy
Rockhaven Zazu
Dam: FC Golden Beauty of Roedare
Sandy of Nutwood
Lady of Roedare
Rockhaven Queen

```
                    Foxbury Peter
            Speedwell Nimrod
                    Marion of Wyatt
        Sire: Speedwell Reuben
                    Rufus of Kentford
            Speedwell Lola
                    Snettish Lady
    FC RIP
                    Eng. Ch. Cornelius
            Corney of Rivey
                    Ballingdon Lady
        Dam: Speedwell Tango
                    Michael of Moreton
            Sheena of Ricketts
                    Abbots Rachel
```

```
                                    Ch. Speedwell Pluto
                            Ch. Rockhaven Rory
                                    Ch. Rockhaven Amber
                        Sire: Ch. Toby of Willow-Loch
                                    Speedwell Boine
                            Rusty Heger
                                    Onyx of Emley
                        GOLDWOOD TOBY, UD. (1st UD)
                                    Ch. Speedwell Pluto
                            Ch. Rockhaven Rory
                                    Ch. Rockhaven Amber
                        Dam: Goldwood Ditt
                                    Ch. Kelso of Aldgrove
                            Ch. Sprite of Aldgrove
                                    Rorina of Aldgrove
```

```
                    Ch. Finderne Gold
            Ch. Cragmount's Peter
                    Goldendoor Taffy
        Sire: Ch. Sunset's Happy Duke, OS
                    Ch. Tigathoe's Music Man
            Glen Willow's Happy Talk
                    Tigathoe's Phi Beta Kappa, CD
    CH. MISTY MORN'S SUNSET, *CD, TD, OS
                    Ch. Golden Pines Ace Hi
            Ch. Cragmount's Double Eagle
                    Ch. Cragmount's Tiny Cloud
        Dam: Amber Lady of Tercor Farm
                    Ch. Golden Pine's Easy Ace
            Ch. Cragmount's Golden Wallis
                    Ch. Rozzy-Duchess
```

```
                            Duke of Little Falls
                    Golden Kit
                            Sally
                Sire: FC-AFC Brandy Snifter
                            Duke of Gun Lake
                    Rustelle of Aitkin
                            Silver of Aitkin
            POIKA OF HANDJEM
                            Ch.-AFC Lorelei's Golden Rockbottom, UD
                    Ch. Little Joe of Tigathoe***
                            Ch. Gold Button of Catawba**
                Dam: Ch. Torch of Handjem***
                            Tonkahof Kilroy
                    Princess Kilroy
                            Golden Showers
```

296

FC-AFC Brandy Snifter
Poika of Handjem
Ch. Torch of Handjem***
*Sire:* Duke of Handjem***
AFC Gunnerman's Coin of Copper
Shenandoah of Stilrovin, CD***
Stilrovin Kathy-K***
**FC-AFC RIGHT-ON DYNAMITE JOHN**
Theron
Tex of Golden Anno Nuevo
Toy of Golden Anno Nuevo
*Dam:* Autumn's Aspen Gold Kandy
Sherrydan Tag* (UK)
Brackenhollow Sheila
Less of Springbrook


Ch. Finderne Gold Cloud of Kent
Ch. Cragmount's Peter
Goldendoor Taffy
*Sire:* Ch. Sunset's Happy Duke
Tigathoe's Music Man
Glen Willow's Happy Talk
Tigathoe's Phi Beta Kappa, CD
**AM. CAN. BDA. CH. CUMMINGS' GOLD RUSH CHARLIE**
Ch. Golden Pines Aces Hi
Am. Can. Ch. Cragmount's Double Eagle
Ch. Cragmount's Tiny Cloud
*Dam:* Am. Can. Ch. Cummings Golden Princess
Am. Can. Ch. Golden Pines Easy Ace*
Cragmount's Easy Lady
Ch. Rozzy Duchess


Ch. Sunset's Happy Duke, OS
Am. Can. Bd. Ch. Cummings' Gold Rush Charlie, OS
Am. Can. Ch. Cummings Golden Princess, OD
*Sire:* Ch. Gold Rush's Great Teddy Bear, OS
Golden Pine's Tiny Tim, OS
Ch. Golden Pine Glorybe's Angel, OD
Ch. Golden Pine Glorybe, OD
**CH. GOLDWING TRUE BEAR, OS**
Ch. Sunset's Happy Duke, OS
Am. Can. Bda. Ch. Cummings Gold Rush Charlie, OS
Am. Can. Ch. Cummings' Golden Princess, OD
*Dam:* Ch. Goldwing Rhythm-N-Blue, OD
Golden Pine's Tiny Tim, OS
Ch. Golden Pine Just-A-Minute, OD
Ch. Golden Pine Glorybe, OD


Jolly Again of Ouilmette, CD***
FC-AFC Bonnie Brook's Elmer
Nancy's Golden Dawn*
*Sire:* Dual Ch., AFC Tigathoe's Funky Farquar
Major Drum***
Tigathoe's Chickasaw***
Ch. Tansy of High Farm***
**CH. ALMADEN SUNDOWNERS SEQUOIA, UD, WC, KH**
Ch. Golden Duke of Trey-C*
Ch. Ronakers Golden Orion, UD**
Ch. J's Kate
*Dam:* Sundowner's Bronze Sherry, CDX
Ch. Butte Golden Aubrey
Shandy Russet Aubray, CDX*
Stilrovin Hiyu O'Brien

Am. Can. Ch. Sundance's Rainmaker (Ch. Wochica's Okeecho-
bee Jake ex Ch. Sun Dance's Contessa), owned by Penny and
Tony D'Alessandro and bred by Lisa Shultz, is another BIS
Jake son. He was shown by Robert Stebbins. *William P. Gilbert*

Am. Can. Ch. Shawn's Golden Boomerang*, Am. Can. UDT, WCX, Can. TDX (Jascha
Golden Gargoyle ex Shawn's Golden Horizon), owned and trained by Betty Drobac
and handled by Connie Drobac. Connie handled this dog to both American and
Canadian championships at only 13 years. *Martin Booth*

# Bibliography

INFORMATION ON GOLDEN RETRIEVERS may be found in many yearbooks of the various Retriever Clubs in the United States, England, and Scotland.

*Golden Retriever Yearbook,* Golden Retriever Club of England. (1955)

*Golden Retriever Handbook,* The Golden Retriever Club of Scotland. (1958)

*Standard of the Golden Retriever,* Golden Retriever Club of America. (1982)

*Northern England Golden Retriever Yearbook.* (1955)

*Yearbooks of the Golden Retriever Club of America,* 1947, 1948, 1950, 1956, 1957, 1964, 1967, 1970, 1976, 1978, 1980.

American Kennel Club, *The Complete Dog Book*, New York, N.Y.

Gill, Joan, *Golden Retrievers,* Foreword by Elma Stonex, W. & G. Foyle, Ltd., London, England. (1962)

*Hutchinson's Dog Encyclopedia*, London, England. (1935)
Some copies in public libraries.

The Labrador Retriever Club, *Stud Book and Record of Field Trials.* (1949) Compiled by C. Mackay Sanderson with an Introduction by the Rt. Hon. Lorna, Countess Howe. A complete record of Field Trials from 1919-1938 . . . Review of 1946-47-48 Black and Yellow History . . . Field History of Golden, Flat-coat, Curly and Interbred Retrievers.

MacGaheran, J., *Bob Becker's Dog Digest*, 29 and 32.

Sawtell, Lucille, *All About Golden Retrievers*, Pelham Books, Ltd., London, England. (1980)

Sawtell, Lucille, "All About Golden Retrievers" in *Retriever International.* (Fall, 1982)

Stonex, Elma, *The Golden Retriever Handbook*, Nicholson & Watson, London, England. (1953) Mrs. Stonex is, without doubt, the authority on the breed in England since World War II. She has done wider research and writing than any other person in England today. In addition, she is an excellent judge and has bred dogs which have competed both in the field and in shows internationally. Mrs. Stonex has written articles on the origin of retrievers for *Pure-Bred Dogs*. She writes for various English dog publications.

Stonex, Elma, "New Light on Our Retrievers," in *Pure-Bred Dogs,* Vol. 76, Nos. 5, 6 and 7. (1959)

Tudor, Joan, *The Golden Retriever*, Howell Book House Inc., New York, New York. (1966)

## General Information

Charlesworth, W. N., *The Book of the Golden Retriever*, Fletcher & Sons, Ltd., Norwich, England. (1947)

Dangerfield, Stanley, and Howell, Elsworth, *The International Encyclopedia of Dogs*, Howell Book House Inc., New York, N.Y. (1971)

Davis, Henry P., *The Modern Dog Encyclopedia*, The Stackpole Co., Harrisburg, PA. (2nd Ed. 1956)

Deutsch, H. J., and McCoy, J. J., *The Dog Owner's Handbook,* Thomas Crowell Co., New York, N.Y. (1954)

Dunbar, Dr. Ian, *Why Dogs Do What They Do*, T.F.H. Publications, Inc., Hong Kong. (1979)

Fletcher, Walter R., *My Times With Dogs,* Howell Book House Inc., New York, N.Y. (1979)

Gaines Dog Research Center, *Touring With Towser*, Kankakee, IL.

Greenfield, Helen, *Your Dog in the City*, Crown Publishing Co., New York, N.Y.

*Hutchinson Dog Encyclopedia*, Vol. 2, Hutchinson & Co., Ltd., London, England. (1936)

Jones, Arthur Frederick and John Rendel, *The Treasury of Dogs*, Ridge Press Book, Golden Press, New York, N.Y. Mr. Jones is a former editor of *Pure-Bred Dogs—American Kennel Gazette*. This book, showing all breeds, has many excellent and classic pictures, with a beautiful double-page spread of Goldens. Many interesting stories.

Large, Dr. Charles H., *American Kennel Gazette* (Series of articles, starting October, 1932).

Otto, Fred Jr., *Simplified Dog Behavior*, World Publishing Co., New York, N.Y. (1952)

Parks, Mrs. D. Eugene, *Dog World* (Series of eight articles, beginning December, 1946).

Pfaffenberger, Clarence J., *The New Knowledge of Dog Behavior*, Howell Book House Inc., New York, N.Y. (1963) Mr. Pfaffenberger was Vice President of Guide Dogs for the Blind, and did research in dog behavior for them, and under Guggenheim Fellowships. The book suggests when training should take place, and discusses advanced methods used in training both family dogs and those required for more serious work such as leading the blind, hunting, or obedience.

Rehm, Theodore, *American Sporting Dogs*, D. Van Nordstrand Co., Inc., New York and Toronto. (1948)

Schlehr, Marcia, *A Study of the Golden Retriever*, 3901 Academy, Dearborn Heights, MI 48125. (Revised 1982)

Smith, Arthur Croxton, *Dogs Since 1900*, Trap and Toothill, Ltd., Leeds, London. (1950)

Whitney, Leon F. D.V.M., *The Complete Book of Pet Care*, Doubleday and Co., Inc., Garden City, N.Y.

Whitney, Leon F., D.V.M., *Your Puppy: How to Select, Raise and Train Him*, Hanover House, Garden City, N.Y. (1955) The Personal and Family Papers of Skip Page. These include the story of Diedre and the letter from Mrs. Charlesworth to Miss Clark.

## Genetics

Burns, Marca, *The Genetics of the Dog*, Commonwealth Agricultural Bureaux, Technical Publications No. 9 of Animal Breeding and

Genetics, Edinburgh, Robert Cunningham & Sons Ltd., Longbank Works, Alva, Scotland.

Hadorn, E., *Developmental Genetics & Lethal Factors*, Methuen & Co., Ltd., London; John Wiley & Sons, Inc., New York, N.Y. (1963)

Hutt, Frederick Bruce, *Genetic Resistance to Disease in Domestic Animals*, Comstock Publishing Association, Cornell University Press, Ithaca, N.Y. (1958)

Onstott, Philip, *The New Art of Breeding Better Dogs*, Howell Book House Inc., New York, N.Y. (Revised 1962)

Roberts, J. A. Fraser, *An Introduction to Medical Genetics*, Oxford University Press. (1963)

Winge, Ojvind, *Inheritance in Dogs with Special Reference to Hunting Breeds* (translated from Danish by Dr. C. Roberts), Comstock Publishing Co., Inc., Ithaca, N.Y. (1950)

## Field Training

American Kennel Club, *Regulations of Field Trials*, New York, N.Y.

Brown, William F., *Retriever Gun Dogs*, A.S. Barnes & Co., New York, N.Y. (1945)

CoyKendall, Ralf W., Jr., *You and Your Retriever*, Doubleday & Co., Inc., Garden City, N.Y.

Elliott, David D., *Training Gun Dogs to Retrieve*, Holt Publishing Co., New York, N.Y. (1952)

Fowler, Ann, and Walters, D. L., *Charles Morgan on Retrievers*, Larry Pisso Dog Training Supplies, San Francisco, CA.

Johnson, Glen R., *Tracking Dog—Theory and Methods*, Arner Publishing Co., Rome, N.Y.

Kersley, J. A., *Training the Retriever*, Howell Book House Inc., New York, N.Y. (1970)

Spencer, James B., *Retriever Training Tests*, 923 Valleyview Lane, Wichita, Kansas 67212. (1983) Contents include single marks, double marks, triple marks, basic blinds, and suction blinds, training tips.

Walters, D. L., and Ann, *Training Retrievers to Handle*, Interstate Book Manufacturers, Olathe, Kansas. (1979)

## Obedience Training

Benjamin, Carol Lea, *Dog Training for Kids*, Howell Book House Inc., New York, N.Y. (1976)

302

Burnham, Patricia Gail, *Playtraining Your Dog*, St. Martin's Press, New York, N.Y. (1980)

Davis, L. Wilson, *Go Find!—Training Your Dog to Track*, Howell Book House Inc., New York, N.Y. (1974)

Haggerty & Benjamin, *Dog Tricks*, Howell Book House Inc., New York, N.Y.

Koehler, William R., *The Koehler Method of Open Obedience for Ring, Home, and Field*, Howell Book House Inc., New York, N.Y. (1970)

Monks of New Skete, *How to Be Your Dog's Best Friend*, A Training Manual for Dog Owners, Little, Brown and Co., Boston-Toronto. (1978)

Pearsall, Margaret E., *The Pearsall Guide to Successful Dog Training*, Howell Book House Inc., New York, N.Y. (1973)

*Regulations of Obedience Trials*, American Kennel Club, CD, CDX, UD, TD, TDX, O.T. Ch., New York, N.Y.

Saunders, Blanche, *The Story of Dog Obedience*, Howell Book House Inc., New York, N.Y. (1974)

Volhard, Joachim, and Fisher, Gail Tamases, *Training Your Dog—The Step-by-Step Manual*, Howell Book House Inc., New York, N.Y. (1983)

Widmer, Patricia P., *Dog Training Book*, David McKay Company, Inc., New York. (1977)

Woodhouse, Barbara, *No Bad Dogs—The Woodhouse Way*, Summit Books, New York, N.Y. (1982)

**Gait and Conformation Studies**

Brackett, Lloyd C., and Horswell, L. A., "The Dog in Motion", *Dog World Magazine*, series of articles (monthly), August, 1961 to December, 1964.

Elliott, Rachel Page, *The New Dogsteps*, Howell Book House Inc., New York, N.Y. (2nd Ed. 1983) An excellent book which explains the importance of gait in assessing a dog. Mrs. Elliott's book is not only based on the earlier material used in her first book, *Dogsteps*, but on additional research. She has studied canine bone and joint motion at Harvard University Museum of Comparative Zoology where there is a specially equipped laboratory for simultaneously photographing and fluoroscoping animals as they move at a controlled speed on a treadmill. This process is known as cineradiography. Her work has given her scientific information as well as personal observation on gait.

Lyon, McDowell, *The Dog in Action* (reprint), Howell Book House Inc., New York, N.Y. (1963)

Smythe, R. H., *The Conformation of the Dog*, Popular Dogs, London, England.

Smythe, R. H., *The Anatomy of Dog Breeding*, Popular Dogs, London, England.

**The Show Ring**

Brown, M. H., and Mason, B. H., *The New Complete Junior Showmanship Handbook*, Howell Book House Inc., New York, N.Y. (1980) This is an excellent book for juniors. The writing is simple, direct, and easy to understand, with illustrations. It discusses personal appearance in the ring, gaiting patterns, courtesy, and practical points for both handler and dog.

Forsyth, Robert and Jane, *Forsyth Guide to Successful Dog Showing,* Howell Book House Inc., New York, N.Y.

**Home Medical Care**

Carlson, Delbert G., DVM, & Giffin, James M., MD, *Dog Owner's Home Veterinary Handbook*, Howell Book House Inc., New York, N.Y. (1980)

McGinnis, Terri, *The Well Dog Book*, Random House. (1974)

Golden Pine's Suntory Royale, owned by Eileen Oshiro and Nancy Belsaas.     *Richard Oshiro*